The Politics of Peril

ECONOMICS, SOCIETY AND THE PREVENTION OF WAR

The Politics of Peril

ECONOMICS, SOCIETY AND THE PREVENTION OF WAR

Carl Friedrich von Weizsäcker
Translated by Michael Shaw

A CONTINUUM BOOK · THE SEABURY PRESS · NEW YORK

1978
The Seabury Press
815 Second Avenue
New York, N.Y. 10017

Originally published in Germany under the title *Wege in der Gefahr: Eine Studie über Wirtschaft, Gesellschaft und Kriegsverhütung* by Carl Hanser Verlag, copyright © 1976 by Carl Hanser Verlag München.

English translation copyright © 1978 by The Seabury Press, Inc.

Printed in the United States of America

Library of Congress Cataloging in Publication Data

Weizsäcker, Carl Friedrich, Freiherr von, 1912–
The politics of peril.

(A Continuum book)
Translation of Wege in der Gefahr.
Includes bibliographical references.
1. International relations. 2. International economic relations.
3. War. 4. Peace. 5. World politics—1975–1985. I. Title.
JX1395.W4413   327'.09'047   78-4991   ISBN 0-8164-9345-6

Contents

Preface

This is one of three books whose simultaneous publication is intentional. The authors of the other two are Horst Afheldt[1] and Guy Brossollet and Emil Spannocchi.[2]

This book addresses itself primarily to readers who have practical political, economic or military responsibility. This means, of course, that it also addresses itself to readers who are citizens with political interests and thus share in this responsibility through the contribution they make to public opinion. It deals with current economic problems (including the protection of the environment), antagonistic social systems and war prevention on a global scale and in their reciprocal dependence.

This is an attempt. Even vigorous criticism will be welcomed by the author if it stimulates discussion. Today, too many practical decisions are made where the interdependence of the various fields and of the regions of the world is not taken into account. Nor do prevailing economic, political and military theories do justice to such interconnections. Without a certain perception of the whole, correct decision can hardly be made. Precisely because of this increasing interdependence, the coming decades will be a time of growing danger for mankind.

In several areas, this book makes practical proposals or

advances criteria for the judgment of such proposals: there are "recommendations" concerning energy policy in chapter 2, and sections entitled "consequences" of economic policy in chapter 3, and "consequences" of defense policies in chapters 8, 9, and 10. To insure that the reflections would remain accessible to possible criticism by experts in the various fields, the attempt was made in every case to deduce the proposals from the internal logic of the area under discussion. The larger nexus does not enter the arguments as a general theory. Instead, its perception is meant to crystallize through the discussion of the individual problems, and step by step. Only the final chapter explicitly considers that nexus.

The principal emphasis of this book is war prevention, for neither the prevention of local wars nor that of a third world war is assured. Prevention and survival are tasks which make direct demands on contemporary practical politics. The book thus picks up the thread of an earlier study.[3] Its connection with the two simultaneously appearing works is briefly set forth in what follows.

In his new book, H. Afheldt takes our collaborative study of war prevention one significant step forward. The earlier work contained a critical analysis of prevailing doctrines but made no positive proposals of its own. Afheldt now begins with a comprehensive analysis of the entire set of problems and includes a discussion of American and European doctrines that have emerged since 1970. From his analysis, he derives concrete suggestions for both deterrence on the strategic level, and the defense of Europe. Chapters 6 and 9 of this book have been decisively influenced by his ideas. The section entitled "consequences" in chapter 9 contains summary references to his proposals.

The present commander in chief of the Austrian army, General Emil Spannocchi wrote a number of articles in which he outlined a changed concept of defense (local defense by armor-piercing weapons). The current reorganization of the Austrian army is based on that concept. In his book, *Essai sur la non-bataille* (1975), Commander Guy Brossollet makes very similar proposals for the defense of France. The ideas of Spannocchi, Brossollet and Afheldt evolved independently of each other, and the publications of Spannocchi and Brossollet were independent events, though Spannocchi's book was the first to appear. Yet the similarity of their conclusions is striking.

The names of those to whom I owe a debt of gratitude for what they taught me in our discussions would make too long a list to be printed here. I do, however, wish to express my thanks to the members of the Max Planck Institute for Research into Conditions of Life in a Scientific and Technological World, for without their work and advice I could not have written this book. Walter Bonhoeffer and Ruth Grosse were directly involved in its genesis.

1. Paths Through Danger

The coming decades will be a time of increased danger for mankind. That danger need not be fatal. There are paths that lead through it. Our willingness to take those paths hinges upon awareness of the danger. Our ability to take those paths hinges upon our perception of them. This book attempts to sketch the danger and to indicate the starting point of those paths.

But is it really true that growing dangers are coming toward us? We should proceed slowly. Rather than ask first whether or not this is a fact, let us consider prevailing opinion. I do not know whether pollsters have raised this question in the Federal Republic of Germany,[4] but it is my impression that more anxiety and concern is being expressed today both in public debate and in private conversation than ten or twenty years ago. The concerns expressed in Germany might perhaps be conveyed by the following key terms: destruction of the environment, economic crisis, dangers of the Third World, the failure of democracy, disintegration of our civilization, domination by communist Russia, and war. Are these dangers imaginary, or real?

The hypothesis of this book is the following: each of

1

these fears has a basis in fact, points to a real danger. But the emergence of these fears is also a psychological phenomenon that requires explanation in turn. The fears reflect a development in human consciousness which itself has some relationship to the common ground of these dangers. A step forward in human consciousness and a related transformation in the political structure of mankind has become necessary today. Without it, we shall not be able to survive the consequences of this scientific and technological civilization. All the dangers listed are forms of what will happen if this step is not taken. All these fears are hazy perceptions of this one, frequently misunderstood necessity, for fear arises where we fail to do what is necessary.

But what is this necessary step? Should we call it the transition to world-wide solidarity? This formulation may be correct, but it is too vague. We have to go into detail. Most of the chapters of this book will provide detailed discussions of certain of these dangers. By and large, they will follow this pattern. Two questions will be raised: What is the danger in a given case? what paths lead through this danger? In the closing chapter, that question will take us back to the necessary transformation of consciousness with greater precision. As a first step in a discussion of these questions, we will analyze the fears of our contemporaries listed above[5] in somewhat greater detail.

Destruction of the environment. This subject, which has been a cause of concern for scientific experts for some decades, became a topic of remarkably vigorous discussion barely ten years ago. "The limits to growth," "the looted planet," are key phrases. In this book[6], we will examine only one aspect of this concern, i.e., the possible dangers of various forms of energy production, particularly atomic reactors (chapter 2). Many of the concerns that are being raised seem exaggerated to me in their specific detail. There are paths through these dangers. But taking them demands planned action and international cooperation. The dangers that result from technical failure seem controllable while those due to planned violence, war, appear as the greatest. The ecological problem thus points to political problems.

Economic crisis. Stagnation, inflation, unemployment are the concrete preoccupations here, especially now, where fear of a permanent disruption of the structure of the economy is resurfacing after profound economic crises had been avoided for decades. The author, who is not an economist, will attempt to shed some light on the causal nexus of these events (chapter 3). What emerges here is the first instance of a polarity of two concerns which also appears elsewhere. The concern about economic stagnation has its counterpart in the ecological desire to limit growth. The advocate of one side customarily considers the opposing side to be in error. But it is quite conceivable that both concerns are justified. Putting the matter concretely, it may be that over the long run, our economic system cannot solve our problems either by growth or without it. That would mean that the economic system itself must be changed. In the third chapter, we state this supposition in moderate terms. We advance a neutral, a pessimistic and an optimistic version of certain trends and attempt to indicate the actions required if we wish to take the paths the optimistic version sets forth. This may be understood as an immanent critique of capitalism which does not wish to abolish the system but to institute reforms for its survival. Socialist friends of mine would advance a stronger critique because they believe they can offer an alternative. But I suspect that among the steps toward socialism being offered today, revolutionary socialism (chapters 4 and 5) is no solution to the problems of our highly industrialized society but a way of modernizing economically underdeveloped ones. And democratic socialism would entail a desirable modification rather than a fundamental change in our system.

The limited recommendations regarding reform (chapter 3) have much less to do with socialism than with international cooperation. To the extent that they did so, the capitalist national economies of the nineteenth and early twentieth centuries solved their socio-economic problems within the legal framework of the nation-state. Within the conceptual frame of reference of the third chapter, the absence of a corresponding global framework is the principal reason for pessimistic prognoses.

Dangers of the Third World. The parochial thinking of our society usually understands these dangers as an inability of the peoples of the Third World to achieve those things which constitute our cultural superiority over them. Even where this observation is valid, this form of thought is inadequate. Thus it is seen correctly, for example, that hunger is due to population growth, but it is not seen that, in view of the worldwide diffusion of modern medicine, excessive population growth can also be understood as a result of hunger, i.e., each family's worry about the future (see also chapter 3, p. 54). People react with contempt to the powerless Third World, and with indignation and fear to that part of it which is gaining access to power (oil crisis, proliferation of atomic weapons—see chapter 9). It is only plausible that Third World reaction to this form of thought should frequently be its mirror image. Generalizing much too crudely, it blames its immanent problems much too exclusively on external factors, on its continuing economic dependence on us. What is the truth here? The technical superiority of European, North American civilization developed on a wide social base and over the course of centuries. The reason for this special development of a culture which, as late as the Middle Ages, was neither intellectually nor technically superior to other high cultures, is a historical problem that need not concern us here. But it is certainly a fact that the intellectual and material building blocks of technical civilization cannot be recreated within a few decades in a historically different culture, but this can be done over a longer period of time. Different prognoses will be made for different problems. Regarding average economic measurements such as the per capita national product, the present-day standard of the industrial nations should be attainable worldwide in less than a hundred years,[7] if the optimistic version of the economic prognosis is justified. Social justice or, more precisely, the eradication of misery, is apparently being attained more rapidly in China (chapter 5); this is a question of political structure. The great economic and military powers of our time will perhaps retain their preponderance at least as long as a war between them can be avoided. Though possible according to these prognoses, assimilation of the Third World to the civilization of the Northern powers is not for that reason necessarily the path through the danger and the right goal. We will return to this question in the final chapter.

Failure of democracy. A polarization that is occurring in all parliamentary democracies is emerging with disquieting clarity in today's Federal Republic of Germany. Particularly during election years, the Right and the Left accuse each other of being a danger to democracy. What is disquieting is that both really believe this, as one can discover time and again in confidential conversations. What if both were right? If our form of government, which is liberal with certain restrictions, does not solve its functional problems, the temptation to prefer other, allegedly more efficient or just forms, will grow. The protection of freedom against the enemy on the other side will then justify the curbing of freedom in favor of one's own side. This polarization, like all polarizations, is not as symmetrical as indicated here, of course. Both sides represent zeal, qualitatively different values (efficiency vs. justice, for example) which it would be the task of a comprehensive social structure to conjoin. Actually, the problem lies at a deeper layer of consciousness. Where do we get the idea that our system is not solving its functional problems? If those among us who are older think back to the dire times around 1945, present conditions in our country should seem paradisiacal. Part of our discontent is simple ingratitude. We give our system no credit for the problems it has solved. It is also true, however, that this lack of gratitude is a fact, itself the product of our system and a source of problems. Furthermore, the unsolved functional problems are both real and dangerous. It is my judgment that it is not the mechanisms of our political system that are inadequate to a solution of the problem. What is at fault is the state of consciousness of those who should use those mechanisms, and that may in part be a result of the system. For this reason, I did not include a discussion of the constitutional structure of parliamentary democracy in this book. I only take up the question concerning the relationship between this structure and the necessary development of political consciousness (see p. 134 and chapter 11).

Disintegration of the culture. Uninhibited egoism, pursuit of material goods, the creation and idolization of meaningless needs, the systematic unleashing of instincts, the numbing of moral impulses, drug culture, terrorism, ungovernability are all enumerated as symptoms of the disintegration of our culture. It is in this disintegration that one can find the real reason why economic and social problems cannot be solved, for the optimistic version shows us that it should be possible to solve them by reason and good will. The vocabulary of this enumeration is unmistakably conservative, and it is a fact that concern about cultural disintegration is a structurally conservative concern. It sees a fundamental good, i.e., this culture, as both existing and threatened, and thus in need of being preserved. But in most cases, the conservatives are no more aware than the socialists that up to a point, they are allies in this critique. Leftist cultural criticism as practiced today does not reject the bases of our civilization, after all. It merely blames it for betraying them. The common enemy is a condition of society which is factually and ideologically based on the private acquisition of material goods. Both critics are morally motivated. Of course, liberal thought also has an answer which is itself morally based (see chapter 6, p. 134). A book about the paths in and through dangers could begin with a theory of culture and morality, and one could hope that such a theory might permit a classification and clarification of such dangers. For understandable reasons, I did not choose that method. The critique of culture is difficult and *eo ipso* controversial in a pluralistic society. If one were to start off with such a critique, the analyses of concrete questions would be prejudiced and might fail to really convince any reader. I therefore start out with concrete problems. The ambition is to be a more than indifferent partner for experts even where the author has no expert knowledge. I believe that any adequately thorough, practice-related and knowledgeable analysis will take us to the background of cultural and moral questions. We will therefore deal with the questions only in the concluding chapter where their coherent discussion will be based on the results of the preceding individual analyses, and therefore be criticizable in their light. This book addresses itself primarily to persons who have practical responsibilities.

Domination by communist Russia. Fear of the Russians and communists, which has prevailed in West Germany since 1914 or 1917, receded during the Brandt era but is growing once again today. We encounter it at every street corner, in almost every newspaper. As one observes the comments and conduct of those who express such fears, one can easily come to the conclusion that most of these cases involve what is called projection in psychology. Individuals, social groups and nations very often escape from unresolved inner conflicts by searching out the external enemy, the villain. But even though this fear has a psychological function, it readily attaches to something which is fearful in fact. In that case, it is not the concern but only the way of dealing with it which is false. I do indeed feel that Soviet Russian imperialism is a threat, and extended sections of this book discuss it. The threatening facts are discussed in parts of chapters 6, 8 and 11. But what underlies these facts is more important than the facts themselves. It is my opinion that the threat does not derive from a political perversion but is a normal historical process, and we can deal with it only if we see it as such. In my opinion, we must expect a hegemonic conflict between imperialist world powers in this historical phase (chapters 6 and 7). I freely admit that the judgment that Russian imperialism is more dangerous than its American counterpart expresses among other things the interest of the state whose citizen I choose to be. I say that this is my choice because I would undoubtedly have also been free to become a citizen of the German Democratic Republic. This free decision reflects a liberal political conviction. But allowing for the limited degree of stringency that arguments about political theory have, I believe that I can also advance a theoretical explanation why Soviet imperialism is more threatening. The reason is that by its very nature, communism has a closer relation to power than liberalism (chapters 4, 6 and 8). We have to grasp these connections to understand how we can protect ourselves against this threat (chapters 8, 10 and 11).

War. During the first fifteen years after the Second World War, fear of the Third World War was more pervasive than today. Indeed, as far as we can judge, nuclear deterrence has reduced the prospects of a large-scale war since the middle fifties. Of course, local wars have constantly been waged (chapter 9). The probability of a limited war between the superpowers has not decreased to zero. An extrapolation from present trends in armaments (chapter 8) would rather tend to suggest that its probability is increasing. The escalation of a limited war to one waged with all available resources cannot be precluded, and this precisely because, widely held opinion notwithstanding, technical means may be developed which could enable one of the warring powers to survive such a war as the victor. Historically speaking, the settlement of a hegemonic conflict without recourse to war is presumably unprecedented. This does not mean that what is historically normal necessarily happens, but it must be viewed as probable (chapter 6). In contrast to the problem of domination, I see war as a threat that comes from both sides. American policy cannot be absolved of the reproach of having engaged in destabilizing armaments.

During the last thirty years, Europe was well protected from war, presumably because a war here would have been too dangerous for both superpowers. But the possibility of a local war here, or of Europe's possible involvement in a world war, should not be excluded. Caution demands that we reflect not only about ways to prevent a war but also about ways of surviving it (chapter 10). An effective position of deterrence is possible. It would threaten neither the enemy nor one's own side with the destruction of the population and will be outlined in the section "consequences" of our eighth and tenth chapters.

Faced with concrete problems, we will not close our eyes to a pessimistic view of possible consequences, but neither will we accept any such view as definitive. Our analyses and proposals are intended to promote a reformist evolution of existing structures. This position is determined by those to whom this book addresses itself. It is all one can propose to the practitioner with real responsibilities. But the paths suggested here are paths in danger. To miss them could be fatal. And they lead into an as yet unknown world. Coping with it requires more than conservative reforms. We conclude with the necessary transformation of consciousness.

2. Development and Supply of Our Energy Needs

A Lecture

FOSSIL ENERGY SOURCES

Reserves. Fossil energy sources will be able to meet our present consumption of energy, not to mention an increasing one, for only a period of time. This span is short enough to prompt us now to make efforts toward procuring alternatives. To judge these efforts, it is useful to call to mind estimated time scales.[8]

As of 1977, proven reserves of oil amounted to 91×10^9 t, and are sufficient to sustain the 1972 level of oil consumption for 35 years. The reserves considered likely to exist come to 285×10^9 t, and would last for 10 years. Given a 4% rate of increase per annum, both figures would be reduced to 21 and 36 years respectively, and if the average annual rate of increase of 7.5% which obtained during the years 1962–72 is used as a basis, we get a reduction to 18 and 30 years respectively. Natural gas will not last much longer than oil. Estimated global coal reserves of 6.7×10^{12} t would last barely 4000 years if present annual consumption were to remain constant. If current energy consumption were (and had) to be fully sustained by coal, they would last about 1300 years. Given an annual 4% rate of increase, this period would be reduced to 100 years. With an annual rate of increase of 2%, it would be 160 years, and 230 years with a 1% annual rate of increase. 60% of these reserves are in the USSR. If consumption remained constant, the reserves of the Federal Republic of Germany would last 700 years. They would last 200 years if the rate increased by 1%, and 85 years if it increased by 4%. The reserves of the European Community would last about 350 years, and 65 if we projected a 4% annual rate of growth. Experience shows that switching to another principal source of energy always requires technical efforts extending over several decades. The least extensive change we could make and which should be initiated now in view of the figures just quoted would be the return to coal. But if growth continues, a changeover to a non-fossil energy source would have to be initiated in a few decades. The reduction from 4% to 1% growth would only yield a factor of a little over 2 as regards time, whereas the reduction to zero growth would result in a factor of around 10. The common experience that reserves of raw materials are usually underestimated would mean that in the case of zero growth, these time scales would be considerably extended. If past rates of growth were to be maintained, however, such extension would be insignificant.

Environmental degradation. Present environmental degradation due to fossil fuels is less of a subject of public discussion than the feared future danger of nuclear energy. However, using the same mathematical techniques by which possible deaths resulting from the release of radioactivity from nuclear fission are estimated, it was calculated that one 1000 MW power station using coal could kill some 70 people yearly through the emission of SO_2 and other poisonous substances.[9] For years, there have been analogous estimates concerning the harm done by exhaust emissions from automobiles.

In addition, climatic effects will play a growing role in the coming decades. They must be divided into those which are common to all sources of energy (with the possible exception of solar energy, see pp. 24–25), and those which are uniquely characteristic of fossil fuels.

Power stations produce waste heat which affects the climate, and this applies to all energy sources. Globally speaking, the limit this imposes lies in a somewhat more distant future though that future merits consideration today. Depending on varying assessments of the climate, that limit may be reached if the present release of energy becomes 40 or 100 times greater. In the case of continued growth, that point would be reached in about a century, perhaps more quickly. In areas of concentration, the time would be shorter. The increasing global saturation of the atmosphere with dust and CO_2 is specific to fossil energy sources. It is presently unknown whether dust has a predominantly warming or cooling effect on the temperature of the atmosphere (absorption or diffusion of sunlight). What is practically certain is an effect of an order of magnitude that must no longer be neglected. CO_2 has clearly a warming effect. (This is called the greenhouse effect: short-wave radiation is admitted while long-wave radiation is not let out again.)

The steady increase of the CO_2 content of the atmosphere as predicted by models has been indisputably proven in recent years (3% in ten years). Even if current quantities of fossil energy sources continue to be used, but especially if the rate increases, there is the serious possibility that fundamental climatic changes will occur here on earth during the coming century. They may jeopardize the habitability of present culture zones and even a drastic reduction in combustion processes could then no longer change this picture.

NUCLEAR FISSION

Reserves and possible applications. Estimates as to the time for which reserves of fissionable material (uranium and thorium) could supply energy needs depend on two factors: the price one will be willing to pay for extraction from lower-grade ores, and the decision concerning the use of breeders. At current prices, without breeders, uranium will last no longer than oil and gas. But an increase in the price of energy would make profitable the extraction from lower-grade deposits. It is very difficult to estimate today where the limits of profitability lie: the economic situation of future decades is unknown. It is probably not irresponsible to estimate that nuclear energy without breeders is assured for about 100 years, given a 2% growth rate. If breeders are successful, profitable and safe, they will extend the time span by a factor of 100. In that case, they would solve the problem of energy supply, at least for power stations, for the period of time for which we can plan.

Environmental degradation. The concerns emerging today relate to this area. Using the following outline, I polled some experts on this subject. The following questions were raised. What is the safety of

a) present lightwater reactors
b) further developments (especially fuel reprocessing, and breeders)
c) storage of radioactive waste

A) under normal conditions
B) to guard against technical accidents
C) to guard against sabotage
D) in war?

Aa. Present-day reactors in normal use. There is virtual unanimity that reactors are considerably sounder ecologically than power stations using fossil fuels. Remaining radioactive emissions lie far below the normal variations in natural radioactivity which so far have not been proven to affect health. They create thermal pollution, but so do power stations that utilize fossil fuels. Only because of a lower efficiency (about 35% instead of about 40%) do nuclear reactors produce about 20% more waste heat per usable kilowatt hour than do power stations using fossil fuels.

Ab. Fuel reprocessing in normal operations. Here, we enter the sphere of future planning. No one would dare assert that all safety problems relating to this question have been solved. There do not appear to be any problems that cannot be solved in principle, but today there exists a more critical sense for the requirements than just a few years ago. The effects of safety measures on costs will be noticeable but not prohibitive.

Ac. Final disposal in normal operations. There is a growing feeling in the USA that present plans for storing the accumulated waste of several decades above ground should be abandoned. The best method for final storage is still the topic of extensive investigation. The concentration and fixing of the remaining high-level waste in ceramic or glass after that material has been stored elsewhere for decades, and its disposal in deep salt beds arouses the possibly not unfounded hope that this may be a safe procedure in normal operations.

Ba. Technical accidents in today's reactors. There is a very detailed study on this topic, the so-called Rasmussen report.[10] Here, one encounters the fundamental problem of correctly gauging the very small probability of very significant damage. The 10^{10} curies of radioactivity in a 1000 megawatts lightwater reactor would, if released over a city of several million inhabitants, kill or seriously injure a large part of the population and make the city uninhabitable for a long time. The numerical statement concerning the very small probability of such an event always remains something of an exercise of the imagination. The qualitative considerations that enter into the estimate are principally these: the popular conception of an "exploding" reactor that would dissipate radioactivity is not in keeping with any known process. The most serious breakdown possible would be the melting of the reactor core, should the doubly shielded coolant system fail. Even then, it would be unlikely that the molten mass would eat its way through the concrete walls and out into the open. This eventuality is considered as highly improbable, and it is also assumed that the mass would largely remain where it was and not be diffused through the atmosphere. The result would be considerable but certainly limited damage.

It is obvious that assessments of such complex events which have never been observed can remain controversial in many details, even if the greatest care was used. For this reason, and primarily with the object of giving some hint of the character of these discussions, we shall report a few isolated facts. In the spring of 1975, a reactor caught fire at Brown's Ferry because a carelessly lit candle had caused a fire in the insulation material of electric lines. There were no personal injuries, and estimates of property damage ranged between 200 and 300 million dollars. A shutdown of 1½ years was considered likely. The unanimous reaction of the experts was twofold: there are still causes of accidents which had not previously occurred to us; the operator who remained calm ultimately had the means to avoid a catastrophe although several safety systems were destroyed.

The scale of a possible catastrophe is compared with the magnitude of other risks which contemporary technology accepts. If the Folsom Dam above Sacramento in California were to burst, 260,000 people would be killed. Given the high degree of probability of earthquakes in California, the technical probability of such a disaster is computed as one in 100 years. Although the population was expressly polled, the decision to build this dam may have been somewhat irresponsible, objectively speaking. But we should not delude ourselves: our contemporary technological civilization accepts many similar forms of irresponsibility.

In a pitchblend deposit in Oklo, Gabon (Africa), traces of two or three "natural" reactors were discovered. Some two billion years ago, approximately, they were "operational" there for a period of 500,000 years. At that time, the concentration of U^{235} was not 0.7% as today, but 3%, so that natural uranium and lightwater could sustain a chain reaction. These natural reactors produced five tons of fissionable material of which two were plutonium 239. It appears that the fissionable material remained in place.[11] In addition to this (limited) reassurance, the fact that nuclear fission is a normal process in natural history and not only a human act seems to calm many physicists.[12] In spite of the renewed work connected with such an undertaking, complicated investigations such as the Rasmussen Report should be checked by others. The American Physical Society asked three of its most highly respected members, H. Bethe, W. Panofsky, and V. Weisskopf to undertake such a review, which was presented to the society in April 1975, at its annual meeting in Washington.[13] In the review no objection was raised to safety measures and safety estimates relating to the present developmental stage, and short-term developments. But for a long-term development where a great many reactors would stud the country, the safety risk was not considered low enough. Other types of reactors and other energy sources were not compared. "We studied risk, we didn't study benefit."[14]

   Bb. Technical accidents in further development. Safety estimates here are not nearly as complete as in the case of lightwater reactors. Typically, one can hear the following thought: "The logical sequence would be to first await certain results from the Fast Flux Test Facility in Hanford before proceeding with the construction of the reactor in Tennessee. One has to balance the possible but unlikely and certainly limited damage created by a catastrophe in some prematurely constructed breeder reactors against the serious consequences of social instability due to balance of payment deficits for the U.S.A. which would result from energy imports."

   One of the problems that should be mentioned here is the toxicity of plutonium. Experts all voice a certain surprise at the present public excitement about this question. A number of workers at Los Alamos ingested plutonium and have been living with it for thirty years without discoverable damage. Some have up to 400,000 "hot" alpha radiating particles in their lungs without having contracted lung cancer. One individual got lung cancer but not at a point where a "hot" particle was lodged. No one denies the chemical and radioactive danger of these radiating heavy metals but an adequate lowering of the risk is considered perfectly feasible.[15]

Bc. Technical mishaps during final disposal. What is disquieting about this problem is not the technical solution itself, which is considered possible (cf. Ac), but the shifting of the remaining risk onto future generations, and for a period of some 1000 years. "A certain minimal monitoring of final storage areas will always be necessary." (Weinberg)

A and B (Review of the technical risks). The assumption with which I entered into these discussions also turned out to be that of my discussion partners: There does exist a technologically feasible, relatively safe way of dealing with risks that have been technically caused. The problem lies in spotting them in time. The history of development of technical civilization was sufficiently slow at an earlier time so that it was possible to learn from experience. The bridge across the Tay River was too weak. During a storm, it crashed while a train was crossing it, and many people lost their lives. Since then, bridges have been more solidly constructed. Present-day technology owes its success in part to its capacity for preliminary theoretical design. It no longer has to learn by trial and error. Reactor and atom bomb worked during the first trial. Contemporary technology thus engages in constructions that carry greater risks, and greater dangers in case of failure. Weinberg sees a "Faustian bargain" in "an arrangement where man promises meticulous and persistent attention to detail in exchange for an inexhaustible and, in principle, a non-polluting energy source."[16] Someone who knows the Faust legend may feel that the respected reactor physicist portrays the devil as too innocuous when his claim to Faust's soul hinges on meticulousness. But perhaps the devil knows that human beings do not sustain such meticulousness.

The financial consequences of the duty to be meticulous can be discussed on the technical, economic level. Safety measures and the desirable circumspection in the introduction of a great and as yet untested technology increase the price. One repeatedly hears the complaint that the construction of power stations is becoming unprofitable. American experts—and this is an astonishing reaction for the U.S.— express the idea that it was a mistake to turn nuclear energy over to private enterprise. They claim that stable and careful further development can only be insured by turning it back to the government. A technical proposal which is gaining ground is to concentrate nuclear facilities in "nuclear parks." Particularly in the case of advanced techniques which call for the transport of spent nuclear fuels for purposes of reprocessing, for example, this would undoubtedly markedly limit risks geographically, and simplify control. The development of the technology of energy transport—a matter we shall not discuss here—would naturally be part of this.

Ca. Sabotage in present-day power stations. Experts do not deny concern about sabotage but put it in perspective by saying that if proper security measures are taken in nuclear technology, saboteurs will find more rewarding objectives than nuclear installations, and that this applies especially to present-day reactors. A serious reactor accident can hardly be caused by outside interference (except by nuclear weapons, cf. Da), and the police could protect reactors against armed attack. But the sabotage scenarios developed by my discussion partners seemed to me only to envisage the action of gangsters in an otherwise functioning society, not that of revolutionaries in an encompassing crisis. When the possibility was discussed that the reactor crew might not react as at Brown's Ferry, but flee in panic, it was postulated that the security system should be automatized, which is technically feasible. What would happen if the reactor crew itself were to take a hand in revolutionary activity was not fully discussed.

The principal and presumably well-founded consolation was technical: even in the case of a major reactor accident, the catastrophe would be limited, and catastrophes of such an order of magnitude can also be caused in other ways in today's technological civilization.

Cb. Other forms of sabotage. The problem that received most attention here was the theft of plutonium. This is related to the treaty banning the proliferation of atomic weapons. Both the danger of the actual theft of plutonium and the danger that terrorist groups might try to bluff others with the false statement that they had plutonium and atomic weapons made of it in their possession were seriously considered. The conviction was that the control over the movement of fissionable material must be refined to such an extent that a shortage of one kilo of plutonium would be spotted and localized. This poses a difficult though presumably not an insuperable obstacle to further technical development.

But there are factors which relativize this danger. The former designer of atomic weapons, Ted Taylor, recently warned the public of home-made plutonium bombs in the hands of subversive groups. But my discussion partners felt that the mechanical difficulties of this work were considerable and the efficiency of such bombs limited. One may ask whether such groups might not construct other kinds of weapons with less effort, or steal atomic weapons already manufactured. It should be added that, often, the political interest of governments is not served by the secret possession of atomic weapons but precisely by the political effect the public declaration of such possession would have, and possession can be more reliably achieved if they produce such weapons themselves.

All this does not mean that today's world is without dangers, but shows that the production or non-production of nuclear energy would have some bearing on such dangers, yet would not apparently affect their order of magnitude.

Cc. Sabotage of final disposal. Storage facilities for waste products, even when underground, are normally accessible. The belief that they should be guarded by the military is becoming widespread. To answer this cops and robbers scenario, the same skeptical questions that were raised above (Ca) can be asked here. The technical argument that radioactive material is very dangerous and quite heavy carries more weight here also. Anyone trying to steal it would have a very risky and unpleasant transport problem, yet the effect he could obtain would be limited.

A precautionary measure which would prevent almost any conceivable theft would be storage in deep salt beds into which the material would sink as into a viscous liquid. In such a case, however, adequate steps to prevent a later disintegration of the containers due to natural processes would be necessary. It has been repeatedly mentioned but never seriously proposed that the waste might be shot into space.

Da. Normal reactors in war. All cases discussed so far entail some dangers, and it is a social duty to avoid them. But as long as safety regulations are correctly planned and observed during construction, they do not constitute a threat to the existence of a nation or of mankind. Already today, what danger there is lies in the possibility of nuclear war. The question concerning the relationship between reactors and war must therefore be this: does the construction of reactors, especially in large quantities, recognizably or fundamentally increase the danger a war might bring? Experts in the U.S. are generally skeptical here. Essentially, they say that someone who wishes to destroy the country can also, and more simply, do so with bombs. Today's reactors are covered by such quantities of concrete that a conventional bomb dropped directly on such a ceiling, or an airplane falling on it, would not crash through. It is true that an atomic bomb would destroy the ceiling, and I do not know whether it is correct that a second one would be required to cause the reactor core to vaporize. This would cause considerable leakage of radioactivity that would spread all over the country. But someone with bombs which could destroy reactors would also have bombs which would not have to be aimed that precisely to spread radioactivity. It is true, however, that the radioactivity produced by reactors decays much more slowly than that of normal bombs.

But this argument is also based on the strategic situation of the U.S. although those advancing it are usually not aware of it. The country is so large that it can construct its reactors in places which are far away from strategically important locations and population centers. Besides, the only plausible scenario for a war which includes the territory of the U.S.A. is one where large ("strategic") atomic weapons would be used against the country. Whether similar conclusions would also apply to a central European country with considerable population density would at least require study in cases where the military alliance to which it belongs subscribes to a strategy of flexible response. In mobile warfare with tactical nuclear weapons in West Germany, any one of many reactors might also be hit without having been a target. It should therefore be determined whether strategies for limiting damage and nuclear energy production are reconcilable with each other.

Db. Further development of nuclear technology in war. In principle, the same considerations apply here. If a modern mobile war of even short duration is considered a possibility in our country, the production of atomic energy in nuclear parks, if possible beyond the borders, perhaps out at sea (proposed by W. Häfele, see below), is clearly indicated. Quite apart from this, there is the increasing chance that countries which do not have nuclear weapons today may obtain plutonium and develop their own. Particularly in the case of countries that did not sign the Nuclear Non-Proliferation Treaty, one attempts to deal with this problem by providing them only with reactors, but not the technology, or asks them to submit to the international controls stipulated in the treaty. But all such treaties, including the Non-Proliferation Treaty, are terminable and the dissemination of material and knowledge is presumably an irreversible process. For this reason, prior restrictions in this area fall into the same category as disarmament. They can only be implemented when the resources nations agree to do without are difficult to obtain in any event, or of no vital interest to them. The rationale of the Non-Proliferation Treaty is perfectly logical in that it makes it more difficult to acquire nuclear weapons for purposes of prestige. It also buys time. But we must not delude ourselves. A much more profound change in the world-political systems for which the original concept behind the Non-Proliferation Treaty wanted to gain time and which would drastically and globally restrict the legal and material means to wage war, is not in sight. Today, we can only hope that it is not in the interests of states to use nuclear weapons in their conflicts.

Dc. Disposal in war. If storage is far underground, it may not constitute a significant problem in a war.

C and D. Review of the danger of sabotage and deliberate destruction. The sequence chosen here—normal operation, technical accidents, sabotage, war—probably also represents a sequence of increasing danger for the peaceful use of atomic energy. Recognized, technically caused dangers call for technical remedies, and dangers caused by human error ultimately call for human means. Other than police protection which would only be adequate in certain contingencies, my discussion partners could not name any human remedies. Their arguments were pervasively technical, and probably correct: the technology of nuclear reactors makes it appear likely that terrorists and warring states would have recourse to other means of destruction provided by contemporary technology and science. However, as regards the NATO policy of flexible response and the non-proliferation of atomic weapons, this argument cannot as yet be considered self-evident.

OTHER PRIMARY ENERGY SOURCES

General considerations. Coal and nuclear fission are the only alternatives to oil and gas which technology could make available within a few decades, but this is true only if preparations are started now. Although this is not a matter of certainty, there are good reasons to assume that in a few decades, nuclear fusion and solar energy will have reached the kind of technological maturity which would also make them alternatives in large-scale energy production. Geothermal energy is also being considered but the preponderant opinion is that it would be quantitatively inadequate. All other forms of energy known to date, such as water, wind, tides, living organic matter (wood, algae, manure) can be used for specific purposes but cannot begin to satisfy the quantitative requirements of an energy-based economy if its present output is just to be maintained. Since coal and nuclear fission entail the problems discussed, thought is being given to the question whether it might be possible to replace or wholly dispense with them. A historical and prospective study by the International Institute for Applied Systems Analysis in Laxenburg near Vienna[17] stipulates a phasing in and a phasing out period of about fifty years each for market penetration, and symbolically employs a form of energy called "Solfus" which would succeed coal, oil, gas, and nuclear fission. The term "Solfus" refers to the option between solar and fusion energy. Häfele believes that during the next few decades, energy needs will be the guiding criterion for energy policy but that after that time, environmental considerations will become dominant. Someone who makes the more radical demand that the avoidance of environmental degradation should already be the guiding criterion at this time could argue that human experience indicates that the announcement that "morality" will be instituted at some future date is usually an evasion ("tomorrow, tomorrow, but not today"). But if this argument is to be used to terminate the development of nuclear fission and the use of fossil material as the principal energy sources in a few decades, one will also have to demand a radical restriction in the growth of energy consumption, at least for the next few decades, for during that time "Solfus" will not become technologically mature.

Nuclear fusion. It is the prevailing opinion of experts that it will some day be possible to use nuclear fusion, the energy source of the sun and the hydrogen bomb, for peaceful purposes, i.e., controlled energy production. The time span envisaged for reaching the two thresholds, large-scale implementation and profitability, however, is several decades. At the same time, the hopes of then having an unlimited supply of fuel ("water") and an absolutely pollution-free energy production must be qualified. The process with the greatest chance for success, the D-T reaction (deuterium-tritium) requires not only deuterium but also lithium which does not exist in great abundance. Should it become economically worthwhile to extract lithium from sea water— and this is likely—this source of energy would last for 10^5 to 10^6 years on the basis of present consumption, i.e., further into the future than we can plan for today. The radioactivity produced here will not come from the residual products as in fission but from the impact that the neutrons produced during the process will have on the wall material. According to a current estimate, fusion per kilowatt hour of energy would produce sixty times less radioactivity than fission. In addition, the radioactive decay would not be as slow.

Today's energy planning should neither rely on the advent of nuclear fusion, nor deprive us of that option. The form of this energy production will be that of a large power station.

Solar energy. In contrast to nuclear fusion, solar energy is utilizable at this time. As a supplemental energy source which might be used for space heating, for example, it unquestionably deserves intensive development. Should it be developed to a point where it becomes a genuine alternative to other sources of energy, the problem will be its profitable application on a large technical scale. Judging by what we know now, this form of energy is the only one of those available in large quantities which causes none of the previously discussed environmental degradation. Because it utilizes the radiating heat of the sun, it releases no additional heat, and this is an important factor. It should therefore be developed as much as is technically possible. More generally, it should be stated that an increasingly conservative use of energy would mean that the share of solar energy could increase, even in our climate, and in densely populated regions.

But its large-scale utilization encounters problems we are not sure we can solve. At the very least, and on the basis of present knowledge, decades of developmental effort would be required. According to present estimates, incoming solar energy would meet mankind's total requirements. But to satisfy the current needs of the European community, for example, it would have to be collected on surfaces of approximately the size of Belgium. As of now, production costs for such procedures are a hundred times those of conventional power stations. In addition, there will necessarily be political problems since such surfaces would have to lie in uninhabited regions, such as the Sahara, i.e., far away from industrial areas. And the argument that the climate would not be adversely affected is no longer necessarily correct when such large amounts of energy are transferred, even if the technical problem could be solved, for energy is not being released where it is being produced. The proponents of the large-scale technical use of solar energy argue that if development of this form of energy had attracted as much investment as nuclear fission, the problems would already have been solved. It is difficult to refute this, and the problems attending all other forms of energy would appear to justify the initiation of attempts to employ solar energy on a large scale. But success in terms of significant market penetration could not be expected for some decades.

ENERGY CONSERVATION

All arguments suggest that the greatest possible amount of energy should be saved. But how far can this take us? We will first examine some current arguments, and then advance a hypothesis.

In contemporary America, energy conservation is a topic that is always brought up in discussions of experts. A permanent reduction of the annual growth rate of energy consumption from 4% to 2% or 2½% is considered possible. But there are two peculiarities in the American situation. American per capita energy consumption is twice that of Western Europe without a clearly definable factor of 2 in the "quality of life" being apparent. In many respects, use of energy in America has been recognizably more wasteful than in the German Federal Republic (higher gasoline consumption of cars per mile, less adequate insulation of houses, excessive heating during the winter, excessive cooling during the summer). Besides, the United States hopes for energy self-sufficiency, although that hope is questionable. "Project Independence" is a national goal.

The oil crisis in the fall of 1973 resulted in a very rapid and thus clearly achievable 12% reduction in energy consumption. But this does not entitle us to a simplistic inference concerning the possibility of permanent energy savings. It is true that what is at least partly a psychological rather than a substantive connection between this temporary reduction in energy consumption and the recession could perhaps be interpreted as a difficult adaptation to new, energy-saving ways. But every additional percent of energy savings would demand new investments in other technologies, and these are very expensive. It is assumed that in the course of a few decades, up to 50% savings could be realized in the heating of buildings, and perhaps also in automotive traffic. But the counter argument is that this would only mean a temporary reduction in the growth rate of energy consumption even if investment costs in new technologies are not considered.

This takes us to the fundamental question: how far may or must the growth of energy consumption go? A careful scrutiny shows that all customary arguments concerning this question are vague. The only historically justifiable extrapolation would be that growth will continue indefinitely. Every other prognosis or demand entails a radical break with 200 years of economic and technological development. The arguments advanced in this lecture suggest that such a break will become necessary in the coming decades. This statement should not be made lightly. Every current prognosis concerning necessary limits to growth has any number of historical precedents each of which was refuted in turn. For the sake of verification, the argument will therefore be reduced to its simplest elements. It is not based on the fact that resources are limited but rests on the environmental compatibility of energy production and energy consumption. Natural law leads one to expect that limits will be encountered here. The climatological problem ultimately derives from the second law of thermodynamics. But the problem of the radioactivity of nuclear energy might presumably be solved if we had political and social conditions that differ from those historically known. This is an example of the thesis that technical progress not only makes political and social change possible, but mandatory if catastrophes are to be avoided. But as regards the limits to growth in energy consumption, this reflection merely contributes the perspective that other, even more radical breaks with out political and economic history will become necessary. There is small likelihood that this perspective will influence decisions in energy policy that must be taken right now.

Given such uncertainty, people normally turn to estimates of energy *needs*. A frequent answer is that the yearly energy production of mankind must rise by a factor of 20 after which it could remain stationary. The assumption is that the difference between per capita energy production in the U.S.A. and the worldwide average (a factor of 6) would entail an upward adjustment, that a further growth of the global population by a factor of 2 is foreseeable, and that the necessary transition to a significant geographic separation between energy production and consumption would create unavoidable additional losses between primary and secondary energy. However plausible all such estimates may be, they are all marked by obviously wishful thinking. It would be easier to arrive at even considerably higher estimates of need, were it not perfectly well known that population figures and per capita energy consumption will have to stop somewhere. The real problem is the mechanism which will arrest these forms of growth at some point. Conversely, this reflection makes it doubtful that the present level of energy consumption in industrial countries is really in line with legitimate needs. Reference here is not merely to the widespread criticism of the consumer society and the meaningfulness of per capita GNP as a measure of prosperity, but also to the problem of the structure of our technology: is its present expenditure of energy technically necessary to produce the goods now being manufactured, or is it the result of a form of technology that is particularly wasteful in its use of energy? This is most apparent in the non-industrial sector.

We will advance a hypothesis which does not express a firm opinion but is designed to stimulate scrutiny of a problem which economic and technical specialists apparently have not yet posed with sufficient thoroughness. The hypothesis is that it is not for reasons of technical necessity that the nexus between energy consumption and social product is as close as is commonly assumed. In a technical civilization with given technical means, there obviously does exist a close correlation between the quantitative growth of energy consumption and the quantity of products, however that may be measured, and which we shall call the national product for the sake of simplicity. If the technology remains the same, greater production can only be achieved through increased energy consumption. This trivial truth suffices to explain the historical nexus between the two rates of growth. But the proportionality factor is a function of the available technology. The hypothesis states that since the introduction of coal, and to a greater degree since the price reduction in oil, i.e., for many decades, we always developed a technology of abundant energy. A technology of energy conservation need not mean, therefore, that we have to do without material goods. We might use a catch phrase and say that it could substitute information for energy.[18] This means more than replacing the thoughtless use of energy by its intelligent use, as in adequately insulating construction, for example. It would also mean making intelligence a structural part of machinery and the system. Well-functioning and consequently energy-saving machines are an example for the technician, the substitution of telecommunication for travel an example for the manager. That the non-use of certain kinds of goods would also be culturally beneficial is a wholly different matter which will not be discussed at this point.

The extent to which information can substitute for energy is probably not easily decided by engineers who have an overview of contemporary technology. Our present technology is not just a result of imaginative design but was created under the stimulus and the penalties of the market. A long-term change in market conditions through an irreversible, significant increase in the cost of energy would provide a stimulus to the development of techniques that substitute for energy which might become more relevant economically than the stimulus to develop alternative sources of energy which would also be provided by an increase in the cost of it.

But such developments cannot be left solely to the market mechanism. This was clearly the view of the American government when it deliberately and for an extended period kept a ceiling on oil prices because it believed that cheap energy was in the interest of the economy as a whole. The governments of industrialized countries which have promoted governmental development of nuclear energy obviously shared this view for quite some time. Retrospectively, both decisions could be viewed skeptically, and it might be asked whether the market which would have kept energy more expensive and in shorter supply might not have had a more beneficial effect. In contrast to resource planning, however, environmental policy now unquestionably calls for the state to play a leading role, for only the state can protect the consumer from bearing the brunt of external costs which would otherwise be unavoidable in a competitive system. Legislation might be passed which would place the burden on those that cause pollution. The energy problem of the future now presents itself as an environmental problem par excellence. Future climatological effects of present energy consumption, or the radioactive risks of an established reactor system are not a factor in determining the price the private sector sets for its energy, of course. Only the state can enforce the timely inclusion of such considerations. Since it cannot escape its responsibility here, it should also propose economic stimuli for the development of a technology that substitutes for energy. This implies recognition that it will not in the future be the business of the state to insure cheap energy. It is only on the basis of such a fundamental decision that priorities in research programs for the conservation of energy on the one hand, and energy production on the other, and also priorities for shorter-term economic policy can be judged within the framework of the technology that is available today.

The tragedy of our situation is that the governments and the national economies they naturally protect are competitors internationally, and that there is no worldwide authority which would regulate external costs. An individual firm that must compete with others is limited in the ecological safeguards it institutes unless a law obliges its competitors to take identical measures, and the same holds true for national economies. In the absence of international regulations, the national interest practically compels them to pass the burden of the external costs of their present form of production on to generations still to come. The decision to choose the path of salvation or disaster may ultimately lie in this subtle difference: do the governments and their electorate view this need to stand up for their national competitive interests as their right, or as a tragic dilemma. The answer to this question may decide whether the problems will ultimately be solved by the creation of a stable system of international rules, or by catastrophes.

A person advising a national government has to remain aware of the latitude he has. He will propose decisions which can be implemented within the national (or, for us, the European) framework, but it will also be his duty to urge international agreements.

PERSONAL CONCLUDING COMMENT

My study shows that the dangers of nuclear energy cannot be denied, but that they must be seen within the framework of the dangers connected with every significant further increase in energy production, and of the risks resulting from the insecure situation of our world which is inadequately protected from war and, to some extent, from terrorists. That public fear should focus on nuclear reactors suggests a symbolic, psychological element since the atomic bomb, which uses the same energy, has become the symbol of the still unresolved problem of a future world war. The study shows that the substantive concerns of opponents of nuclear energy can largely be put to rest. But this is most difficult where they are tied to the fear of war. In the rationality of the irrational, they presumably symbolize that fear. In every objective examination of controversial issues, it has become customary to ask mistrustfully whose interests it serves. Anyone who looks at himself critically will certainly observe that both his questions and their answers were guided by interests with which he was either consciously or unconsciously identified. To the extent to which one can recognize them, it is thus presumably an objective procedure to admit to such interests.

I was trained as a nuclear physicist and have felt during the last three decades that the peaceful use of nuclear energy is one of the most important and promising developments.[19] Through the concerns of my colleagues who work on reactor problems, worry over its environmental effects has become dominant in my thinking in recent years. That combined with an earlier anxiety about the role of nuclear reactors, should nuclear mobile warfare occur. I therefore welcomed the opportunity to examine this question once more in some detail. As a result of my investigation of it, my concerns relating to the specific problems of nuclear fission reactors have decreased without having disappeared altogether. But my apprehensions about the unsolved political problems cannot be mitigated along this path. On the contrary! What I see increases them. Subjectively speaking, I must admit that I would not be unhappy if all further growth in energy production in the highly industrialized countries stopped. I believe that our economic system would be strong enough to deal by means of technical developments with the associated rise in energy prices. After a transitional period, economic growth without increased energy production might be possible for a period of time if techniques that substituted for energy were to be developed. I well understand the worry that profound social crises might be triggered by this process, and believe that it will prevent the governments of industrialized countries from furthering such development. But I cannot deny that it is my personal impression that this worry as voiced today does not yet go to the core of the problem. For at this moment, it turns largely on the short- and medium-term employment picture. Over the long run, technical progress will necessarily reduce demand for industrial man power in its present form, unless I am mistaken. The labor market can adjust to such a development by the following measures: a planned transition from energy-using to information-using jobs, a shift from manufacturing to service industries, rational distribution of the leisure time resulting from technical progress, and assistance in shifting economic growth to the Third World where that is necessary. These steps lie in the logic of development and will create economic and social crises, particularly if we resist them. I shall discuss these very complex questions elsewhere. I should like to say explicitly that while I consider a major war quite possible during the coming decades, and therefore feel it would be a realistic policy to include consideration of possible dangers to reactors in such a war, I would not expect it to be triggered by the social problems which might emerge during the transitional phases leading to a policy of energy conservation. I believe that the likelihood of war follows from the very old-fashioned argument that there are global problems which demand a global organizational solution (the environmental problems of energy are an example), but that a stable world order will not readily come about without a trial of strength between the candidates for hegemony. Obviously, every effort must be made to avoid a war whose consequences it is difficult to envisage. But this reflection takes us away from energy policy and into different spheres.

I cannot exclude the technical possibility that a policy of very small growth in energy production might lead from the current oil-based phase to a fusion- or solar-energy-based phase without nuclear fission becoming dominant. And it is possible that such a development would not necessarily entail foregoing essential goods or a long-term jeopardy to social stability. But I must assume that this will remain a politically inconsequential personal view. As an adviser to a government and a public which are determined to embark on a different course, I have no compeling reason to persuade them to deviate from it. I think it is a legitimate task to develop a plan for a circumspect navigation along the path of nuclear energy. The choice between salvation and catastrophe will not be made in the concrete decision about this question. Whatever the decision, it will cause considerable difficuties but no direct threat to the survival of an entire culture, to the best of my knowledge. The real decision is one relating to the intentions which lie behind this and other choices.

Specific Comments

On the Rasmussen Report (p. 14). The central thesis of the report is that even the greatest conceivable accident would not discharge all of the radioactivity from the reactor into the atmosphere but would release only a small fraction of it, and even that only into an area of a few miles around the reactor. If this is correct, any reasonably plausible estimate of the probability of an accident would always lead to the result that danger to human beings from lightwater reactors is significantly smaller than the dangers of automotive traffic, for example.

On the report of the American Physical Society (p. 16). It has been published in the meantime. Its criticism of the Rasmussen report raises a number of questions that deserve investigation, but does not in my opinion lead to significantly different conclusions.

On the spread of nuclear weapons (p. 21). It is my present judgment that I did not sufficiently stress this danger in the lecture. (See chapter 10.)

On the order of dangers (p. 22). That dangers arising from human error are greater than those due to technical failure does not apply to nuclear reactors only. The development of technology imposes a historically unprecedented political responsibility on us. That is the reason the technical chapter is the first in this book.

3. Long-term Economic Prognosis

Like any kind of prognosis, economic prognosis is an eminently difficult art. But there are two motives, a general and a specific one, that have prompted the author of this book who has no training in economics to concern himself with the questions of long-term economic forecasting. This chapter sketches the opinions at which he has arrived. The general motif is the nexus between the economic development of today's world, and its political development, and thus specifically the problem of war prevention. Because of this nexus, the economic chapter was included in this book. But this very general connection may easily remain vague and almost undiscussable. The specific motive was governmental advisory work in the area of research and technology policy from which the preceding chapter also derives. The questions which force themselves on our attention and require more specific formulations will therefore be commented on first.

If for no other than purely national considerations, the research and technology policy of a highly industrialized country which, like Germany, is heavily dependent on exports, must be seen under the motto: paths through danger.

Today, we finance the stability of our national economy through our competitive strength on the world market. Conversely, this competitive strength rests partly on that relative, social stability of our system which insures that we can adhere to delivery dates and maintain product quality. But this immanent self-stabilization would not be possible if our exports and production methods were not among the technically most up-to-date. But since up-to-dateness is by definition something that is forever going out of date, a constant planning effort is required if technological up-to-dateness is to be maintained. This is the national, competitive economic aspect of technology policy. But there is also interdependence between technological and economic development. Not everything that is technologically new is also economically new in the sense that it lies along the path of a promising economic development. Technology policy must therefore also try to forecast economic need. Such forecasts also have both a specific and a general aspect. Specific, because the future of particular products and of sectors of the economy must be determined. The question about the future of certain fundamental structures of our economic system is a general one. Only this general question can be discussed in this chapter.

To facilitate discussion, we will first formulate specific assumptions which are stated as theses. They refer to the problems of the world market[20] insofar as it includes the "First" and the "Third" Worlds, economic growth in these regions and the demand for manpower. In order to define more adequately a complex question, we will restrict ourselves in two ways. The interaction with the socialist state economies of the "Second" World will only be touched upon. And discussion of the possibility of large-scale war will be reserved for later chapters.

The suppositions will be stated in three versions: a neutral characterization of developmental tendencies, an optimistic and a pessimistic version. The hope that our room to maneuver will include a choice between the optimistic and the pessimistic version will be discussed. "Our" actions, however, cannot be the isolated action of the Federal Republic of Germany or even the European Community, but only a relatively homogeneous action on the part of the governments of the highly industrialized, capitalist countries. During a historical phase such as the present, however, where our country finds itself in a relatively strong economic position internationally, the policy of the Federal Republic of Germany could have a triggering effect.

Suppositions

Neutral version.
1. The economy of all countries will continue to be as dependent on the world market as it is at present, and perhaps that dependence will increase.
2. The growth rate of the industrial sector, and perhaps also the growth rate of the per capita GNP will have a significantly lower average value in the economy of the highly industrialized countries than in past decades.
3. In the industrialized countries, technical progress and the growing importance of a world labor market necessitate a reallocation of work and decreasing demand for unskilled labor, and presumably for labor generally.

Optimistic version. It is the basic assumption of the optimistic version that trends indicated in the neutral version are recognized and actively taken advantage of to implement what is in any event a desirable restructuring of all economies that share in the world market.
1. The average growth rate of the world economy remains high, particularly as a result of the necessarily more diversified economic development of the Third World.
2. The decreasing growth rate of industry in the industrialized countries is used to qualitatively restructure their economy. Socially unnecessary, environmentally harmful and globally non-competitive production is halted. In particular, people will learn to husband energy.

3. The high mobility of the labor force is used to redistribute the decreasing demand for labor. The result will be socially balanced reduction in necessary work hours, and the growth of socially meaningful services.

Pessimistic version. The fundamental assumption here is that an attempt will be made to fight trends, and that this attempt fails.

1. The attempt to use tariff barriers, nationalization, etc., to make national and regional economic spheres independent of the world market fails, leads to a weakening of that market, and thus to progressive worldwide poverty.

2. The attempt to maintain lines of production against the tendency of the world market leads to inefficient production and decreasing competitive strength of the sector concerned. Secondarily, it entails an increasing rate of decrease in the growth rate.

3. The tendency to maintain jobs leads to growing structural unemployment through the process described under 2.

Discussion of the Neutral Version

It is obvious that a judgment concerning our alleged room to maneuver between the optimistic and the pessimistic version will largely depend on the question whether the trends set forth in the neutral version do in fact exist. Discussion will therefore turn to them.

THE WORLD MARKET, ESPECIALLY ENERGY

The world market is perceived by industrialized countries under a three-fold aspect: as a world market for products, as a global source of raw materials, and as a world labor market.

The world market for products or, more precisely, global trade as a market for the sale of industrial products, will be a theme throughout this chapter. Particularly in Germany, we are extremely conscious of our current dependence on export sales. The interrelationship between the three aspects of the world market is therefore a matter of public debate, although it is true that a certain narrowing of perspectives is involved here. During times of a worldwide market crisis as was experienced in a pronounced form in 1974–75, for example, a desire for a decreasing dependence on the world market becomes manifest. Efforts are made to stimulate the domestic market on which national economic policy has more of an influence. But this can only amount to quantitative shifts since we remain indissolubly linked to the world raw material market, and thus have to finance the import of raw materials by the export of industrial products. Given today's technological development, our industrial domestic market is also dependent on foreign raw materials. Our national labor market finally is so dependent on our industrial exports that a trend toward decreasing exports must quickly be reversed because unemployment rises. To do this requires the technological progress mentioned in the introduction to this chapter, which means a technical development which will entail a structural increase, not a decrease, in our dependence on the world market. It is a fundamental thesis of this chapter which must be proven step by step that this increasing dependence on the world market is not just a specifically German development but a result of worldwide economic development and the technological progress that is interdependent with it.

We will first consider the world raw material market. Due to the oil crisis of 1973, awareness of their dependence on it had the effect of a shock on the consciousness of all industrialized nations. There are very good reasons why the oil or, more generally, the energy market should be in the forefront of discussion. The oil problem, taken by itself, will continue to exist for a few decades, i.e., until supplies visibly decrease and alternative forms of energy production and—hopefully—energy-saving technologies have been developed. To avoid new mistakes, it is useful to ask in retrospect how the oil problem could arise in the first place.[21] Because the market price for oil was low, the economy of the industrialized countries created for itself a one-sided dependence on this energy source. This made it conomically possible for the oil producers to form a cartel. The cartel then was actually formed under the political solidification which is based on the common conviction of Third World elites that they are being economically exploited by the First. This conviction continues even though the major oil producers are now becoming members of the "Club of the Rich." It thus creates a permanent climate for a readiness to engage in further militant action when that becomes economically possible. If the First World wants to avoid being pushed onto the dangerous path of military force (which, in major cases, would require tacit Soviet acquiescence), it has to count on the continuation of this climate as long as the development set forth under 1 in the optimistic version has not become generally visible. That is the reason this development is now vital for the industrialized countries themselves.

Energy economy is discussed in detail in chapter 2. Here, we will merely give a brief resume of the consequences. Energy-saving technology should be given the highest developmental priority since it is true of any possible energy source that growing energy consumption creates problems that are difficult to solve. All fossil fuels exist in limited quantities, and the environmental damage they do has thus far been underestimated as compared to nuclear energy. In view of the presumed global climatological effect of CO_2 emissions, energy needs growing exponentially and on a scale that has prevailed up to now should not continue to be met by the combustion of coal. In the case of nuclear fission, the dangers caused by technical inadequacies have been overestimated by its opponents. But as long as we have no confidence in our ability to deal with war and guerillas for a period of centuries, this form of energy continues to present dangers that are difficult to gauge. Nuclear fusion is pie in the sky for the time being and will bring with it its own safety problems (radioactivity of the wall material), and encounter limits of applicability (production of electricity). As of now, solar energy is economical at best as a supplemental source, for space heating. It may be that the future lies here, but that hinges on unsolved technical problems. Generally speaking, however, all exponentially rising forms of energy consumption will finally become climatologically prohibitive, if only for thermal reasons.

This resume relates to global energy consumption. Dependence on the world market of primary energy sources can probably not be eliminated by Germany or, more generally, by Western Europe. As regards oil, this is known; the same is true of natural gas. Our coal would last longer but it is not competitive on the world market because the large-scale development of deposits to which access is difficult would become necessary. We also have to buy uranium and even if reactors are quickly constructed, energy from fission cannot become the principal energy source before the year 2000. If fusion comes at all, it will be even later. Solar energy on a large technical scale will come later still, if at all, and make us dependent on energy imports from countries with high levels of irradiation (such as the Sahara). But the economic and foreign policy consequences of the continuing or increasing dependence on the world market here discussed will occur before the year 2000.

The only countries which can at least try for independence from the world market are the three superpowers (two present, one potential): the United States, the Soviet Union, and China. All other supliers of energy depend on industrial imports, all other suppliers of industrial goods on energy imports. Perhaps these three powers are superpowers because of their relative independence. The U.S. is far and away the most powerful economically, yet it is precisely for this reason that it is probably utopian to expect to attain full independence from the world market. The U.S. role is not that of an island of self-sufficiency but of the center of the world-wide capitalist system, a certain tendency toward introversion notwithstanding. In this role,

the United States has incessant political and economic in-
centives to exploit, defend and increase its global power—
and these are the three interconnected functions of any
power (see chapter 7). It is unlikely that they will stop yield-
ing to these inducements which result in interdependence,
not autarchy.

It seems likely, on the other hand, that concerns about a
possible cartel of producers of mineral raw materials which
arose in industrialized countries subsequent to the oil crisis
were exaggerated. The preceding decades during which
prices for raw materials declined slowed down the development and application of new raw material technologies,
beginning with prospecting. The subsequent price rise led
to a world-wide intensification of such techniques. The
present prospect for the coming decade is for a surplus
rather than scarcity of the most important mineral raw materials. And harmony of political interests among producers
of raw materials exists only among a few of them.

DECLINING INDUSTRIAL GROWTH RATE

A shift of growth from the industrial to the service sector
has been observed in all highly industrialized countries. Up
to this time, the Federal Republic of Germany has not substantially participated in this trend and it is therefore not
superfluous to call attention to it. The trend must be seen as
a natural consequence of technological progress. In the historical order of the satisfaction of needs, industrial production of goods precedes modern services, and it is more
easily accomplished through technical progress.

In addition, the expectation of a decreasing, indeed a
vanishing growth rate of the total economy as measured by
per capita GNP, for example, has found many adherents.
Depending on the motives behind it, this expectation can
be attributed to two frequently unconnected views. There is
the opinion a) that growth *should* come to a halt and b) that
growth *will* soon come to a halt.

The view that growth *should* come to a halt has become

popular primarily through the ominous ecological prognos-
tications of the Club of Rome. More profound cultural and
moral arguments in favor of that position have been advanced by Ivan Illich, among others.[22] Among the public,
the fear of the social consequences of an actual zero growth
caused by the 1974–75 crisis deprived this view of much of
its force. The expectation that growth *will* soon come to a
halt was created among some critical observers when they
looked at the "stagflation" of the late sixties. Because of the
profound slump of the last few years, this expectation manifested itself as fear. Signs of a recovery of the world economy in 1976 led to a quickly revived hope that the crisis had
been nothing more than a normal recession which had been
aggravated by the explosion of oil prices. The optimism that
had prevailed during the decades since the end of the war
quickly returned. All of these easily explained changes in
public opinion prove almost nothing concerning the truth
or falsity of the two theses under discussion, however. We
will attempt to test both of them. The thesis a) that growth
should come to a halt will be taken up in the discussion of
the optimistic version, section 2. We will turn first to b), the
stagflation argument.

For the sake of a shorter description of the inflation of the
last one and one-half decades, we shall stress a single causal
nexus among the complex causes of the phenomenon.
Those who make them usually perceive rising demands for
wages as a way toward a more just distribution of consum-
able income. But as regards the economy as a whole, the indisputable high-priced consumption of the well-to-do is not
seriously affected by this since it constitutes a significantly
smaller part of the income of entrepreneurs. In actual fact,
an increase in wages as a proportion of the national income
means a reduction in investments. It might be mentioned
here that the statistically proven rise of the wage quota is
primarily due to the fact that employees make up an increasing proportion of the gainfully employed. But even if
this structural effect is allowed for, the wage quota still

tends to rise, though less steeply. If entrepreneurs either voluntarily or involuntarily accept a decline in investments, the growth rate of the economy declines. It may be assumed that the English workers today are worse off than their German counterparts precisely because, since 1945, they have been more successful in pushing through social redistribution. If, on the other hand, entrepreneurs accept an increase in wages but no reduction in investments, they must raise prices. Should the government countenance the monetary consequences of this development, inflation results, which means that the increase in wages was pointless. If one asks why such a transparent mechanism cannot be arrested, one must look at the bases of political psychology (as in the case of the oil cartel, although the details are quite different). That we live in a class society, though an attenuated one, is obvious to any wage earner. While the average worker does not lean toward revolution, his wage demands will nonetheless appear justified to him. Governments depend on the electorate and on interest groups. Precisely because their dependence is apparent, they even find it difficult to confer public legitimacy on reasonable measures.

In spite of this, inflation could probably be brought to a halt if the economy were purely domestic. An economically strong country with relatively well-functioning social mechanisms for negotiation, like the Federal Republic of Germany, had impressive successes in this area, and it is conceivable that other governments will also master the problem. But the role of the world market during the worldwide inflation of the last few years is obvious. We will not discuss here the initial role of the U.S.A. Allowing for all differences, oil prices have been subject to the same sort of processes as wages during the last few years. Being economically weaker partners, the oil producers had to accept them initially. With the growing importance of oil, the producers became increasingly conscious that this price was too low. They strove for a redistribution of the money oil brought in. A favorable political constellation permitted a drastic increase in prices through cartel formation. The oil consumers now perceived this increased price as too high. They could react to the additional burden on their balance of payments only through inflation, i.e., a factual decrease of the price of oil. But precisely this gave the oil producers a justification for further increases, or at least the refusal to lower their prices. The present relative stabilization of the oil price, in any event, is due to the fact that both consumers and producers are interested in a price level which makes it possible for alternative sources of energy to come on the market over the longer term, and this in turn has something to do with the limited oil supplies.

The inflationary effect of the international oil crisis was more abrupt and violent than that due to domestic labor disputes. Compared with the internal elements of national domestic markets which can be regulated, even today's world market generally shows an "early capitalist wildness." This is not surprising since there exists no regulatory world authority which could assume the role the state plays in the domestic market. On the world market, national states are partners in, rather than regulators of, the competitive struggle. We will encounter this phenomenon repeatedly as we proceed.

What then is the relationship between inflation and stagnation? In the most recent past, the two phenomena occurred together. The term "stagflation" is first of all a demand that theory explain this empirical nexus. As regards the domestic economy, it would seem plausible to look to the labor market for an explanation. An irreversible increase in the level of demand on the part of wage earners leads to a reduction of investments as described above. This cannot wholly be made up for by inflation, particularly when the government succeeds in slowing it down significantly. What we thus have is not just stagnation or inflation as we suggested in a simplified manner above, but their simultaneous occurrence. Successful cartel formation by both employers and wage earners shifts the struggle increasingly into the political arena. What is decisive here is the public legitimation the two partners and, between them, the government, which increasingly has to shoulder the burden of political decision, can obtain. Legitimation problems, however, are ultimately problems of legitimacy, i.e., truth problems. It is impossible to avoid addressing the question as to who is more in the right when there is a dispute about a growth imperative and a distribution imperative, or as to whether the conflict itself derives from an inadequate insight into the public interest, which would mean that objective truth lies with neither of the contending parties. This question may also be seen as central to the following parts of this chapter.

WORLD LABOR MARKET

Today, even optimistic prognosticators dare not prophesy that unemployment will be eliminated in the foreseeable future although they do predict renewed economic growth. A return to the low unemployment figures of the past few decades is promised, if at all, only for that distant future to which people normally assign events in which they do not really believe. This disparity between growth and employment prognoses results initially from a simple extrapolation of present trends. If one asks about the cause of this trend, one should first note that real unemployment is significantly more sizable than statistics indicate. Much of the renewed demand for labor can be satisfied by eliminating shorter work hours and increasing overtime. It can therefore be expected that the recovery of the labor market will be delayed. Beyond that, however, there is a more formidable barrier, for part of the expected economic recovery is based on investments which aim at the rationalization of production, i.e., the saving of labor power. For the entrepreneurs, this goal is the natural consequence of high wages. In short: because of the increased price of this commodity, demand for labor is probably irreversibly lower now than before.

Such simplified verbal accounts of the causes of the development of our economy are customary in public debate but do not do justice to the interdependencies of the system. It cannot be the task of this work, a popularization, that it set forth a quantitative model of the labor market, and everything that is being said here is said with the understanding that it may be modified by such a model. We will, however, stress some rather more political nexuses of our labor market which are usually neglected in economic models. Job security is perhaps the politically most explosive subject of current economic policy. When governments have no adequate understanding of the factors at play here, or when they do but cannot communicate it to the public, there can be catastrophic political consequences.

Guaranteed full employment is almost the principal criterion by which the public judges the correctness of an economic policy. But job security is actually one of the weakest links in the economic and social policy of industrialized countries. A glance at economic history or at the Third World today shows how little it can be taken for granted that this demand can be met. I remember how struck I was in 1945 when I read Beveridge's programmatic book *Full Employment in a Free Society*. We should briefly look at this question from a historical and philosophical perspective. In pre-capitalist societies the right to work was never a universal demand. This idea did not even occur to people because work was not considered a good, but a bitter necessity. There was, however, a moral claim to *maintenance* by the local community. Capitalism progressively destroyed these communities. In exchange, social legislation later formalized a claim to maintenance by the state. That economic crises went hand in hand with fluctuating employment had to be accepted as inevitable. It required Keynes' optimism that such crises could be permanently overcome to produce Beveridge's idea of guaranteed employment. In post-war Europe, there was actually an exceptional need for labor because an economy whose fundamental structures were unscathed spent a decade rebuilding what had been destroyed, and an additional decade catching up with America. During this entire time, the rate of unemployment in Europe was lower than in the U.S. The Beveridge model has never really been put to the test. The present stagflation crisis is not one of the classical cyclical crises to which Keynes' theory applies. The guarantee that large-scale unemployment can be avoided is no better than the guarantee that this crisis can be dealt with. For this reason, we have to isolate the consideration of the labor market from the national economic framework that was appropriate in earlier times. What we must study is the world labor market.

During the past few decades, the world labor market evidenced itself in certain Northern European countries (including West Germany) by the importation of an army of foreign laborers from the Mediterranean countries. This development has peaked and actually reversed itself during the last few years. Not only the two previously mentioned factors—the catching up that was necessitated by the war, and the decline in demand for labor due to rationalization—are responsible for this. A third, important factor is that on a worldwide scale, labor-intensive production is being shifted to countries where labor is cheap. Technically, this has been made possible by inexpensive production and transport methods. That people prefer this technical possibility to the utilization of foreign labor in their own country has its reason in labor law: it is not possible to pay foreign workers the low rates that obtain in their country of origin. One can offer them inferior housing and inferior work but one cannot pay them less than one's own workers. Whenever production is labor-intensive and can be done elsewhere, rising wages in industrialized countries are driving production into the Third World. Up to now, this has not been a quantitatively significant phenomenon. Current production by German firms abroad amounts to about 7% of domestic production, and a third of this may occur in underdeveloped nations. But even this contributes more than

1% to the present unemployment rate of 5%. It is also possible that production abroad will grow. Disregarding failures that always occur, we can say that those enterprises which can produce abroad have a competitive advantage. Because they can survive a crisis more easily, their contribution to the total economy of the industrialized country, and therefore production abroad as a proportion of total production, may increase.

If the world labor market could be described as a single open market, as free of politically, geographically and historically conditioned restrictions, an even greater shift of production to countries with low wage scales could be expected than is seen today. All realistically conceivable shifts of production will not begin to exhaust the potential labor supply in the Third World. It is estimated that there are as many able-bodied adults in cities of over one million inhabitants in the Third World as there are industrial workers in all of the highly industrialized countries of the West. They are partly unemployed and partly employed at wage scales which average about one sixth of the wage rates of the industrialized countries. This average represents a mean between still much lower and significantly higher wages. Qualified industrial workers in the Third World are often themselves a kind of worker aristocracy. Although detailed prognoses are difficult in so complex a situation, the causes for the trend of a progressive shift of production to the Third World are apparent and massive. Whether this will actually happen depends on reactions to this trend in both the First and the Third Worlds.

These reactions are closely tied to social policy. We will try to define its scope in the optimistic and the pessimistic version. In countries such as West Germany, job security is the area where the social struggle against the tendency set forth in the neutral version will most surely be kindled. The pessimistic version predicates that this struggle cannot be won. Should that be true, it is all the more important that an optimistic version of the prognosis exist.

Discussion of the Optimistic Version

If one merely asks what development would be rational, it is almost a priori obvious that there must be an optimistic version of the trends envisaged here. We shall soon advance reasons for the view that it is only technological progress and the consequent rise in prosperity that make these trends possible. We will be led on to the pessimistic version by another question which concerns the identity of the economic, social and political representatives of such a development. It therefore seems expedient to now separate these two questions and to first inquire into the rational goals of this development.

THE WORLD MARKET

Whatever theory of underdevelopment one may subscribe to, it cannot be denied that even after the end of the colonial system, economic dependence of the Third World on the First has been pervasive. The Third World was primarily a supplier of raw materials for the economies of the capitalist industrialized countries. Technical progress in both the extraction and transport of raw materials, and the increasing share of fabrication and processing in the cost of the manufactured product also caused a lowering of raw material prices that extended over a number of decades. The terms of trade of Third World countries in the world market had an inherent tendency to deteriorate. Growing skepticism in industrialized countries toward development aid—because it was alleged that this only cured symptoms—was correct at certain points but obscured the fact that our own economic behavior toward the underdeveloped countries was a cause of the incurability of the disease. While impoverishment increased in some cases, there also occurred technological progress, however, and the economy and political self-consciousness in the underdeveloped countries improved. The optimistic version assumes that this progress may, though slowly, remedy underdevelopment.

The argument concerning the trend rests primarily on the market mechanism. During the last few years, the position of the producers of raw materials has reversed itself; it has become stronger. The causes for this lie in an at least temporary scarcity of raw materials and the political will to form cartels. The scarcity of raw materials is not due to a decrease of supplies because they were exploited, but to an increase in demand resulting from the economic growth of the industrialized countries, which means they are ultimately due to technical progress. And it is also the technical progress in transport and manufacturing which makes possible the creation of a world labor market. But precisely to the extent that technical progress furthers it, the continued development of the raw material and labor market will not end the economic dominance of the technically more progressive countries.

The optimistic version does state, however, that according to old liberal theory, the market will ultimately promote the economic well-being of all that participate in it worldwide, and that any attempt to inhibit its effects would be counterproductive. But this does not mean that the world market requires no regulation of the sort that has been in place for some time in the domestic markets of liberal countries. And here the question of control mechanisms arises. Not only theoretically, but also as regards their political implementation, this is an enormously difficult problem.

We shall first consider the concerns with which both sides view the consequences of the development of the world market. In the industrialized countries, small entrepreneurs and workers in certain sectors suffer from the consequences of foreign production. In the textile industry, for example, we see the formation of lobbies that include entrepreneurs and unions and aim at import restrictions. Conversely, public opinion in the underdeveloped countries is largely correct in its perception that real power over the production of raw materials and of modern industry on their soil lies in the hands of the multinational corporations of the First World and the governments protecting them. It complains about the transfer of profits into the centers of the capitalist system. Tendencies toward nationalization are the natural upshot of this kind of perception of the world market. These defensive mechanisms which are the mirror image of each other and are directed against what is today a spreading world market are themselves ambivalent. We must distinguish their negative from their positive aspects. The former will be discussed in the pessimistic version. They are the strangulation of the contributions the world market can make to growth. The positive aspects in the industrialized countries will be taken up in the section, "Limits to Growth". What is of primary importance here are the positive aspects in the Third World.

A comparison with the development of the labor market in the capitalist domestic economies of the nineteenth century may be useful here. The large supply of labor power (the "industrial reserve army," as Marx called it) led to the exploitation of the workers because such was the law of the market, and that exploitation made Marx's immiserization prognosis appear plausible at that time. It was the *creation of a political will* on the part of the workers which gave them a negotiating position which finally achieved for them more humane conditions of work and a quasi-petit-bourgeois well-being. It then became apparent that higher wages were not damaging but beneficial to the growth of the economy because they represented increased purchasing power. This causal analysis of the complex historical process which gives the greatest weight to the creation of a political will on the part of the workers could of course be answered by the equally plausible counter argument. It would present the creation of purchasing power as the result of an increasing productivity in industry and the possibility of an economically effective political will as the result of this new purchasing power. The former perspective is in line with the way the workers' movement perceives itself, the latter with the perception of the entrepreneurs. An objective theory of social processes must always demand of itself that it make comprehensible the perception of a process by the various parties participating in it, and thereby justify it in terms of each. It is in an analogous fashion that we should view the political cartel formation in the Third World for purposes of changed terms of trade: presumably, and over the long term, it will tend to expand the world market on whose future we depend as well. With respect to the world labor market: if the world market flourishes at all, it may be assumed that over the long term, job security in the industrialized countries will also hinge on a significant rise in wages in the Third World.

But the formula "terms of trade" does not exhaustively define the conditions of a healthy growth of the world economy. The somewhat superficial and misleading title "limits to growth" has again made us aware of the negative aspects of industrial society, and the peoples of the Third World have every reason to resist our exporting all of these liabilities to them. The transfer of high-technology industries does indeed create growth, but also significant social inequalities. *Intermediate* technologies which are especially suited to regions where labor power is cheap would be socially important today. It is often said that the nations should learn to increase their demand for them and to let a profitable market develop in this fashion. But in the actual market of the Third World, many such attempts have already failed. A criticism which makes things too easy for itself believes that the reason for this lies in the preference for large-scale prestige projects, but this is not the case. Rather, it is a typical market phenomenon. Large, capital-intensive centralized technology benefits from economies of scale which a deliberately labor-intensive, decentralized production does not enjoy. The political system in China finds it much easier to implement intermediate technologies than social idealists could in the capitalist market.

One of the most significant problems of the Third World, particularly in Southeast Asia, is *population growth*. Experience so far suggests that the large number of children will stop only when they are no longer considered necessary for the economic security of the parents. Only two models for this exist: adequate general well-being, or the Chinese method of replacing the family as the economic unit by the commune. But it will hardly be possible to introduce the Chinese way of doing things to the Indian subcontinent, for example, without causing considerable political convulsion. Perhaps such convulsions have become unavoidable. Otherwise, the only chance remaining to an optimism of constant development will be the effort to permanently raise and keep the growth rate of the national product in these countries high above the growth rate of the population. Such an effort is in the vital interest of the world.

•

LIMITS TO GROWTH

At least as a psychological cause, the level of technical progress can also be detected in back of the stagflation crisis. As long as production techniques are known but capital and consumer goods are scarce, the argument that more growth is required is convincing, even in tariff negotiations. Once prosperity has been attained, the problem the economy poses is perceived as a problem in distribution. The growth imperative loses its urgency, and is no longer carried through for that reason.

The optimistic version tells us that this is the path of reason, that growth in industrial society is in fact no longer the most important goal, that what really counts is not to undergo its limitation as stagnation, but to make it serve plans for a *better quality of life*. This thesis, like many advanced here, is popular, but that does not prove it correct. It requires discussion. The thesis becomes more pointed when it is understood as a criticism of the present and a warning about the future. Concerning the present, it tells us that the "affluent society" does not create true prosperity, or what is meant by the real quality of life, but mistakenly includes meaningless consumption and destructive forms of production as part of its prosperity. This claim can be articulated more clearly. Radical cultural criticism must be distinguished from the immanent critique of an attained quality of life, and criteria must be used which an industrial society that believes in prosperity would acknowledge. It is my belief that fundamental cultural criticism is an indispensable phase along the road to a balanced judgment about contemporary problems. But this book has the inverse structure. We predicate that its readers know, and have responsibilities for, concrete problems in our world, and spare them an introductory passage through fundamental criticism of this sort. Only the final chapter will open up a perspective on its indispensability. By then, the reader will be oriented about those problems of our world which remain unresolved when their discussion is merely immanent. At this point, we therefore confine ourselves to the immanent criticism of our present quality of life.

Such a critique must pick up the already somewhat obsolete discussion concerning the meaning the GNP has as a measurement. Economic science did not introduce the GNP as a measure of prosperity but as a measure of demand. To use it as a measure of prosperity makes sense only under conditions of scarcity where demand corresponds to unquestionable needs, and then only in an adequately insulatable domestic market. In the affluent society, its use as a measure of prosperity primarily serves purposes of political psychology which requires simple success criteria. A detailed quantitative analysis based on a multiplicity of social indicators and a judgment of the overall economy based on its result should be demanded so that this simplification can be corrected. The optimistic consequence of this for the market economy would be that dissemination of the find-ings in popularized form would reorient demand.[23]

The importance of an analysis which does not criticize growth but rather its simplistic measurement is also neces-sary to answer the question whether the capitalist market economy can be stabilized at all at "zero growth." The kind of stabilization that has occurred so far during periodic crises or recessions always had one variable parameter, which was precisely the growth rate at any given moment. It frequently happens in self-regulating systems that stabili-zation occurs via a relatively short-term variable parameter. A moving bicycle, for example, achieves stabilization through small shifts in the angle of the front wheel. Neither when it stands still, nor when the handlebar is fixed, is it stable. Of course, the stability of a complex system is dif-ficult to see through mathematically, and for the moment we only have the simple *argumentum ex eventu:* up to now, the capitalist system has been stable with growth. Its stabil-ity without it is yet to be tested.

A warning as regards the future was made a matter of public awareness by the Club of Rome.[24] Economists reacted with justified criticism to a number of simplifica-tions made by Forrester and Meadows. Particularly the claim that a scarcity of raw materials was impending was disputed. Prospecting, substitution and recycling will sig-nificantly delay the advent of scarcity. The market reacts to scarcity by price increases, and the resulting adjustment in demand. Another justified criticism concerned the use of measurements which did not even bring out the fundamen-tal difference between highly industrialized and economi-cally underdeveloped regions. The new report by Pestel and Mesarovic[25] takes account of all of this criticism by dividing the world into ten regions, and by making flexible assump-tions concerning all factors that have economic effects. It may thus be admitted as a possible model of a nuanced approach which now will have to be subjected to further critical evaluation. The results of such evaluation can only be hypothetically anticipated here in rough outline.

Of course, a prognosis based on flexible assumptions seems less dramatic than the relatively rigid models of Forrester. But the central thesis of the Club of Rome shows a surprising resistance to variations in assumptions, and this not only in the hands of its already convinced adherents. Time and again, it becomes apparent that if relevant measures are applied to the economy, the coming century will not see the exponential growth of the last two hundred years. Depending on the measurement and the region, the temporal barrier will be attained either sooner or later, but it is never many decades away. So far, we have seen this in the sketch of the energy problem (p. 40), and the threat posed by population growth in Southeast Asia (p. 54). While on a global scale they are still some time into the future, the climatological effects of energy consumption will soon become a threat in areas of concentration, such as the Federal Republic of Germany, for example. To demand detailed studies concerning environmental degradation and its avoidance is not original nowadays, although it may not yet be superfluous. But overall integrated studies of economic development under these new limitations are much more difficult, though indispensable. Prophets of doom find the courage for such encompassing investigations more quickly than others. Usually, they provoke a kind of criticism which is even less discriminating than their own prognosis, if that is possible. A study of economic and technological development under the conditions of the limits to growth, but in an "optimistic version," would be more essential than anything else, a study, in other words, which would encourage discriminative action.

ADAPTATION OF THE LABOR MARKET

We shall concentrate here on the adaptation of the labor market in industrialized countries to the changed demand for labor. This adaptation must contain three components: transition to a more qualified labor force, transition from manufacturing to services, reduction in the hours of work. In the third assumption of the neutral version, it was maintained that the reduction in the demand for labor in industrialized countries would apply primarily to unskilled labor. This is a plausible but not a self-evident result of technological progress. The mass unemployment expected by the critics of early capitalism did not occur. What has happened is that the average level of competence of the worker rose over the decades, and growing productivity created a demand for products that were previously either too expensive, or unknown. Today, the mobility of the world labor market also primarily affects the less skilled labor force. This applies not only to the foreign workers in northern Europe during the last two and one-half decades, but also to the shift of production to the Third World. But in both cases, the utilized labor force became and becomes progressively more qualified in many cases. Over the short term, shifting production abroad unquestionably means that demand for work within the domestic economy declines. If we apply classical market theory to the world market, however, purchasing power in the Third World would have to rise, and that would create demand for products manufactured in the First, and therefore also act as a stimulus to the labor market there. According to market theory, both sides would thus profit if production is shifted to areas where labor is cheaper. Of course, in a free market, this would also mean that wages for equal work would move toward equality in the various countries. But there are strong political forces which prevent or significantly slow down this process of adjustment. They lie primarily in the differing political power of the workers in the First and the Third Worlds. The unions in the industrialized countries can largely prevent a downward adjustment of wages. But precisely as a result of the numerically enormous supply and the multitude of countries, the labor market in the Third World is a buyer's market. For the time being, the highly mobile modern industry of the First World can shift its production into ever new regions of low wages. In the industrialized countries, this phenomenon must lead to sustained pressure on the demand for labor in those sectors which can be moved abroad. The laws of the market are remorseless: "the market does not forgive."

The optimistic version demands that we view all of these processes not as misfortunes but as opportunities. If it is the legitimate desire of the industrial workers in our countries not to work for the low wages paid in other countries where such work can also be done, the rational effect in the world market is that they will not do that work in the future. To deal with this contingency, there is the possibility of moving into other kinds of work which either cannot be done abroad or are not being done there today. This could be work in other sectors of the industry and will demand higher qualifications in many cases, i.e., there will be a transition to more qualified personnel. It may also be work in the service industries which by their very nature are tied to the society where the services are being rendered.

It is to be expected that all of these structural changes will not eliminate the long-term trend toward the *reduction of work hours*. This trend is part of those effects whose causes can be perceived in a twofold way. It became a reality because the political will of the workers made it one, but it was technical progress that made it possible. That the reduction of necessary labor time results from technical progress becomes self-evident when demand does not increase. But over the centuries, the labor time saved because of technical progress has always, and to a very large extent, been utilized in the production of new goods. The fact that a progressive reduction in labor time occurred nonetheless is connected with the decreasing marginal utility of creating new needs. Society will do more work to fight obvious distress than it will to satisfy new needs. Today, however, a new socio-psychological motif arises: the reduction of necessary labor time also has decreasing marginal utility. The creation of needs was one of the principal engines of economic growth. In industrial society, it went hand in hand with sustaining the need to achieve which replaced the feudal status symbol of idleness by the bourgeois status symbol of performance. The mobility of the labor force which necessarily resulted from the constant structural change of the growing economy creates a greater capacity for response and adaptation but it deprives men of the security of paternalistic conditions. The loss of one's job now becomes a real social threat. The combination of these motifs brings it about that industrial society does not want to face its ineluctable fate, the decreasing demand for labor.

The optimistic version must be based on the restoration of the old consciousness of values, according to which liberation from the compulsion to work is a blessing. This creates a psychological and an organizational problem. The psychological problem is the more profound one. It manifests itself first in the question of how the great cultural value and the experience of happiness and identity based on the *need to achieve* can be preserved in the new phase. This is one of the unsolved problems in the psychology of culture that modern society faces. If our society cannot deal with it, it will create trouble. But it would be burying one's head in the sand, were one to escape these problems by the creation of economically unsustainable, superfluous work. To the degree that public consciousness addresses the fact of decreasing hours of work, it will be possible to solve the organizational problem. In analogy to the distribution problem of consumer goods, it might be called the distribution problem of labor time. The debate concerning the correct form the reduction of work time should take to achieve a reduction of unemployment has been initiated. Whether it would be best to reduce the work week, increase holidays or pension workers at a younger age is already being discussed today. All these considerations lead to the specifically "postindustrial" problem of what to do with leisure time.

This problem transcends the economic context of this chapter and will be touched upon once more in chapter 11. But one further analytical comment will be made here. With technical progress, the concept of work changed its meaning. But the conscious change in the meaning of this concept has not yet caught up with the real change. Philosophically, material production is the production of form, for the quantity of material is not increased. The large growth of the service sector relates almost exclusively to the processing of information.[26] But the production of information can also be seen as the production of form under certain concepts, philosophically speaking.[27] Meaningful human life which includes leisure time that allows for the continuing experience of meaning ("real happiness') is also a conscious forming of life. Precisely on high cultural levels, in the lives of artists and scientists but also in the case of pedagogues, pastors and politicians, the distinction between work and leisure hardly exists. Here, work is experienced meaning. That it should be necessary to cut back industrial production means that such work is "alienated." Alienation in the profound sense in which Hegel used this term, however, also contains the productivity of the negative, like all of Hegel's concepts. To understand our problem, we shall have to look at the work character of information processing, the meaning of work, and also the evolutionary meaning of alienation. This is a philosophical task. In practice, we certainly will not escape the redistribution of labor time.

WHO ARE THE AGENTS OF THIS DEVELOPMENT?

All reflections in this "optimistic version" contain an appeal to that form of reason that perceives the shared overall interest of global society. In the common sense of the "man on the street," there is always present some part of this reason, albeit without precise knowledge of causal connections, and usually without a strong motivation to act. But all organized agents within the nexus of global society are representatives of special interests. That is the reason some of the problems of the future which are perfectly capable of rational solution appear almost hopeless in practice. Those agents of today's economic development which can bring (an always limited) measure of influence to bear on its course fall into three categories: entrepreneurs, employee unions, and governmental agencies.

Today, the smaller entrepreneurs are actually engaged in a defensive battle. While I assume that many of the smaller firms are going bankrupt or are losing their independence, as so often in the crisis-filled history of free enterprise, it is also true that the type of entrepreneur and the size of the enterprise they represent will continue to occupy an economic niche which will partly be filled by new establishments. The somewhat complicated idea from the theory of competition that leads to this assumption can be expressed in a biological metaphor: it is true that the big fish are constantly devouring the small, but this does not mean that the number of small fish need necessarily decrease.

But those that are economically most successful and seen as most representative by the public are the "multinationals." If the world market is our economic destiny today, they will have to be called the only economic agents in today's world whose organizational form answers the demands of modernity, and that is the *ability to act across borders*. Here, an old strength of the capitalist system reveals itself anew: at any given moment, private enterprise can usually develop modern organizational forms more quickly than anyone else. The affective resistance such success always arouses does not invalidate the fact that these firms are today the most efficient representatives of economic growth in the Third World. It is also true, however, that the strengths of capitalism are here, as always, tied to its negative effects (which are referred to as its "contradictions" in

Marxist terminology, a language which is difficult for a logician to assimilate). The survival of firms in the competitive struggle requires that the interest of the firm be given the first priority in all decisions. The unequal growth and frequently increasing misery of that part of the population that is not needed for this growth, and the economic dependence of entire nations on foreign decision-making centers, are the unavoidable consequences of this kind of development.

The hope that the market itself would compensate for these negative consequences as development proceeds is at best a partial truth. The complicated process which is the target of the frequently raised reproach that profits are transferred from the country in which they were earned to the home country of the firm may serve as an example. In our country, we are not particularly sensitive to this criticism when Third World members raise it against our firms, but very sensitive when American firms (or, more recently, oil producers) gain a foothold in our own economy. Actually, a certain transferable profit is the natural basis of any international business contract. There would be no world market without such possibility. If the prognoses attempted here are correct, there is the long-term prospect that such profits would increasingly be reinvested in the Third World. But this does not mean that the population, and to some extent the government of the country where the profit is made escape their role as the dependent partners in such contracts. Anyone who does not believe this should recall the hysterical public reaction to private investments by foreigners in West Germany.

The historical parallel to the development of the domestic economies of early capitalism which we have mentioned previously teaches us that the unbearability of the capitalist system was mitigated or removed as a) tariff partners, i.e., workers, became capable of political action and b) to the extent that the governmental framework made possible the implementation of social and later also of regulative mechanisms. But in today's world market, neither the workers nor the states are efficiently organized on an international scale. The problems of the world labor market have already been discussed. The short-term perceived interest of unionized labor in the industrialized nations conflicts with the interests of the underemployed labor force in the Third World. A truly open world labor market would make possible a certain rise in average wages in the Third World over the long term. Today, this only happens in more or less isolated instances in certain Third World countries. Our workers should not only perceive this development politically, i.e., in the sense of the solidarity of the working class, but also as the only way of preventing a further long-term decline in their own rate of employment. But it is extremely unlikely that they will disregard their own, very real, short-term interest unless they are thoroughly enlightened about these complex interconnections. An effective international solidarity of workers' organizations can therefore not be expected for the time being.

Even in fundamentally liberal countries, governments are assuming an increasing share in production and enact social regulations. In this sense, all of them today draw certain consequences from the experiences of capitalist development over the past two centuries. But many problems can only be attacked through international cooperation. Where natural interest groups are involved (as in the case of the oil producers, for example), cooperative action does occasionally occur. But generally speaking, one may wonder whether the absence of however loosely unified a governmental framework for the entire world market can be compensated for by any kind of international agreements.

The problems of the state economies of the major socialist powers which have otherwise been ignored in this chapter will be touched upon here. Contrary to Marx's prognosis, it is only in underdeveloped countries that radical socialism came to power through internal action. In these countries, it took over the role which fell to capitalism in the economically more highly developed Western European countries: to transform a "feudal" social and economic structure into a modern one. This complicated starting point makes a structural comparison of the two economic systems conceptually difficult. Economically, the "First" World is largely independent of the "Second" at this time. What justification socialist states have when they blame their unsolved economic problems on being islands in a capitalist sea is an open question. There is no easily recognizable sense in which the tensions between the West and the Soviet Union derive from their economic relations or contrasts nor, more specifically, from the opposition of their social systems. What is fundamental here is the unavoidable foreign policy conflict of two imperialisms (chapter 6). The coming decades could entail an increasing participation of socialist state economies in the world market. From the point of view of the First World, there is an obvious economic interest in such a development. The opening up of large markets is very attractive; in addition, a shift of production to socialist countries has the appeal for the capitalist that the negotiating partner there is not an independently organized labor force but a politically firmly established bureaucracy. It is attractive to shift production to countries where strikes are no threat. But for socialist state economies, participation in the world market is ambivalent. A socialist economy has never yet succeeded in developing to a level where it could compete with its natural capitalist trade partners, as for example Russia with Western Europe, or China with Japan. That these state economies might attain the same degree of economic power as the entire capitalist system seems wholly out of the question for the foreseeable future, even when one looks at those prognoses which are most optimistic for socialism, and most pessimistic for capitalism, provided no political change modifies existing power relationships. In this situation, economic self-sufficiency is the presupposition of the political independence of the socialist system. The Marxists in power there see more clearly than

Western liberals that political rule is dependent on the economic system. China strictly adheres to this insight. For the Soviet Union, which today is still stronger economically than China, and probably already under greater pressure to satisfy the consumer demands of its population, economic participation is a greater temptation. It is in the interest of Western capitalism to further such participation, for in the direct contact of the two economic systems, the material and structural preponderance of the West would presumably come into play. But all of this is predominantly a political question to which the following chapters make more of a contribution than the chapter on economics.

Discussion of the Pessimistic Version

The pessimistic version is based on the expectation that the only people that can act, the representatives of special interests, will be unable to make the overall interest of world society prevail over that of their own clients, even where those in leading positions see this overall interest with some clarity. Such has been the normal condition of world history up to this time. The sequence of crises and catastrophes progress has had to overcome is the result of this normal state. At an earlier date the whole whose overall interest was still a reality comprised less than all of mankind. It is therefore still difficult today to conceive the present worldwide interdependence of interests, and to turn it into an effective motive for action. But it is also true that the extent of this interdependence deepens the dependence of all its members on the weal of the whole, and that it makes a malfunction in it more dangerous. There are thus reasons for supposing that future catastrophes will be greater for all participants than past ones, unless timely prevention becomes possible.

WEAKENING OF THE WORLD MARKET

Several of the previously listed agents of today's development have an understandable special interest in forms of action which contradict the categorical imperative, i.e., a stake in procedures which would be harmful to the interests of all participants, were they to become general. The harm here referred to is the weakening of the world market.

There is no question that the growth of the world market is in the interest of the multinationals. In this limited sense, the overall economic interest of mankind presently coincides with the special interests of these firms (optimists such as Hegel and Marx would therefore have to count these firms among the present-day agents of historical progress). As described above, however, the expanding world market is harmful to the interests of smaller enterprises and of a large number of workers in the First World, and large parts of the population in the Third. Import restrictions in the First World and nationalization in the Third are the natural defensive reactions.

Of course, the weaker countries are vitally interested in participation in the world market. This is not a self-evident thesis. The *dependencia* theory which originated in Latin America sees the origin of underdevelopment precisely in dependence on the capitalist world market. It points out that certain domestic industrial developments which served as import substitutes flourished in Latin America between 1930 and 1950, precisely the period when political crises in the Northern world temporarily weakened its world market position. We do not deny the causal nexus between dependence and unequal development but doubt that isolation from the world market could be a long-term remedy for underdevelopment. The significant examples of independent economic development in Japan, Soviet Russia and present-day China Probably do not prove this. In the first place—and this argument is in line with the *dependencia* theory— such developments presuppose the political independence which was the pre-modern historical legacy of these three old imperial countries and which they managed to preserve. They did not need revolution to become independent but needed independence to become revolutionary. In the second place, the kind of success aimed for and attained would have to be examined in all three cases. Japan integrated capitalism into a feudal social structure. Today, it bears up under the world market because it has been adapting to its capitalist structure for one hundred years. As regards Russia, it is empirically difficult to refute the thesis that its economic growth since 1917 corresponds on the average to the extrapolation of pre-1917 development, and would thus not have been fundamentally different, had the country participated in the world market and been politically independent. Besides, Russia is mutatis mutandis like Japan in that it integrated a modern economic structure, a socialist planned economy, into a traditional administrative structure of an absolutist-bureaucratic type. The Chinese development is the most difficult for an outsider to judge. On the one hand, it seems to combine traditional hard work and efficiency with a relativization of prosperity goals whose attainment seems a matter of course under capitalism and to many of its socialist critics. It is understandable that this system can see itself as a model for the world. But within the time frame of our prognosis, it appears unlikely that it can be transferred to the Third World. Its implementation stands and falls with the autarchy to which Maoist China has assigned first priority, and with good reason. If such autarchy can be created at all, it would only be in economic regions of the size of the Indian subcontinent or all of Latin America, and it may be assumed that the already existing degree of participation of these regions in the world market precludes the subsequent creation of autarchy. In any event, the majority of present Third World governments are interested in relative independence, but independence within the worldwide system of trade. We may therefore assume that the weaker countries will continue to view their participation in the world market as being in their own interest.

It seems likely that import restrictions in the economically stronger countries are more harmful to the world market than nationalization in the economically weaker ones. According to classical economic theory also, the market should not be dominated by oligopolies. Small states with nationalized enterprises are to be viewed as individual partners of the world market, as it were, and they contribute to the desired multiplicity of suppliers, though experience shows that state enterprises function less rationally than private ones. A symbiosis of multinational private firms, national private firms and national state firms can be imagined as favorable for the market economy.

This symbiosis rests on a politically narrow base, however. A pessimist could easily sketch the following vicious circle: the inequality between that part of the population that profits from the world market, and the part which suffers, leads to a revolutionary potential in the Third World such as we see it today. The representatives of the revolutionary movement come, in most cases, from those parts of the population that benefit from the world market. They are intellectuals, perhaps also members of the industrial proletariat working for the world market. But the system dominating the world market will guarantee that local revolutions will fail economically, and thus ultimately politically as well. There are heads of large firms today that say that direct investment in the Third World is unprofitable because political conditions are unstable. And certainly these firms recognizably prefer politically safe areas. But those are the countries where revolutions can be suppressed with some measure of dependability, which means they are primarily military dictatorships. Such dictatorships are in the objective economic interest of international capitalism, and precisely for that reason, connections with capitalism are in the objective political interest of military dictatorships. This objective interest is sufficiently strong to prevail politically, and it is irrelevant in this connection whether certain firms

cooperate in certain coups d'etat or not (though it does interest those who make it their business to look for this sort
of thing). But it is also true that military dictatorships generally cannot deal with the growing modern consciousness
of their subjects, and therefore often cannot deal with objective problems either. Then, long-term political stability
does not set in, and a foundation for undisturbed economic
growth is lacking.

Particularly during the initial phases, the precarious economic growth in the Third World needs a market in the
First. This market is only guaranteed for scarce raw materials. At least while industrialization in economically underdeveloped countries starts up, the world labor market can
exist only if the goods produced in the Third World (either
by multinationals or nationally) can be sold in the First. But
these goods compete with those produced in the latter. Precisely during a stagnation crisis, there is considerable temptation to eliminate this competition by import restrictions
in order to insure job security. The assumption is that such
a step will deepen and make unavoidable a long-term stagnation or shrinkage of the world market. How long the intent of the superpowers to avoid war could be sustained in
face of such political unrest is uncertain. At this point, the
pessimistic version of the economic prognosis connects
with the problem of the *danger of war*, which was not considered here.

SHRINKAGE OF THE DOMESTIC ECONOMIES
OF INDUSTRIALIZED NATIONS

Up to this point, our reflections advanced reasons for the
plausible thesis that measures to insure job security and
stimulate investments must take account of the world market to succeed. Political lobbies which want more usually
only take the world market seriously as it relates to trade
within the First World. If the Third World reminds the rest
of the world of its existence, as in the case of the oil cartel,
the reaction is anger, not to say indignation. Whatever

one's personal view of such an attitude may be, one might have to put up with it as a political adviser, were it not self-destructive. This will be explained by using the example of protecting labor-intensive forms of production when the wages paid are higher than those prevailing on the world market. There may be strong and other than narrowly economic reasons to maintain a form of production that is no longer profitable in global competition. The agricultural support policy of industrialized states is an example. The motive for governments is not simply that farmers constitute a voting bloc. In addition to what is now the anachronistic argument that a healthy society needs them, there are other reasons which modern consciousness can understand, such as the maintenance of a measure of autarchy in food production during times of crisis and, more recently, the ecological benefits provided by farming. Such reasons make it necessary to strike a balance between the cost and the usefulness of support payments.

With the exception of the argument concerning votes, such reasons become significantly less persuasive as regards industrial production when it is no longer competitive vis-à-vis countries with low wages. Traditional arguments for protective tariffs can be relevant during the start-up phase of new industries, but hardly for the retention of outdated ones. Judgments will have to be made on a case by case basis. The real danger is that it is politically so easy to resist competition from economically weaker countries. With a strong partner that does not need protection, such as the U.S., there will be considerably greater reluctance to engage in a trade war than with a weak one which needs to have its production protected. What must be stressed here is that the argument that one does not need weak trade partners is not only cynical but presumably economically incorrect. It is certainly true that we can produce all goods if we pay the wages customary in industrialized nations and deny the cheaper products from the Third World access to our markets, but only if we could altogether dispense with trade with the Third World. A single indispensable raw material, like oil at this time, changes the situation. We are obliged now to take the economic and political viability of our trade partners into account. The attempt to exclude them from our markets (and to exclude the financially strong ones from our capital markets) would presumably have catastrophic consequences on both sides of the tariff barrier.

As formulated here, the argument is insufficiently nuanced, if only because it refers to the "Third World" as if it were a unit. A more refined analysis should be undertaken by experts. But it is also possible that the argument will be too readily applauded by some because the Federal Republic of Germany is so dependent on exports.

Even without a more detailed analysis, however, I would not hesitate to say that the attempt to stimulate the economy would fail if it were limited to the domestic economy of the industrialized part of the world. If powerful political interests push it through because it is in their short-term interest, the result may well be a crisis which will cause a shrinkage of this same domestic economy. It is not clear whether such a crisis would be temporary.

STRUCTURAL UNEMPLOYMENT

It is a trivial truth that such a development would jeopardize the very jobs it seeks to protect. Of course, we have learned from the study of economics that a certain measure of structural unemployment represents an incentive for industry to modernize, and that means to invest. The pessimistic version would maintain that especially a markedly conservative policy of job security would be destructive in the present worldwide economic system and thus produce the evil it attempts to avoid.

Consequences

The reflections set forth in this chapter are still too general to allow the consequences to be presented as specific recommendations for economic policy. Generally speaking, we would advise an economic policy which attempts to create the preconditions of the optimistic version of our prognoses, which means that it would accept the developmental trends set forth and avail itself of the opportunities inherent in them. The basic presupposition is made that it is desirable to maintain the capitalist world system, which means that it must also be protected against immanent dangers. Such a presupposition is not self-evident. A great part of the intellectual youth, and to a much greater extent in the Third World than here, places its hopes for a better future on the elimination of this system. For this very reason, this book may well be viewed as an error of today's older generation a few decades hence. I shall therefore discuss the only current promising alternative, revolutionary socialism, in the next two chapters. My conclusions will be that the viability of this alternative as elaborated in our time is problematical in the Third World, and that it is no alternative in the First. At most, it is conceivable though not certain that the Third World might develop better with it than in today's capitalist world system. Today's power relationships make it appear unlikely that the influence of the capitalist world system in the Third World could be terminated except through a major war (see chapters 6 and 9). It is my view that the introduction of this system in the First World would represent a serious regression, not only morally, because the radical restriction of the freedom of speech is part of it, but also functionally. As regards the latter, the conviction rests on a view which is admittedly difficult to prove, and holds that our highly complex economic and social system which developed during a liberal period of history cannot remain functional without freedom of thought and speech. I will advance no reasons here for this view but shall make some comments in the eleventh chapter.

But this does not prove that our system can survive if such freedom is preserved. The optimistic version attempts to set forth the economic conditions necessary for survival. In conclusion, they are being restated here as theses:

1. The world market must grow, not shrink.

a / It makes no sense for the industrialized countries to strive for autarchy, nor should they do so. Import restrictions, particularly vis-à-vis Third World countries, are counterproductive over the long term.

b / Multinational firms are one of the elements that bring modernization.

c / The economic independence of Third World nations is also in the long-term economic interest of the First World.

d / International governmental regulations and organizations are vital if the world market is to function. They are a weak substitute for, and at best the precursors of, a world organization that can enforce its decisions but does not exist today.

2. Economic growth is no end in itself but a means that must be judged discriminatively.

a / In the industrialized countries, a smaller growth rate in the GNP must be accepted. The resulting qualitative restructuring of the economy must be seen as desirable, and should be promoted.

b / The growth rate in the Third World can and must remain large. Social justice in its distribution is not only a moral demand. Over the longer term, it serves growth itself, and it serves stability and thus growth indirectly.

3. A reallocation of labor time should be pushed forward.

a / Current wage scales in a number of sectors are incompatible with job security in the industrialized countries. A transition to other, more highly skilled forms of production, to services, and reduction in total work hours are desirable.

b / It is in the long-term interest of workers all over the world that rates of employment and wage scales in the Third World rise.

4. The Hope of
Revolutionary Socialism

The immanent criticism of the capitalist world system which seeks to stabilize it is confronted by a wholly different critique of the same system, and that is the critique of radical socialism. It considers a stabilizing reform of capitalism as neither desirable nor possible in the long run. For it, the path through danger looks entirely different from what it does for liberal or social democratic economic policy makers. In the worldwide economic crisis, socialism sees the chance to overcome a system that is meant to perish. It sees the danger in the desperate actions the system will take to save itself, and which will take the economic form of increasing exploitation, the political form of fascism and, in the extreme case, war against the precursors of the new, socialist world. For them, the path through danger lies in revolutionary action, wars of national liberation, and in the development toward socialism in those countries where revolutionary socialists have attained power. We would not be taking the search for paths through danger seriously if we failed to duly consider the alternative these forms of thought and action represent. I will criticize this alternative and not subscribe to it. But this stand is backed by years of effort to think through the internal logic of this mode of thought. My criticism of it tries to remain "dialectical," i.e., it does not criticize its weaknesses and imperfections but attacks its strong points. It tries to show, in other words, that it is the very correctness of certain fundamental ideas of radical socialism which enables one to recognize that the difficulties it incurs are essential to its very nature and not merely passing failures.

Of course, this is not a book about social systems but primarily one about economic, foreign policy and military questions. For a thorough criticism of both capitalism and socialism, a more penetrating and more widely based analysis would be required (see *Fragen zur Weltpolitik*, pp. 38–39). For this reason, this chapter will confine itself to the thread of a single theoretical train of thought, the question whether the hope of revolutionary socialism—that domination can be overcome—is credible according to Marx's own insights. The following chapter (5) offers what may be called an aphoristic case study, impressions from what I take to be by far the most interesting, radical socialist country today, China. In the seventh and eleventh chapters, the theoretical question is pushed somewhat further.

It is one of the strengths of Marxism that it does not give a detailed picture of the future, and that includes the final goal, and the path toward it. It can therefore employ flexible tactics. And it is also consistent theoretically. According to the dialectical schema, the future has to crystallize from the contradictions of the present. The result of this labor cannot be anticipated by present thought.

But it is equally true that Marxism derives much of its persuasiveness from an anticipation of the future, however vague. It sketches a picture of the final goal, the elimination of the rule of men over men, more specifically a classless society and the withering of the state. It also sketches a picture of the road toward that goal, the proletarian revolution and the dictatorship of the proletariat that emerges from it. Bourgeois adversaries of Marxism frequently envy it for its clear design for the future. Although in a manner that is not always apparent to them, even non-orthodox Marxist socialists often show that their thinking is governed by these ideas. It could easily be shown, I believe, that their analyses of the problem of present-day capitalism, for example, are based on the same facts but draw conclusions that differ from those of a non-Marxist analysis because the criterion underlying theirs is that real events must be measured against the socialist hope.

An examination of socialist hopes is therefore also important for a judgment of the present time. We confine ourselves here to a critique of the path, i.e., the concepts of proletarian revolution and of the dictatorship of the proletariat. But this critique will be preceded by a short comment on the unsolved task of a clearer definition of the final goal.

The concept of domination denotes a complex phenomenon where at least three components can be distinguished. They might be referred to as order of rank, function, and power; but these terms are themselves in need of explanation (see chapter 7). I am not aware of any anthropological, historical or systematic and theoretical reason why this structure of behavior should have to continue for all time to come. The long-term hope for overcoming the domination over men makes sense to me. But I shall omit here a more detailed discussion of an idea which requires careful qualification (chapter 11). Today, in any event, this hope lies in a distant, wholly veiled future.

But the hope that a proletarian revolution will overcome the phenomenon of domination seems demonstrably false to me. I admit that there are situations where a socialist revolution may be a necessary and indeed a desirable event, and may serve the interests of men. But I maintain that it contributes nothing to overcoming domination since it forces the revolutionaries themselves to create an equally stable domination. This is precisely what distinguishes it from bourgeois revolution, for while the latter has not overcome domination, it has contributed to its dismantlement. It can be seen that this assertion directly contradicts Marx's hope.

Marx adopts and transforms an Hegelian idea about world history. He assumes that there exists in every historical phase a class whose special interest is sufficiently close to the overall interests of society to become the agent of historical progress during that particular phase. A revolution occurs when one class supplants another in this historical role. Revolution could be a bloodless replacement. But in reality, it will almost invariably be violent because the ruling class does not voluntarily surrender its rule. In his description of modern times, Marx operates conceptually with three classes: the feudal nobility, the capitalist bourgeoisie, and the industrial proletariat. He does, of course, make distinctions within the classes and recognizes the peasants as a class unto themselves. But it is precisely these three that he makes the agents of historical dynamics. This results in the model of two successive revolutions: the bourgeois and the proletarian.

I maintain that this model derives from wishful thinking with understandable motives, but that it will not hold up under a more careful scrutiny of its concepts, for the coincidence of the specific and the class interest has a wholly different meaning for the bourgeoisie and the proletariat.

The victory of the bourgeoisie over the nobility was the victory of an urban over an agrarian culture. Since the Middle Ages, the cities had been in the hands of the burghers and not in those of the landed nobility. The burghers always were in control of the material and intellectual means of their own culture, and when that culture had acquired economic preponderance over agriculture, they finally also took over political power. Since the Middle Ages, the bourgeoisie has never been a functional servant of the nobility.

The industrial proletariat, on the other hand, has always been the most dependent estate. It was a product of the bourgeois economy, a slave army of capitalism, as Marx correctly pointed out. It had no control over the machines it operated, for as technicalization progressed, its intellectual command over them decreased more and more. Its material control, on the other hand, remains purely negative: it could strike. In contrast to the bourgeoisie, its class interest was not the attainment of real, integrated power, but liberation from misery and dependence. What the proletariat has been able to achieve is precisely in line with this: its integration into bourgeois society in the petit-bourgeois role. So far, a successful proletarian revolution against the bourgeoisie has never occurred in an industrialized country. Nor has there ever existed a dictatorship of the industrial proletariat. Our earlier reflections make it appear unlikely that the two will ever become a reality. At the beginning of industrialization, the industrial proletariat is too weak for revolution, and in the later phases, it lacks adequate revolutionary motivation.

The socialist revolutions that did occur are something altogether different. In Marxist terminology, they are antifeudal revolutions which took place before there was a bourgeoisie capable of a bourgeois revolution. They are ways toward the modernization of economically backward countries. If it were permissible to look for parallels in periods of western European history, they would functionally correspond to mercantilist absolutism seizing power from the feudal nobility. They are sustained by intellectual cadres (descendants of the old nobility and of the bourgeoisie which is numerically too weak) who are supported by the revolutionary potential of peasants. The natural result of these revolutions is a centralized bureaucracy. The Russian revolution capitulated to the inner logic of this development. With a heroic effort probably sustained to a considerable extent by Mao himself, the Chinese revolution tries to escape this fate. It seems that today, the only conceivable counter-model to the historical necessity I predicate here is the Chinese way. What follows refers to that model, but I shall first discuss non-Chinese experience.

While the parallel between today's socialist states and bureaucratic absolutism results from an objective structural necessity, it is not in keeping with the intentions of the revolutionaries, who see bureaucracy as a degeneration of socialism. Not only Mao, but names such as Tito, Dubceck, Nyerere, Allende and even Castro refer to attempts to better realize socialism today. The programmatic development of the Italian and French communist parties at least takes account of the loathing of Soviet absolutism that prevails in western countries. Today's socialists are contemporaries of a liberal bourgeois society with representative democracy and an egalitarian ideology. Modern rationality and the good and bitter experiences with the market economy and the capitalist form of production, none of which existed under the European absolutism of the seventeenth and eighteenth centuries, have left their mark on them. Besides, local cultures vary considerably. It is possible that in a nation which for millennia has been as industrious and spontaneously orderly as the Chinese, experiments in decentralization are feasible which in Russia would be doomed to failure.

But I maintain that this abundance of corollary phenomena does not invalidate the structural necessity which pushes socialist but not bourgeois revolutions not to dismantle but to take over and to stabilize domination, indeed to increase it. Socialists who observe the phenomena pointing in this direction often excuse them by saying that genuine socialism can only be implemented after the capitalist world system has been overcome. Before that, socialism in one country is not really possible; all that can be hoped for is rule by men with socialist beliefs. For the capitalist world system compels all national economies involved in world trade to adapt to the competitive forms of capitalism, at least in the sense that the state is the entrepreneur, which would mean state capitalism. Even a country that can sustain autarchy is subject to the constraints of the capitalist system since it is obliged to maintain adequate military strength and internal political control, and the accompanying structure of domination if it is to protect itself.

I believe there is some truth in this thesis but that its formulation is distorted by hopes. Today more than ever before, capitalism is indeed a worldwide system which imposes certain structural characteristics even on societies that ideologically and power-politically are adverse to it. In line with what has been said, one may formulate the impossibility of radical socialism in our world as follows: there does not exist a social formation which has enough economic power to take over political rule from the classes that have been integrated into the capitalist system, as the bourgeoisie once took it from the nobility or the king. Socialist revolution can therefore only come about through internal action, through tightly organized minorities, cadres, or from the outside, i.e., by the military victory of a socialist over a non-socialist power. It is pure wishful thinking to believe that the force which brings about such a revolution would later automatically have the majority of the population on its side. Even where it need no longer fear counter-revolution, it must fear new coups d'etat, for its basis of legitimation is that of a minority that has attained power through violence. In addition, there is a psychological argument: quite independently of what may be their ideological commitment to freedom, professional revolutionaries that have been schooled for years to think in terms of power are little suited to divest themselves of it, once they are victorious. And their successors are the bureaucrats trained in their service.

The only power which might take political control away from capitalism in the foreseeable future is thus the military of the major socialist states, the Soviet Union and, over the longer term, China. Objectively, the expectation of a worldwide socialist revolution is thus presumably tantamount to the expectation of a world war. And such war is likely, quite apart from the opposition between the social systems (see chapter 6). Prognoses that go beyond it hardly seem possible. Yet we should ask what development is likely, should it be possible to prevent war.

It may be assumed that modernization of the economy and the mentality will continue in the socialist states. This would probably mean an increase in the size and the self-confidence of that segment whose role in production would be functionally similar to that of the bourgeoisie in the European eighteenth and nineteenth centuries. It may be assumed that this segment will develop a desire for freedom that will be similar to that of the bourgeoisie at an earlier time. Liberalization would thus be the long-term destiny of socialist states, and in that sense it would be an approximation to a dismantling of domination. But, as Marx pointed out, the actual seizure of power by the western European bourgeoisie had its economic basis in the legal institution of the private ownership of the means of production. At least in the Soviet power sphere, the absence of this legal institution of private property is the chief support of the existing "absolutism," which means that it is the principal impediment to political progress. An intelligent interpretation of Marx would have shown that the elimination of such private property is an obstacle to progress, at least in a pre-bourgeois society.

When governmental service no longer suited him, a feudal statesman would "retire to his estates." In the ideal case, a bourgeois politician could live on his interest, and the present-day American politician or high-ranking civil servant frequently comes from the private economy and returns to it when he so wishes. When an academician enters public service as an administrator or member of Congress, his position is usually kept open. In Anglo-Saxon countries, this may be at a private university, for example, and it is to this "retreat" that he owes his independence. But the total dependence of every member of the political leadership stratum on the benevolence of the men at the top of that same stratum restricts the room to maneuver, the chance to

gain acceptance for diverging views and interests, more se-
verely than was true of barons and bourgeois under the
absolutism of the eighteenth century. In bureaucratic socialism, there is thus no class whose economic situation would
predestine its members to become agents of a movement
toward individual freedom. At best, they may act in concert
to implement collective interests.

Marx's theoretical construct, the succession of feudalism-
capitalism-socialism, has a clear meaning precisely when
one looks at the creation and safeguarding of political freedom. In this schema, it is the role of the capitalist bourgeoisie to push through, secure and teach those freedoms which
will benefit the masses, once the socialist phase has been
reached. Revisionist Social Democracy thinks and acts precisely as this logic dictates. The idea of a dictatorship of the
proletariat derives from a wholly different, revolutionary set
of arguments. I feel that Marxism could combine these ideas
only "dialectically," which means by admitting a contradiction within the doctrine. So far, history has not "sub-
lated" this contradiction but always realized only one side
and precluded the other. In developed capitalism, we have
social evolution without revolution and therefore no supersession of the fundamental capitalist structure. Socialist revolution, on the other hand, has so far been successful only
in those countries where the real experience of bourgeois,
constitutionally guaranteed freedom was unknown, and it
did not contribute to the creation but only to the obstruction of this freedom. If one tries to carefully detach the crust
of wishful thinking from Marx's analyses, that is pretty
much the historical result one would have had to expect
from them. The Maoist hope of replacing the bourgeois
profit motive by the spontaneity of the masses, and of having it secure an economic structure that would sustain freedom seems heroic to me, as I said before. But pending a
better understanding of it, its chances of success do not
strike me as significant. Doesn't an excess of idealism here

ignore the significance of the motive for economic activity as both Adam Smith and Karl Marx understood it?

This criticism of the utopian hope of revolutionary socialism does not mean that at least for the modernization of economically underdeveloped countries and those with a pre-capitalist social structure, socialism may not be the most radical path and have far-reaching consequences as a model and a power system for this reason. Where it can base itself on an adequate measure of autarchy, it offers the chance of avoiding certain aberrations and dangers of a dependent capitalism. The morality to which it makes its appeal, however, is one which divides social groups into good and evil people, i.e., polarization. As far as one can see, polarization contributes to an increase rather than to a reduction of the danger of war which already exists without it. In part at least, this is due to the unabashed arbitrariness with which the large socialist powers concretely implement the division into good and evil people, and frequently do so in exactly opposite ways.

Neither present-day socialism nor capitalism are tending toward the withering of the state. The pessimistic prognoses for both international relations and the world economy would be considerably less well founded if global interdependence could be given an organizational framework similar to that of the state. It may therefore be assumed that crises will either continue to be destructive, or that the creation of such a framework will be hastened. For the span we can project, the real problem of freedom will therefore be freedom within the state, not freedom without it. This will probably continue to be the case as long as the world economy is dynamic.

5. Reflections on China

After a Four-Day Visit (October 29 to November 2, 1975)

> The son of Heaven received the chief of the western barbarians and talked to him about the German philosophers Kant, Clausewitz and Häckel. The chancellor of the Federal Republic was impressed how the Chairman concentrated on essentials.

China is a developing country. Vice Premier Teng Hsiao-ping said so in his welcoming address. Some Germans who had come along were uncertain at first whether this was a way of disguising the claim to great power status, or modest self-knowledge. But it was meant honestly, as the simple truth which it is no loss of face for a Marxist to speak. According to statements by its present rulers, China had been a half-feudal, half-colonial country which was exploited partly by its own feudal class, partly by foreign capitalists. Chairman Mao Tse-tung said that today it is helping itself, proudly confident of its own power.*

Conditions in and achievements of present-day China should not be compared with those of the Soviet Union, let alone with those of the western industrialized nations, but with those of other developing countries. Seen from that perspective, much in its economic and social development seems exemplary. But in part, such achievements are perhaps only realizable because of the autarchy enjoyed by a tightly governed giant empire that can isolate itself from all

---

*This chapter was written before Mao Tse-tung died.

undesirable contact with the outside world. As regards details, I can only restate what I heard from experts. My reflections will be introduced by a few direct impressions.

During arrival and departure at the airport, thousands (in Peking perhaps 5000) paper-flower-waving children standing in formation. Some of them were doing dance figures. They were almost exclusively girls, with colored ribbons in their hair, divided into companies each of which was dressed in cheerful clothing with the color varying from one unit to the next. Many of them wore a uniform, bright makeup, and were rhythmically calling out the welcoming slogan. We always walked slowly along the entire front, the inside of a rectangle open on one side. In Nanking there was a very acrobatic, popular lions' dance in the center. Who can resist the impression of a thousand children's eyes? Especially the smaller ones were obviously having fun and we exchanged many smiles. We did not see them line up or disperse.

In Peking, there are large, straight streets cut through the labyrinths of old, twisting alleys. Those of us who had known the old Peking were profoundly depressed by the Stalinization of the city. I had no such memories, and felt spontaneously and invariably more at ease than in Moscow. In Nanking, whose charm has not been destroyed, the old China hands in our delegation revived. Urumchi, the capital of Sinkiang (Eastern Turkistan) has been almost entirely rebuilt during the last twenty-five years and consists of quickly constructed, regularly placed one-story brick and mud buildings where we could not imagine living. There are small mosques among the rows of houses, we saw Turkish Uighurs who move with more dignity than the Chinese who enjoy laughing, a large museum with splendid educational exhibits of products of local origin, and a well-stocked department store. But to buy one of the bicycles there requires putting money aside for a long time. Altogether, one has the impression of the decent frugality of a developing country.

Along the outer lanes of Peking's main streets, I saw as many cyclists as in Holland and Denmark during my youth. Along the inner lanes, tolerable automotive traffic. Our government vehicles did not have to respect any traffic signals. In Nanking we crossed the Yangtse bridge which was shown us with pride. It connects north and south, and while we were on it, we saw a train on the lower and a freeway on the upper level, but not a single car except for our convoy. In Peking, I also took walks through small streets. The people seem relaxed, adequately fed, with all clothing in identical style (although functionaries have more carefully tailored suits of finer cloth which are quite smart and trim). All women wear pants, there is no hesitation about exchanging glances, and a good deal of laughter or unstylized smiling (very different from Japanese politeness). General impression: they do what is necessary and what they are asked, but do not overwork. The diligence of the Chinese living abroad is not in evidence here. And this is not surprising, for the Chinese abroad work for themselves, those here for official ideals. Everything that related to the organization of our trip functioned with breath-taking punctuality.

Near Peking, we visited the people's commune "Red Star," an agricultural production unit which comprises some ten thousand people. It is certainly a model commune but equally certainly no Potemkin village. Anyone who has seen developing countries can appreciate the happy mean of these clean, precise institutions, far above misery but intentionally not luxurious or fancy. Experts generally told me that the small family is intact, that large families no longer exist and that kinship ties seem to have become inconsequential. The commune is the framework of life in the country. It seems that the problem of population growth is being mastered here, and that the two-child family is the rule although the prosperity needed for such development elsewhere is far from having been attained. Not wealth but security seems the precondition for renouncing the large number of children.

I visited the deputy chairman of the revolutionary committee of Tsing-Hua University (technical university) in Peking. He described the changes the Cultural Revolution had brought to the university. Before, students studied up to six years, and the longer they studied, the more they lost themselves in specialties without practical value. Now, they study for three years, with time off for work in agriculture and industry. From the very beginning, they thus learn the practical meaning of their work.

Here, reflection sets in. Other members of the delegation visited another university with humanities and German language instruction, and were horrified by the primitiveness of what was learned. "This used to be a real university. Now it is an elementary school." I also asked myself, and the dean, how much students could learn in about two years, the time that remains when the services they perform are taken into account. In the library, we saw the collected works of Gauss and Weierstrass which had been acquired at an earlier time and which probably none of the students now at the university can read. I was shown electronic instruments which the students had helped build. It is my impression that the technological equipment works, but it did not become clear to me what kind of research it is being used for. I thus had certain reservations, but the introductory remarks of the dean that study had been inadequately related to practice before, and that it was necessary that it be both practical and broad-based is something almost every university in any developing country I have seen outside of China might well take note of. When one considers that China has many decades to develop, one might well argue that Mao's program means first things first. Inequalities of income over a range of three to one are comparable to those among salary and wage earners in highly developed capitalist countries and thus significantly smaller than in other developing countries. During an early phase of economic growth, the consistent socialism here enforces a degree of equalization which it took the union movement to achieve in advanced capitalism. To provide a healthy diet for the masses is more important than quick progress in sophisticated technologies. It seems that the Chinese had sufficient psychological strength to do without prestige projects. In the West, the present state of industry was reached via many intermediate steps where pools of trained craftsmen and schooled technicians always existed. The destruction of the elite universities in favor of the elementary schooling of the masses could be a phase that will benefit long-term growth.

Of course, the visitor cannot even guess at the suffering of the intellectual elite that for decades has been forced into total silence, i.e., lying, if it wished to survive. Mao wants to create the new man. This will require decades or centuries and thirty cultural revolutions. The new man is the person who spontaneously puts the well-being of society, the whole, ahead of his own interest. There is no sharp distinction here between egoism and the decision of one's own conscience, and this is deliberate. The party is always right and prevails even over the well-meant individual action of revolutionary fighters. What is the new man? Is he Chinese, Marxist, modern in a global sense?

I have the impression that Mao fights Confucius because he is so much like him. The motivation of both is intensely moral. Because it transforms it into a moral institution, Confucianism can accept domination. Respect is rendered heaven, the emperor, the father, the husband and the older brother. Confucius looked for a prince who would put straight moral concepts. Had he found him, he would have led him to hegemony. "It's all over. I have never yet seen one who loves moral values as much as the beauty of women." For three years, Confucius was minister to the king of one of the states into which ancient China had been broken up, and that state flourished. A neighboring prince sent the king female dancers. For three days, the king stayed away from government business, and Confucius took his leave. Mao does not teach kings but the masses. It is inconceivable that he should not be an irreversible turning point in Chinese history, for the masses are being imbued with his teaching, they are becoming literate, and are forced to think. Many things suggest that after the death of this remorseless taskmaster, they will relapse into a more comfortable life. All experts say that the Chinese can keep up a pretense for decades. But the sloppiness that will set in then will not be the same as the old.

Is this Marxism? Whatever he may have said about them, the three philosophers Mao discussed with our chancellor represent a significant choice. My constant Chinese companion from the Foreign Office said: "Kant was an idealist philosopher, wasn't he?" But the necessity of world history, its dialectic, is material. Häckel's *Welträtsel* was read all over the world when Mao was young. The book is monistic, optimistic, proclaims a biological theory of evolution and combats religious myths. The ever-present personal god of the Christians is a contradictory anthropomorphism, from Häckel's point of view, a "gaseous vertebrae." An essential difference between Mao's version of Marxism and European and Russian Marxism seems to be an intensely Chinese dynamization of concepts. Europeans create classes and members, deduce sentences from sentences, and then apply them practically. Hegel's dialectic, of course, turns against this "abstract" thought. But European Marxists have such an inveterate belief in logic that their attempts to think dialectically usually remind one of a frog attempting to fly. According to M. Granet, every Chinese word is dynamic, a demand, every Chinese sentence contains an imperative or a polite optative. Abstract theory does not really exist in this language. The highest concepts, such as Tao, Yang and Ying, heaven and earth, music and custom, are not the most abstract but the most powerful. This is presumably a highly nuanced version of the original nature of human language compared to which the European separation of concept and thing, fact and value, is and ought, theory and practice, represents a new level of abstraction. One must read Mao as a Chinese to understand his elementary application of Marxism. Western Maoists should also consider this: their form of a theorizing individualism that escapes into action would not be put up with for twenty-four hours in Mao's China.

Like Kant, Clausewitz also is a figure that illuminates significant contrasts, though not because of the usually misinterpreted sentence about war as the continuation of diplomacy by other means, which was meant to establish the primacy of politics over the military, as all communist parties also demand it. But Clausewitz formulated the theory of Napoleonic strategy, the decision enforced in open battle. This is a tactic Napoleon could afford because his armies were made up of draftees. But the armies of the preceding feudal and absolutist era were too expensive and had to be used sparingly. *"Seul un chef maladroit livre bataille."* [28]

Mao could not field a superior army but wear down the enemy through guerillas if he also gained the political sympathy of the peasant masses. His strategic writings are very intelligent, relate very precisely to the actual situation, and are understandable for any junior commander. An expert told me that Mao's originality in world Marxism lay even more in his dynamization of the military by pervasive politicalization than in his substitution of the peasants for the industrial proletariat. The army functions because the smallest units can act independently. The appropriate comparison is not to a machine but to locusts.

Banners with the inscription "We support the European peoples in their fight against hegemony" were strung across the streets of Peking. In theory, it is the Americans and the Russians that are today's hegemonists, but what is really meant is the Russians. Skeptical interpreters immediately perceive the foxiness of such slogans. According to them, the criticism of the two leading competitors as hegemonists is the best camouflage for one's own claim to hegemony. And Soviet pragmatism is the natural ally of pragmatic communists in China as well, and therefore the most dangerous enemy of Mao's domestic political program. But such reflections are only seen in proper perspective if one grasps the relative banality of what is correct in them. No successful politician, and certainly not Mao, can ignore the relation of causes and effects in the power struggle. But the attempt to believe what people say, i.e., to see it with their eyes, always seems more instructive to me. For decades to come, the developing country that is China will not be a contender for world hegemony. The structure of the power system compels states to accumulate power to insure survival, and this is the same compulsion which Marx described for the capitalist competition among private entrepreneurs. All historical parallels indicate that this accumulation will some day lead to war. It is in China's vital interest not to participate in this race. For a long time to come, its atomic weapons are meant to be defensive, deterrent, like those of France. Mao's moralism fits in with this assessment of China's interests. The coincidence of the universal and the particular interest (here: an end to the worldwide race for hegemony, and China's exclusion from that race) defines, according to Hegel and Marx, the role of the current agent of world-historical development. The Soviet Union betrayed this role which now falls to China.

The betrayal of the Soviet Union is a profound Chinese trauma, and probably especially a trauma for Mao. Why did the Russians try to keep down the Chinese in decisive steps of their development? The fear of a future Chinese preponderance is one of three Russian nightmares, perhaps the greatest. Fear almost always prompts irrational action. Unless it is prepared for the most horrible eventuality, the extinction of the Chinese people, Russia would probably not be able to permanently subjugate China. A Maoist-schooled China cannot be governed from the outside, and destroyed atomic weapon centers can be rebuilt. Russia embittered China without depriving it of its power. After this visit, I am less inclined than before to believe that a Russo-Chinese war is likely in the foreseeable future. It is my feeling that China is important for us. It seems to me that in today's world, it represents almost the only major attempt to solve problems in a way that substantially differs from ours. That this attempt is inapplicable to our circumstances does not lessen its objective interest.

After a Second Visit (March 1976)

Four months after the first trip, I went back. We were shown industrial works and scientific institutes, in other words, something of China's modern sector. We were not shown the most advanced things everywhere. Occasionally, one could infer that more modern steel works, large computers, more advanced reactors existed in the country. It seems plausible that all these have something to do with military developments. Even so, the trip was instructive enough. As regards the technical and scientific apparatus we saw, the various experts in our delegation estimated that they were somewhere between five and twelve years behind the level achieved by the most highly developed countries. When one considers that all of this is being produced here without foreign aid, and that scientific institutes normally build their own equipment, this is a remarkable achievement. As was pointed out to us time and again, bitter experiences lie in back of the "confidence in one's own strength": the trauma of the American embargo after Mao's seizure of power ("after the liberation") and the more profound trauma of the total Russian withdrawal in 1960 ("when the Soviet Union tore up agreements that had already been signed").

How will technical development proceed? Will China be able to close the gap? Where development now lags by ten years, will it be by five or fifteen in ten years, zero or twenty in twenty years? As regards industry, I dare not make a judgment. In the natural sciences, the chance of further closing the gap would seem to depend on certain political conditions. There is unquestionably a pool of good, indeed of great talent. A glance at the intelligent faces of the scientists in the institutes, or into the alert ones of the people one sees as one strolls through the streets of Shanghai would almost validate such a judgment. The role physicists of Chinese origin, such as Lee and Yang, play in the United States is a more persuasive argument. But the non-Chinese world develops very rapidly these days, especially in technology. Basing oneself on the interpretation of Mao's line, one could imagine that China would view this competition as a temptation, that it would, in other words, not measure its progress by the technical progress of the rest of the world but by the equilibrium of its own internal structure, the raising of the consciousness of the masses. But this may well be a somewhat abstract perspective. In actuality, it would seem that people take seriously the proclaimed goal of making China a completely modern industrial nation by the year 2000. One may have secret doubts about its attainability, but not its desirability. If one accepts the goal, it would seem to me that in the scientific domain, there would be two political conditions which this system might not find it altogether easy to meet: tolerance for the modest elite consciousness of scientists who feel the need not to be judged by external success criteria and wish to be left alone, and the furtherance of unrestricted international contacts. The second condition is this: for a productive scientist, there is no substitute for the chance to exchange views with and be criticized and stimulated by his best colleagues anywhere in the world, at any time, and for as long as he may wish. The excellent assortment of periodicals in some of the academic institutes we visited hardly makes up for such a lack of unrestricted contact. No Chinese scientist told me this, but I am convinced that the laws of optimal scientific productivity do not become inoperative in China.

To inform oneself politically, it is useful to visit a number of plants in succession. On the wall of the reception rooms, one either sees the four European beards of Marx, Engels, Lenin and Stalin and, facing them and twice as large, the one Mao. Or, if the portraits of the classics hang elsewhere, there are huge landscapes with mountains and a rising sun, or an azalea branch blooming under the snow. The welcoming speech, never less than fifteen minutes long, contains optional elements but an obligatory core: everything that happens here happens in the way we learned it from Chairman Mao Tse-tung. Because of the great Cultural Revolution, production rose significantly, and the subsequent campaign—the criticisms of Confucius and Lin Piao—had the same effect. Scientists did not fail to mention that before, they did all their theoretical work at home, behind the closed doors of their institutes, but that they now go into the factories and out into the countryside to pursue some of their research there where they learn from the masses and get ideas which otherwise would not have occurred to them (in the excellent biochemical institute of the Academia Sinica in Shanghai, for example, research into the early hormonal diagnosis of liver cancer among the population at large). The principle of Three in One is carried out in all plants: the masses, i.e., the workers in the factory, the leading political cadres, and the technical experts all collaborate closely. In their work, the class struggle is the principal element and technical progress and economic stability come next. The consciousness of the masses is trained in this way and insights that derive from practice everywhere lead to improvements at work. Just now, we are gathering all our strength to fight off the wind from the Right which is aiming at a revision of previously made decisions. Once that problem is overcome, there will undoubtedly be another significant increase in production. Comrade X will now explain the organization and work methods in our plant.

The reader of this account can only get some idea of the impression this litany makes if he reads that part of the preceding paragraph which reports the speech at least five, or, better still, ten times to himself. The degree of permissible variation extends at most to the rearrangement of two sentences. Down to the last detail of their formulation, the experiences of all plants in the entire People's Republic of China are clearly identical. The perplexed Western listener naturally wonders disrespectfully what reality stands in back of this ritual, and he tries to politely ask his Chinese host. We also questioned many male and female workers. Their answers were always unaffected and obviously precise. Conversational style is candid and relaxed. Laughter is valued. After the inspection, the management always invited a detailed discussion of their operation.

I shall try to summarize the picture that crystallized after many such hours of questions. It may be assumed that all the structures of authority and privilege peculiar to an old culture were still quite marked before the Cultural Revolution. In the sciences, theory had priority over practice; in the plants authority lay with management, privileges with the technicians, and obedience was for the workers. Workers now participate in decision-making committees (such as the "revolutionary committees" for example) through elected representatives. After extended discussion of suitable candidates, the number of men nominated is the same as is later elected and confirmed by higher, governmental authority. West German workers would not be willing to accept that small a measure of participation in decision-making, we thought to ourselves. We do not credit the claim that the Cultural Revolution and other campaigns resulted in increased production. Judging by everything we heard, the very opposite is the case. The visitor who is willing to take seriously the Cultural Revolution propaganda because it was necessary or at least made sense to change the social structure, to develop the consciousness of the masses, to raise overall levels, to link theory and practice, encounters the kind of difficulty that always arises when one has to deal with implausible arguments that may serve a good cause. But that is a point where he comes up against the internal disputes between the two "lines," and he cannot maneuver his partners into the impossible situation where they have to admit their adherence to what has been officially condemned. Once, in a plant of many tens of thousands of workers, we asked the chairman of the revolutionary committee: "Do you have any followers of the Wind from the Right here in your plant?" "No," he answered with a beaming face. "Not a single one?" "No." "And in the city?" "None." The visitor hears the really fundamental arguments only in polemical reflection, the considerable openness about all details notwithstanding. He must develop an ear for nuances.

A second visit four months after the first gives considerable insight into the political mechanism. The first time, we were received by Teng Hsiao-ping as the representative of the sick Chou En-lai, and all China experts believed he would be the successor. Though never referred to by name, it is perfectly obvious that he is the exponent of the "Wind from the Right," which wishes "to revise judgments that have already been made." He does not appear in public, and no one knows whether he still performs his official duties (including that of chief of staff of the army). What is involved here is the profound opposition between a doctrinally socialist line committed to the class struggle, and functional stabilization. From the very beginning, the history of the Peoples' Republic has shown a periodic fluctuation between functional stabilization and socialist mobilization which alternate over an eight-year span.[29] Mao personally is almost always clearly associated with the revolutionary side, and this applies even more markedly to his wife, Chiang Ching. Prior to the Cultural Revolution, Liu Shao-chi and Teng Hsiao-ping, who were subsequently removed from office, were the representatives of functional stabilization. The return to power of the latter is traced to the quiet and intelligent efforts of Chou En-lai. Chou's death was the decisive event of these four months.

The writer of this book naturally shares Western prejudices and has a spontaneous sympathy for functional stabilization. Precisely for that reason, it is a lesson in self-education to present the arguments for Mao's line in a way that makes them accessible to Western thinking, which means that they must first be taken seriously. In the Soviet Union, functional stabilization, i.e., the stabilization of bureaucratic rule, has prevailed. The freedom-loving Westerner finds this apparatus of domination repellent and lifeless. But the arguments against such rule do not merely derive from liberal emotions; they are themselves functional. A stabilized machinery of domination finds it easy to implement its insights but all the more difficult to learn something new. Undisputed rule makes the rulers stupid. "Victory makes stupid," Nietzsche said after 1870. The search for truth needs the atmosphere of free discussion. Isn't Mao correct to cite Soviet conditions as a deterrent example? "Stalin took the Soviet Union along the path of hegemonic ambition, he armed it with nuclear weapons," he told our chancellor Helmut Schmidt. Asked whether he cannot back away from this development, Mao answered: "No. Anyone who has chosen this path is compelled to walk it to the end." "But, Mr. Chairman, I see portraits of Stalin everywhere in your country. I thought you admired Stalin?" "Seventy percent of Stalin was good, thirty bad. We adopted what was good."

But what is the reality of Mao's counter-model? We will again begin with impressions, and let rational reflection follow. Unfiltered impressions often contain perceptions which correct our established concepts. Four words came to my mind when I closed my eyes for a moment, and asked myself: "What is this China really like?" I then thought of the adjectives "engaging," "unmysterious," "ambiguous," "pragmatic." Can I interpret the mixture of what is learned and what is perceived in these four adjectives? "Engaging" is not specifically a reaction to Mao's China, but to China generally. It contains a personal component for which I am not obliged to account but which is not mine alone. China experts usually love the country. I mention this in order to make clear that everything I criticize here is not said to rationalize a fundamental resistance (which is very common among Westerners) but comes from direct involvement.

"Unmysterious" requires an explanation. It need not be emphasized that we cannot discover how the power struggle between the two factions is being decided. Nowhere did we have the sort of freewheeling political discussion between individuals that may take place in Germany after people have known each other for five minutes. But I cannot rid myself of the feeling that what remains hidden for us in official China are unmysterious mysteries. The principles used in arguments are of a highly simplified, popularized rationalism. Mao is a master of simplification. In his case, simplification appears as the brilliant achievement of a person who is capable of highly nuanced perceptions and balanced consideration and who is educating a people by transforming the judgments he has formed into practicable guidelines. But when these guidelines are followed, believed and rattled off, they seem of an unmysterious primitiveness. One is actually ashamed of engaging in debates with this sort of intellectual equipment. I heard that young European Maoists who had come to China attracted unfavorable attention because when they saw the wall inscriptions criticizing Teng, they wanted to discuss the correctness of the reproaches contained in them.

"Ambiguous" compensates for the perception of a lack of mystery. The simplest judgment in China is always more than that judgment. It is acting in a situation. What is important is not to understand an opinion, but to understand the situation within which this opinion has some effect. The litany is important, not its content. The term "ambiguous" is perhaps a typically European reaction to a Chinese form of action. That statements should serve life means that statements are ambiguous from the point of view of the traditional, theoretical truth concept of Europe.

"Pragmatic" is again one of the conventional assessments

Europeans make about the Chinese. But conventional assessments reflect a reality. Perhaps I have just interpreted Chinese pragmatism to a degree—and in line with the reflections that were made after the first trip.

The great political leaders of a nation often have qualities that are typical of it, and they have others which are its opposite. The combination of the two is a prerequisite for extraordinary success. Mao leads China by making excessive demands on it. Where is he taking it? As a Chinese, he is taking it into the modern age via socialism. As a Marxist, Mao lays claim to a socialist consciousness which is correct for the entire world. This does not keep him from conducting Machiavellian alliances in power politics; it does not prevent him from urging the Federal Republic of Germany to pursue a policy of German reunification, advice which, if acted upon, would necessarily lead to armed conflict with the Soviet Union. "Only a true believer has the psychological strength for such Machiavellianism," one of the best-informed Americans told me. But let us get back from the attempt to understand China as much as possible on its own terms (although we must use European concepts to understand traditional Chinese conduct) and return to our own, direct questions. Is Mao dealing successfully with the problem that is characteristic of victorious revolutionary socialism, the reestablishment of entrenched domination? There can be no doubt that he sees it although, being a Marxist, he does not formulate it as we do. For him, the road toward the creation of the new man is a long one. Why does he believe that for a long time to come, revolution will have to recur periodically? The class struggle is the principal element. Classes which appropriate the means of production must be broken time and again. We shall try to express this more abstractly, and without using specifically Marxist concepts. Victory leads to rule, stable rule decreases the capacity to learn, decreased learning capacity provokes crises. Because of a homogeneous geography and good historiography, Chinese history is easy to survey. If one looks only at the most extended rhythms, one sees that for millennia, centuries of successful rule and cultural achievement alternated with centuries of gradual decay and chaos until a new central government was established. But what Mao, a modern rationalist, is looking for is not cyclical movement but progress which he describes in Marxist terms such as liberation from exploitation, i.e., the overcoming of class rule. Is there something we can learn from him, structurally speaking?

The Cultural Revolution shows that Mao deliberately and methodically created social crises for which there was a potential but hardly a necessity at this particular time. Undoubtedly, what was involved here was an internal power struggle, the re-establishment of Mao's position as leader after the economic failure of the "great leap forward" of 1959 had caused him to lose influence vis-à-vis the stabilizing, "revisionist line of comrade Liu Shao-chi." But ultimately he did not lose control over the crisis. After the power of certain individuals and their apparatus within the party had been broken, the military reestablished order. And after the Lin Piao crisis, Chou En-lai reestablished the position of the party and the experts. Crises triggered by those at the top are ambiguous events. If successfully engineered, they prevent the explosion of the kettle by a timely release of steam, and also and simultaneously bring necessary modifications to the structure of the system. But such action walks the line between jeopardizing the survival of the entire system, and curing symptoms. It seems to this observer that Mao achieved a flexibility which has so far avoided the ossification that has set in in Soviet Russia. But for that reason, individual freedom, particularly for those who think independently, is no greater but probably even more restricted than in Russia. All reflections about the pragmatic meaning of ambiguous statements do not do away with the fact that, for the Western observer, the litany comes under the heading of lying on command which is characteristic of successful revolutionary socialism. A physician from the West who visited a Chinese hospital during the time of the Cultural Revolution found himself alone with a Chinese colleague in an elevator between two floors for a quarter of a minute. The Chinese embraced him with tears in his eyes. The elevator stopped and the Chinese colleague smiled as before. In the Soviet Union, it is the very rigidity of the structure that at least creates niches in which a relatively undisturbed private life for intellectuals is possible (or the existence of another, not primarily political type).

We believe that good politics is not possible without truth, and the continuing search for truth impossible without freedom, and Mao may have an awareness of the problem involved here but probably no solution to it. The concrete struggle against the "Wind from the Right" centers around the question of whether performance should also be furthered by material inducements, or wholly by the appeal to socialist consciousness. Mao, who insists on the purity of the social and moral motive and allows the tendency to grant material inducements to be stigmatized as a deviation toward "capitalism," seems closer to utopian socialism here than to the insights of Marx. Neither Mao's conceptual framework nor his practice provide an answer to the analyses of the preceding chapter. It is possible, indeed likely, that a new era of greatness for China has dawned with the Maoist revolution. And the self-destruction of the Western system (in which Mao includes the Soviet Union) might some day force China to assume the hegemonic role which Mao rejects for sound ideological reasons. But his China has not solved the specific problems of modern society which we are facing. It seems to me that he still has to confront them.

The quasi-philosophical formulation of these problems may be the assimilation by China of the Western concept of truth, combined with the self-criticism of this concept under the aspect of the primacy of praxis over theory. In most cases, Western liberals are not even aware of this problem. They normally have a concept of truth as facticity, which neither comes up to the Greek level of the primacy of theory over isolated insight, nor understands the dynamic and pragmatic use of statements as a genuine possibility of thought, as the Chinese typically do. If China wishes to become modern, it presumably will not be able to avoid adopting the concept of truth of Western science. It is only in this way that the kind of self-correction possible in the liberal system will become accessible to it. Perhaps the "lack of mystery" of Maoist China is precisely a still very primitive stage of a resolutely modern form of thought. What is traditionally Chinese is hardly present in it. At best, one can discover its formal trace in the ways modern thinking is used in present-day China, as in the "litany," for example. But it is also true that in the dialectic deriving from the Hegelian tradition, Marxism imported into China a self-criticism of the prevailing Western concept of truth, although in the form given it here it is wholly inadequate. It would be an error to believe that a direct path leads from Mao's essay on contradiction to the really due self-correction of the modern concept of truth. China will no more be spared the passage through contemporary Western rationality than we in the West will be spared a self-correction which cannot come from the outside. But of course, these philosophical themes are not the subject of this book.

6. Five Theses
on the Third World War

At least in the vague form in which it is initially being stated here, almost everyone knows the truth contained in the following theses. Because of the fear of the actions it would urge on us, this knowledge is usually suppressed. Being suppressed, it does not become clear awareness, and therefore does not result in action. Since necessary and possible political action is not taken, the result will be the event we fear.

Theses:
1 / The Third World War is likely.
2 / A policy which prevents war is feasible and is being attempted today.
3 / This policy encounters obstacles which are rooted in social structures.
4 / To overcome the obstacles confronting a war prevention policy requires a comprehensive transformation of consciousness.
5 / A war prevention policy must be conducted in such a way that it facilitates and does not impede the transformation of consciousness.

This book attempts to make vague theses precise. To do so, it must make a number of specific assertions which will be contradicted by a variety of people. Such contradiction is welcome, for it is indispensable to the formation of consciousness.

On the connection between the theses: they move in a double loop. The elucidation of the first will initially state the general reasons why war is likely. These reasons are sufficiently apparent to the statesmen of the major powers to motivate them to conduct a policy which attempts to prevent major war (second thesis). The social causes of the probable failure of such a policy lead back to the point of departure: war continues to be likely (third thesis). An author of political books has no choice but to address the consciousness of individuals if he is to overcome these obstacles. The indispensability of a transformation of consciousness (fourth thesis) takes us back to the starting point for a second time. A policy which harbors the illusion of having none digs its own grave if it prevents the transformation of consciousness needed for survival (fifth thesis). The present chapter will discuss these theses by illustrating them with views current today. The following chapter (7) tries to find a deeper conceptual base. Then, three chapters (8–10) concerning the concrete problems of war prevention follow. In the final chapter, we return to the basic question of a change in consciousness.

The Third World War is likely.

1. *It is likely because the compulsion to engage in hegemonic competition in a system of sovereign major powers which has always led to major wars in history continues to exist today, without abatement, and with the identical structural consequences.*[30] *This is a very general thesis and a conservative argument.*

To justify it as stated would require a political theory of power systems which I would not wish to impose on the reader at the outset. I therefore choose the opposite course. I examine the specific reasons which are advanced in support of the view that such compulsion does not exist today or that it will not lead to war, and postpone the sketch of the basic theory (see chapter 7).

A person who believes that the competition between the major powers will not lead to war either has faith in political developments, or in the deterrence provided by large weapons.

2. *A change in political consciousness, a change in social systems and the techniques of classic diplomacy are necessary today to prevent war. None of these means by itself is adequate today.*

How they are to be used will continue to engage our attention throughout the balance of this book. Here, I shall list those indications which suggest why none of them will suffice by itself.

A change of consciousness as regards war as an institution is emerging in our century. For millennia, mankind has known war as an ineluctable evil or even as the source of power, glory and freedom, and as a test for human beings. Today, the rationalist conviction that war must and can be eliminated for good has spread among intellectuals and "the man on the street." Usually, this conviction suffers from the ignorance of the conditions necessary to give it practical effect. People accept or further political, social and economic structures which push toward conflict, and ultimately toward armed conflict. When it does break out, they blame the politicians and the military as individuals when they should blame the dynamism of the system which such individuals are almost always subject to, however good their intentions. People permit themselves an attitude of fear and aggression, and are surprised by the unavoidable conflicts which a society of individuals with such attitudes produces. Peace advocacy which fails to see the social and psychological causes of war is no real change of consciousness; it is merely a symbol of the longing for peace.

In our time, the hope to prevent war through social change emerges in three forms: as convergency hope, as liberal hope, as socialist hope. All three are important but inadequate.

Convergency hope sees the cause of the tension that may produce war between the great powers in their ideological opposition and demands that both sides make the conscious effort to overcome this opposition. In so doing, it falls in with a strong feeling among the masses and the intellectuals: why should we kill each other because our social systems and beliefs are at variance? The seventeenth- and eighteenth-century themes of religious tolerance resurface in a political and social framework. One might cite the common problems of modern industrial society as a real structural change that harmonizes with this conciliatory intent.

The suspicion that these important motifs are inadequate to assure peace is confirmed by a glance at the causes of major wars, or the tensions that threaten them. In the First World War, the progressive Western democracies and autocratic Russia were aligned against Germany which resembled the West but had internal political structures and a consciousness that were more conservative. Among the causes of the First World War was the Eastern European, Balkan hegemonic conflict between the two conservative empires, Russia and Austria; the hegemonic conflict between the two modern industrial nations, England and Germany, as it related to world trade and colonial expansion; the conflict of two similar nationalisms, France and Germany. In the Second World War, the identical coalition resulted from Hitler's power politics. There are times today when the tension between the leading communist powers, Russia and China, seems almost more difficult to allay than that between the present competitors for world power, Russia and the United States. As one views history in this fashion, power conflicts appear as less avoidable than ideological ones, or at least one might say that the talk about opposing ideologies or social systems is too superficial to get to the bottom of the antagonisms. Liberals and socialists are therefore justified in speaking of the concrete forms of political and social systems. This is a step toward a form of thought appropriate to world-internal politics.

The liberal hope wants to extend the success achieved in regulating domestic political conflict by representative democracy to the overcoming of wars. It can hope for this in three stages: through the victory of the liberal form of state and society in the sovereign nations; through a network of transnational liberal structures; through a liberal, federated world government.

The first step, the hope to prevent wars by a collaboration of democratic governments and peoples rests on the appearance the North American and Western European world has presented for some decades. Today, a war between these politically and technologically most advanced nations seems out of the question. But this hope cloaks two illusions. One of them revealed itself after the liberal optimism of the time shortly after the Second World War when it became apparent that the societies in which parliamentary democracy had achieved stability were almost entirely those in which it had come into existence, and it became manifest how difficult it is to transplant this type of society. This sobering experience continues to obscure a second illusion: it is by no means clear that a victory of the liberal system in Russia or China would sufficiently mitigate the antagonisms of interests and sentiments. The internal peace of the Western world is being stabilized by common capitalist interests and the common political fear of the rest of the world. While it is conceivable today that a peaceful world might some day have the internal political organization of a federation of representative democracies. But there is no reason to assume that such a form of organization would be enough to bring peace.

The second step, the hope for transnational liberal structure, is more realistic today than the first. It can point to at least two facts: liberal, i.e., worldwide capitalist economic interests, and the transnational community of sentiment among intellectuals. But both are ambivalent.

It is true that worldwide capitalism has an interest in maintaining that degree of peace which world commerce and the multinational mode of production require. A closer tie to the Soviet economic sphere would be an additional peace factor in that sense. But it also creates opposing interests and conflicts and is not strong enough to stand up to the profit motive of the armaments industry. Liberals will find it difficult to refute the Marxist analysis which makes capitalism responsible for the wars of the bourgeois era. Besides, and at the very least, today's transnational capitalism lacks the regulatory mechanism which the government framework creates in a national economy and which, however inadequate, does promote the creation of a democratic will and bureaucratic supervision of the unregulated growth of economic interests. According to liberal economic theory, the market needs the state for all non-profit-making activities. Worldwide capitalism cannot compensate for the absence of a liberal world state, to put it mildly.

The community of sentiment among intellectuals is ambivalent from a liberal point of view because while it contains the liberal component of the demand for freedom of opinion, it either remains politically inactive or is predominantly critical of capitalism, which means that it tends toward socialism. In any event, it is merely a leaven for world peace, though an important one. It always combines the constantly reproduced internal dissent and consequent political weakness with the indispensable principle of free and open discussion.

The third level, hope for a liberally organized world state, is wholly utopian today as a road toward peace. Who will create it? It is also true, however, that during the discussion of the two preceding levels, it was the liberal world state which showed itself to be the logical result of the liberal initiative. The fathers of liberal thought during the Enlightenment lived in more or less absolutist states with a functioning bureaucracy and police. In face of what was at that time a modern state based on the military, they had recourse to older ideas about liberty, to what were privileges in medieval reality. They generalized them, proclaimed them as human rights, and implemented them with the help of the bourgeosie that had risen to economic power and was striving for free trade and political power. Precisely because a stable state existed and the goal was to shake off some of its chains, the liberal tradition has not always taken adequate account of the need for governmental stability. The worldwide analogue to that development, however, would be the establishment of an absolutist world state through war, and its subsequent liberalization. Such an event may be our fate but it cannot be our goal. (As the implicit background of certain ideas concerning armaments, it will be taken up again below.) And even liberal states will not voluntarily surrender their sovereignty, for otherwise at least Western European political unity would more easily become a reality.

The socialist hope for peace also transfers a principle of domestic policy to what has been foreign policy up to now. Socialist criticism states that the capitalist economic system refuses to grant man his substantial, i.e., his economic freedom. The competitive struggle for capital accumulation inherent in this system creates crises which in turn produce wars like the two world wars of this century. According to this thesis, a third world war is likely. It will be triggered by a capitalism that cannot overcome its crises, and will be waged against the socialist states. If the private ownership of the means of production were to be eliminated, the socialist hope tells us, the causes of wars and therefore wars themselves would ultimately disappear. In its critical part, the analysis attempted in this book parallels the Marxist one to the extent that it places the causes of war not in subjective failure but in an objective compulsion that inheres in the system. To be creditable, the two analyses cannot content themselves with the general assertion that such necessity exists, however; they must point to specific cases. The difference between the two analyses is that the one attempted here understands the social form of the disposition over the means of production as merely one of the aspects of the phenomenon we have referred to as power. In such an account, capitalism would be merely the form within which the bourgeoisie was able to accede to power, and its disappearance would not mean that power struggles would come to an end. At the same time Marxist doctrine contains a plausible refutation of utopian prognoses. According to it, it is not the business of theory to develop futuristic projections but to criticize those present contradictions from whose supersession the future unfolds. But the expectation that war will be overcome if its economic causes are removed is a prognosis that must submit to an examination of its likelihood in the light of our experience. This takes us back to the reflections of the fourth chapter, but we will now trace the same three steps as in the case of liberalism.

The first step would be the expectation that socialist nations would not wage war against each other. But the history of the socialist bloc up to this point shows no decrease of the potential for internal conflict. The power struggles of the bureaucracies and the ideological conflicts which are especially virulent in all movements of the Left lead to enforced pacification of the weaker by the stronger and leadership conflicts among the strong which barely avoid war. Within the framework of the means at their disposal, the foreign policy of socialist states has so far followed the classical pattern of power politics. This is accentuated by the traditional, power-political cast of the Russian empire. But beyond that, there is an explicit connection between revolutionary socialism and the exercise of power which manifests itself in the one-party system and the contempt for representative democracy. The hope that this habit of thinking in terms of power and the use of violence would suddenly be supplanted by peacefulness with the victory of the revolution is wholly unconvincing psychologically. That the exercise of power finds its justification in a good cause is an age-old ideology to which enthusiastic groups succumb time and again, and always with identical consequences. What offers hope for peace is not a number of socialist states but at best a future socialist world.

On the second level, the transnational one, the socialist analysis has the strength that it sheds light on world capitalism as a unified system. That this system will continue producing economic crises and limited wars as it has for the last two hundred years, seems likely. But it appears to have suffered no impairment of its growth potential if we abstract from occasional crises, and to be more efficient than the largest socialist state economies. It is possible that transnational counter-movements may act as a corrective by making it more just, as the union movement did, but they will hardly be able to transcend it. Its weakness is the increasing difficulty of legitimation encountered by its political superstructure, and it is this very factor which makes plausible the expectation of armed conflicts. The final struggle between the leading capitalist and the leading socialist power might then turn out to have been the most correct aspect of Leninist-Stalinist prognoses.

That a socialist world organization will be attained without war is as utopian as the expectation that a liberal one will. It should also be said that the world state is not as logical a consequence of revolutionary socialism as it is of liberalism (under which I am subsuming Social Democracy, although that may be somewhat too simplistic). According to Marxist doctrine, the state will ultimately wither. The inhumanity of communist bureaucracies may seem even more striking because the socialist ideal of autonomous social action made no provision for them. But as the economy keeps growing and becomes increasingly technicized, government planning will become more, not less, necessary. It can be assumed that neither the doctrines of economic liberalism nor those of socialism (with the possible exception of the Chinese) have so far understood the social consequences of economic growth, and that they are therefore helpless vis-à-vis real developments, including those that are making for war.

If the two major doctrines cannot bring world peace, we are led back to the question whether the means of classical foreign policy can preserve it to the extent it exists today. Classical foreign policy acknowledges the competition for power among states as a fact and attempts to preserve peace where it is in the interest of the state that engages in such policy. But it can only preserve world peace if all participating large powers feel that peace is also in their own special interest. One might assume that such is the case today. And it does appear that American and Russian policy during the last few years has been governed by a manifest interest in preventing war. But at least in the case of a key figure such as Kissinger, such a policy presupposes as its motive force the consciousness of the continuing probability of a future world war. If the analysis attempted here is correct, that probability has its roots in the very structures of classical foreign policy.

The formula of classical foreign policy to prevent war is "si vis pacem, para bellum." Every potential enemy is to be deterred from war by the threat that he would lose it or win it only at unacceptable cost. This system would only be stable if defense is militarily so superior to attack that everyone would be safe from everyone else, and also safe from any possible coalition. But because every partner tries to be superior to the rest, this system invariably leads to arms races. If only because that is economically unsustainable, such activity usually ends in war.

If we use an ideal-typical simplification, history teaches us two methods by which competition between sovereign powers can be settled: the concert, and hegemonic war. In the concert, classically in the system of five major powers, the "pentarchy," changing coalitions mean that none of the parties achieves hegemony. But in its classical forms, as in ancient Greece and modern Europe, for example, the alliance was stable only when wars regularly recurred. War was a necessary test of strength, and recurred once during a generation on the average. A hegemonic war to the finish usually broke out where less than five threatening powers existed and a coalition that was dependably superior to the strongest partner could no longer be formed. It usually ended with a definitive victory which was frequently achieved by a power that had originally been judged peripheral, as in the case of ancient Rome. Today, the domination of the world by Europe has been transformed into the hegemonic conflict between what were once peripheral powers, the U.S.A. and Russia, while a new peripheral power, China, looks on. For political reasons, this conflict might already have led to war. It may be assumed that the increased destructiveness of weapons has been the most important inhibiting factor.

3. *In and of itself, the size of weapons does not guarantee the avoidance of a world war.*

This thesis merely defines the trivial starting point of the analysis of the system of deterrence but not the form it takes in the arms control concept, which will be discussed in the next section. It addresses itself to the popular but false consolation which suggests that war is suicidal and will therefore not be waged. The equally popular counter-argument cannot be definitively refuted and states that even a suicidal war can be triggered by technological failure or an act of madness. Today, the likelihood that war will start in such a fashion may be considered small, although it remains an open question whether it is sufficiently so to allow one to live with it permanently. The stronger but publicly less-well-known argument is that a war with modern weapons need not be suicidal. The technical possibility of a first strike capability, i.e., a first blow which will adequately disarm the adversary, may become a reality with any new generation of weapons. Technically, it is perfectly conceivable that both sides will some day have this first strike capability (as, for example, with MIRVs against land-based missiles only) so that the side that started the war would also win it. Today, the pessimistic prognosis is irrefutable: the Third World War will occur when it can be won.

Up to now, nothing has been set forth that is not known in principle to the statesmen of the major powers. It is against the background of such knowledge that efforts to prevent war must be tested.

A policy which prevents war is feasible and is being attempted today.

If we view the overall situation, it seems incomprehensible that sound common sense should find it impossible to prevent the catastrophe that is a world war. Reason is the capacity to see the whole. The arguments adduced so far show that the automatism of individual interests does not prevent war. For millennia, man has been trained in the habit of war; it is the way the greatest individual interests settle their tests of power. Reason today has to attempt something historically unprecedented: it must overcome this way of settling conflicts. As a result of the last two world wars, the pentarchy of the European cultural sphere (England, France, Germany, Russia and the U.S. in 1914) was transformed into the U.S.-U.S.S.R. duopoly. The following are two theses on the problem as it presents itself today:

1. *The first task in preventing war lies in the stabilization of the Russo-American duopoly.*
2. *The duopoly is unstable over the long run. It must end in war or a pluralistic power structure.*

Both theses are not self-evident. The central problem is the tension between the two. As a result of a deliberate albeit wavering policy of the two superpowers, an at least temporary stabilization of the duopoly has occurred during the last three decades. The alternative of a major war between the two was thus avoided. That there were no additional alternatives can be formulated in two further theses:

- A policy which attempts to assure victory for one of the world powers by non-warlike means is no peace policy.
- The peaceful transition to a pluralistic structure hinges on the prior stabilization of the duopoly.

Our argument will deal first with these supplementary theses, then turn to the military and diplomatic means of stabilizing the duopoly, and infer from them the reasons for believing that the duopoly is unstable over the long run.

Abstractly, it is easy enough to imagine how one of the superpowers might achieve victory without war. It is usually described as the worldwide victory of the social system it represents. In most social spheres, as in elections and economic competition, there is such a thing as a victory or a defeat the defeated can live with, and no blood is spilled. Historical experience also teaches us that there are nations which once were major powers but no longer are, and that the well-being of their citizens need not suffer because wars were lost. That we can hardly expect a major power to acknowledge defeat without attempting to avert it by war shows the extent to which the system of sovereign powers has become an anomaly within modern societies. But this anomaly is today's reality. As we analyze the system of deterrence, we will note that its functioning is in fact predicated on this anomaly. A policy which, though perhaps subjectively sincere, tries to assure victory for one of the world powers without war risks war on the threshold of peaceful victory. This will be studied below in its strategic detail. Such a policy is thus no alternative. It is the more cautious form of a policy of war even if it isn't aware of it.

The transition to a genuinely pluralistic power structure presupposes a reduction of the power the duopoly can commit. Such a reduction may be voluntary or compulsory. During the phase of antagonistic bipolarity (cold war), this reduction was partly achieved involuntarily, by the reciprocal deterrence of the superpowers. Since that deterrence included the incalculable threat of escalation, it created a kind of paralysis in the use of available means. The Vietnam War became so expensive and unsuccessful for America because partly for legalistic convictions, partly because of this paralysis, it did not dare use the simpler means of direct conquest. But this self-induced paralysis of the military preponderance of the duopoly will only last as long as the two superpowers do not agree to do away with it. Where their common interests are at stake, they have the means to make those interests prevail. A stable concert, a new pentarchy, which would include the United States, Western Europe, Soviet Russia, China and Japan, presupposes that the two military superpowers find their permanent common interest in not using their military superiority against one of the members of the pentarchy. While it is true that such a condition would not be the same thing as world peace, especially vis-à-vis the Third World, it would mean a long-term avoidance of a major world war. This will only happen if the two superpowers feel threatened by none of the other three powers, or by each other, militarily or as regards their domestic policy. The sense of not being threatened for the foreseeable future is tantamount to the stabilization of the duopoly. This takes us back to thesis 1.: the prevention of a world war requires first of all the stabilization of the duopoly; it requires cooperative bipolarity. How is such stabilization possible?

Strategic deterrence is the supporting pillar of the stabilization of the duopoly. We shall first examine the doctrine of strategic deterrence in its theoretically pure, abstract form. In this form, it is characterized by three elements: symmetry, stability, pure bipolarity. Symmetry is the underlying concept, while stability and pure bipolarity are weaknesses that inhere in this concept.

The symmetry of deterrence is the element that will cushion the threat of increasingly effective weapons. The formula of a change from quantity to quality which is usually employed somewhat haphazardly has a meaning here. But perhaps it would be more correct to speak of the possibility of a new structure that would be realized by going beyond a limit value. The limit value is that employment of weapons which would eliminate the enemy nation as a functioning industrial society. Quantitatively, and according to a formula that was probably coined by McNamara, this would mean the death of more than a quarter of the population and the destruction of more than half of the industrial potential. This was already attainable by the weapons arsenals existing some ten years ago. It should be emphasized, however, that a saturation effect sets in above this limit value. Those parts of the population and industry which can more easily be destroyed are those that are spatially concentrated. Even a tenfold increase in the use of weapons would not exterminate the entire population and destroy all of industry. During the last ten years, the Soviet Union has implemented air defense measures and dispersed its industry far and wide in its very large territory and presumably protected itself to a considerable extent against this threat.[31] The idea of the total disappearance of mankind through nuclear war presupposes a wholly different, extreme use of weapons which is guided by the intent to inflict total destruction. But it is also true that a nation which has been eliminated as a functioning industrial society will no longer have the means to recover its previous condition, and without external help, subsequent catastrophes (starvation and disease) will cause greater loss of human life after the attack. This is said to convey a more precise sense of the possible quantitative effects. We now pass on to the possible qualitative change in the structure. The whole point of stabilizing deterrence through the threat of a nuclear attack lies in its symmetry, and more precisely in second strike capabilities, as American military theoreticians worked it out toward the end of the fifties. If each of the two powers can survive the first enemy strike and destroy the other by a counter strike, the first strike offers no advantage. There would thus be no inducement for it, and no reason to fear that the enemy might launch one, which would mean that there is no inducement to launch a preventive attack. What is the meaning here of a change from quantity to quality? The old form of deterrence through armaments (*si vis pacem, para bellum*) required a quantitative superiority over the enemy and therefore led to arms races and periodic wars. This system had a limited stability only because defense was superior to attack.[32] In the case of nuclear weapons, *attack is far superior to defense.* Even an efficient ABM system is much more expensive than the weapons it protects, and such a system may be not possible. At first glance, this seems to eliminate stability; a guaranteed victory would be the reward for a first strike. But if second strike capabilities survive the initial attack, we get a guaranteed symmetry of deterrence, and stability along with it.

The term stability may first of all refer to a strength of the system. Once it has been stabilized, it need not be developed further. If one puts one's trust in it, it means that one renounces the possibility of achieving a military victory through a first strike but has traded this for the advantage that one need no longer engage in an arms race to insure the possibility of this victory. But this stability is also a weakness. Deterrence through strategic weapons solves the problem that lies in keeping the enemy from using strategic weapons but, initially at least, that is all it solves. From a formal point of view, it might seem that the same situation between the two enemies has been produced as if strategic weapons did not exist. We will list the chances and problems of a system of deterrence according to points of view which will show that this formal way of looking at the problem is false. They concern (a) psychological unreliability, (b) instability vis-à-vis technological progress, (c) the problem of limiting damage, and (d) the relationship to possible limited wars, i.e., to third powers.

These points of view refer to the various problem areas in which it becomes apparent that strategic weapons are not the only weapons in the world. They do possess the curiously psychological unreality of representing a power that threatens all of life and which only a tiny minority of those living today has ever seen. Even the author of this book never saw a nuclear bomb although he was trained as a nuclear physicist. Vis-à-vis a skeptic that denies the existence of these bombs (like that of the emperor's new clothes in Andersen's fairy tale), he could not argue that he had seen them. But when one traces the real plans and modes of action of all people to their ultimate consequences, one observes that they keep coming up against the limiting conditions which the existence of these weapons establishes. In the language of escalation, this can be expressed as follows: whether the threat of escalation toward an ever more massive use of weapons is limited because capacities are, as was still true in the Second World War, or whether escalation increases almost continuously to the use of lethal weapons which the demand for self-preservation excludes, is not the same thing. The chances of a policy that prevents war by deterrence lie in the possible effect stability at the highest level will have on the lower ones. The danger of this interaction of levels is that the lower levels undermine the stability at the highest levels. This will be discussed in terms of the four points of view listed above.

a. Psychological instability becomes apparent in the fact that technical failure or madness of one of the actors cannot be excluded. This would mean that the first strike would be triggered by irrational agencies. But even if we assume rationality, deterrence cannot be wholly relied on. For the deterrence effect actually rests on the calculation that behavior will be irrational, and this is not unlikely, psychologically speaking. On page 117 we noted that with the exception of the system of sovereign powers that compete for hegemony, the peaceful recognition of defeat is a learned form of behavior that promotes survival. If such behavior could also be relied upon in the case of armed conflict between the superpowers, deterrence would lose credibility. Let us imagine that power A unleashed a first strike against power B. B has 70% of its population and its military leadership left, but it no longer has the means of feeding that population. In this situation, is it rational for B to really launch a second strike? How does that improve the situation of its population? A second strike is not rational, but it is plausible. There are reasons for it in the psychology of behavior that go far back to the animal kingdom. Caution prevails when the superior enemy merely threatens, but pointless resistance is offered when he attacks. Already in the behavior of animals, this is a deterrence factor (see chapter 7, p. 148). Throughout the millennia of wars, this was a form of behavior that favored survival. At the very moment when the era of wars is to be left behind, it becomes irrational. The consequence is that even deterrence through "mutual assured destruction" (called MAD by its opponents) is not wholly reliable. Ultimately, it is merely deterrence through an incalculable risk, although it is true that no one will readily test the magnitude of that risk. It is against the background of this insecurity that its other strengths and weaknesses have to be examined.

b. Instability due to technological progress. How are second strike capabilities to be assured? A counter force blow which would eliminate the second strike capability of B or reduce it below the necessary level would give A a superiority that could be used for blackmail so that the "countervalue" strike might no longer be necessary. Unless a political situation of mutual trust can be created where the development of counter-force capabilities is no longer even envisaged, such a development must be forbidden either through controllable or other creditable treaties, or one must make timely technological preparations against it. Technical measures could consist either in defensive measures against counter-force strikes (hardening of bases, ABM protection of bases, the camouflaging of bases by rail movement or submarine) or in the development of new second strike capabilities against which a defense does not as yet exist. It is therefore at this point that the incentive to an arms race arises. SALT essentially has the goal of limiting this race. At the moment, we have the triad of land-based missiles, sea-based missiles, and strategic bombers. Its purpose is a greater guarantee of safety through diversification. SALT I precludes not only the ABM protection of cities, which is viewed as destabilizing (see c, below) but also the stabilizing ABM protection of land-based missiles. Greater accuracy and an increased number of warheads (MIRVs) will presumably leave land-based missiles unprotected in about five years. Antisubmarine weapons are being developed against sea-based missiles so that their immunity ten years hence may no longer be taken for granted. Bombers are also becoming increasingly vulnerable to missiles. In sum, the situation is that we will have reliable second strike capabilities for roughly ten more years, and that it is not certain that that will be the end of their reliability, but that continuing technological development threatens a continuing arms race whose result might be the loss of the present stability. The avoidance of this race requires reliable political agreements. The technical stabilization of war prevention must have a political base.

c. Compared to the prevention of war, the limitation of damage is the more traditional concept. Along with the age-old logic of preparation for war, it crops up time and again. The argument seems almost irresistible: we want to prevent war. Should it break out, we want to be able to minimize the damage to our population and economy. Who would not be in favor of such limitation if it were possible? But one must understand that this means that in abstracto, the principle of a change from quantity to quality, of symmetrical deterrence by the threat of practically lethal countervalue blows, goes by the board once again. If the damage in B which the greatest blow A can inflict can be limited by measures in B, then A will simply no longer threaten B with a lethal blow. B can conduct war unless a threat other than a lethal blow will effectively deter it. Using the age-old argument that A will not start a war it cannot win, B will claim that it is its very capacity to limit damage which will deter

A. But this argument is no longer symmetrical. Superiority can once again come into play. The natural limitation the pointlessness of overkill capacities imposes on armaments becomes irrelevant. If war can thus be waged once more, everything will depend on which side is the stronger, just as it always has. Motives for an arms race have once again been created. The familiar causal chain: armaments— economic burden—political crisis—war as a way out, can once again take its course. In short, if war can be waged, it will.

Such a far-reaching thesis must be discussed more concretely.[33] Since about 1960, the U.S. has proclaimed a doctrine of symmetrical deterrence but actually conducted an armaments policy of superiority in strategic weapons. Not until the late sixties did the Soviet missile buildup put an end to this. McNamara himself strove for a counter-force capability when he first came into office, and later others demanded it when he had changed his mind. They argued for the limitation of damage. The consideration that a war which could be waged would in fact be waged some day was pushed aside by the conviction that America's superiority constituted a guarantee for peace since America did not want war. Even if it is subjectively sincere, such a conviction is not compelling. One can imagine situations where America might feel so threatened that it starts a war it recognizes to be possible. The Leninist thesis expects that capitalism will start a war because it can no longer manage its crises. On page 111, the establishment of a world hegemony, perhaps a kind of world government through war, was mentioned as the possible background of some armaments conceptions. Planners who want to make sure that America can survive a war forced on it at every level of escalation would have to lack imagination if they did not ask themselves if, after this war, the world would not be readier than it is today to accept political forms which would make American hegemony possible. Anyone who considers such plans, however, must not forget that wars usually become more devastating than was foreseen. If the ability to limit damage increases the probability of war, it presumably also increases the expectation value of damage (expectation value= size of damage x probability of its occurrence, all possible cases being taken into account).

It is understandable that the Soviets do not feel reassured by American confidence in peaceful U.S. intentions. Besides, Russia's thinking was always more conservative than America's. Greater importance was given to limiting damage and counter-force capabilities. There was the argument that this was much closer to the traditional ethics of war than the taking hostage of the peaceful population through a system of deterrence. The abstract idea of overcoming war by the heightened effectiveness of weapons was seen as fundamentally perverse. Nor was such an idea necessary if one hoped that a change in social system would do away with war. The actual consequences of this perfectly natural feeling were destabilizing, however. The ABM system that protects Moscow and which the Americans called Galosh gave the U.S. the principal impetus to develop its own ABM sites and MIRVs which are designed to penetrate ABMs. SALT I eliminated the ABM element of this destabilizing development. But it is doubtful that this can also be done with future weapons systems.

Another measure to limit damage which even today casts an uncertain light on stability is civil air defense measures. Soviet civil defense was mentioned above (p. 119) and will be discussed in somewhat greater detail in chapter 9 (p. 169 ff). E. Wigner and E. Teller (quotations in chapter 9) are of the opinion that the "assured destruction" of the Soviet Union is not wholly assured even today because this civil defense exists. This is a controversial point among experts but it would be irresponsible not to take seriously the skeptical view of these authors.

In addition to counter-force and counter-value, the increasing accuracy of missiles would permit a third form of deterrence which might be called "counter-government."

The decision to go to war is not made by peoples or soldiers but by governments. We will discuss this in greater detail in chapter 9. I shall confine myself here to mentioning the possibility of an armed threat directed against the governmental machinery of the enemy. Given present-day defense systems, it is precisely the governments which have the best chance to survive. It is an old, popular wisdom that one is less willing to inflict injury on oneself than on those one governs. Lichtenberg picks up this bit of common sense in an aphorism which tells of a country where during times of war, the king and all his ministers had to sleep on a powder keg with a lit candle nearby. Since that time, wars no longer take place in that country, he writes. One has to strip the argument of the malicious and melancholy sarcasm about evil governments which so readily attaches to it. If the theses of this book are correct, governments are subject to constraints which always produce events such as war, even when those in charge do not wish it. (When a friend congratulated Sir Edward Grey after the August 1914 session of the House of Commons because he had obtained the consent of all parties to a declaration of war on Germany, he merely said: "I hate this war."). The point of counter-government deterrence would merely be the creation of a restraint that would deter governments from war. The counter-argument that especially Americans advance is that after the first strike or exchange of strikes, nothing is more urgently needed than governments on both sides that can act to end the catastrophe as expeditiously as possible. In principle, this argument is correct, and we will deal with it in the section on the problems of guidance and control in chapter 9. But even it shows the tension between limiting damage and deterrence. It does not believe that deterrence can be relied upon, and therefore tries from the very beginning to minimize the consequences of a threatened strike, which means that it returns to the traditional logic of war. This may well be realistic. But then it is also realistic to expect that this war will take place some day.

d. In the abstract formulation of the doctrine of deterrence set forth so far, limited wars have not yet been considered. This problem highlights the weakness of static strategic deterrence. During the fifties, the Americans had the doctrine of massive retaliation: every transgression of the enemy was to be punished by a large nuclear strike or, rather, the enemy was to be deterred from any and every transgression by the threat of such a strike. Leo Szilard answered a Russian who told him that Dulles had to be mad if he actually meant what he said: "I see that Mr. Dulles was successful. He made you believe he may be mad. That's his kind of deterrence." The doctrine was abandoned when it was argued that it allowed the enemy a "salami tactic," i.e., transgressions in such thin slices that none of them would motivate a massive retaliatory strike. What this really means is that one cannot day after day credibly threaten an act which one would prefer never to commit. But then symmetrical deterrence solves at most one-half of the problem, the avoidance of massive strikes, but offers no protection whatever against the salami tactic. It is against this background that the doctrines of limited deterrence and flexible response came into being. Initially, these doctrines reestablished the old logic of war on the level of smaller weapons. Through the threat of escalation, the attempt was then made to combine the ability to use weapons on a limited scale, and the system of deterrence. The NATO doctrine of flexible response claims to be not primarily a doctrine about war, but a doctrine of deterrence. On every level of escalation, the enemy is denied possible victory by the threat of escalation to a higher level. This cannot be made logically consistent with the claim that strategic weapons reliably deter their use by the other side. Deterrence in this system rests in principle on the incalculable risk of a threat which is self-contradictory (chapter 10).

In a constructive policy of war prevention, a strategic deterrence that is viewed as sufficiently dependable would have to "radiate" downward before it is too late (i.e., before one's own side is weakened by technological innovation). Stable disarmaments agreements which limit the use of weapons would also have to include limited wars. They would have to affect economics, social and foreign policy and would have to produce other forms of problem solving since the system would make it impossible to settle conflicts by war. But development is probably tending in the opposite direction. Unresolved political conflicts make for limited wars. The superpowers find it unacceptable to renounce the option to conduct such wars. Options to escalate are seen as indispensable because they are to safeguard the possibility of waging limited wars to prevent escalation by the other side. By limiting damage, the option of a strategic strike must also be kept open, and this means that strategic deterrence itself is undermined.

This abstract consideration becomes more concrete when one includes the weakness of strategic deterrence mentioned on p. 120, its pure bipolarity. In actuality, deterrence occurs in the dynamic sphere of national and social plurality, for it is supposed to stabilize the duopoly as the basis of world order. The political form of this world order was itself originally meant to be duopolistic, as the polarity of two systems of alliances. But partners to the alliances move independently, and independent powers establish themselves outside of them. When superpowers honor their obligations vis-à-vis their allies, they either become involved in limited wars, or must be able to threaten them. Disarmament or a reduction in armaments on the part of the superpowers in their reciprocal dealings encounters the barrier that the superpowers wish to remain superior to all others. Thesis 2, as stated above, concerns itself with this problem: the duopoly is unstable over the long term. It moves toward war unless it can transform itself into a genuinely pluralistic world balance. We will consider the most obvious concrete examples.

The reduction in armaments of the United States and the Soviet Union which might be the hope of SALT II cannot, in the Soviet view, be taken so far as to shift the power relationship between the Soviet Union and China in China's favor. A technical solution of this dilemma would be the distinction between long- and medium-range missiles. The United States and the Soviet Union can threaten each other from their respective countries only by long-range missiles. The Soviet Union would retain the option of medium-range, land-based missiles against China. If the China problem stops being an obstruction to a SALT agreement, the problem of Europe will necessarily come to the fore.

Actually, it is probable that neither the Chinese nor the European problem are susceptible of a long-term solution within the duopoly. The deterrence of China by land-based medium-range Russian missiles cannot prevent China from undermining the Soviet position in the communist bloc and the Third World, nor does it pose an obstacle to China's attainment of nuclear power status. Both processes may take decades, and these decades are a reprieve for the duopoly. If the Soviet Union wished to prevent China's attainment of parity, it would have to wage a preventive war. Such a war might be limited either to a counter-force strike against the Chinese nuclear forces or attempt the political conquest of China. The former would probably merely postpone the problem. The Soviet Union would sacrifice its moral credibility without permanently incapacitating the enemy. But short of genocide, the latter alternative is hardly conceivable. A country of such enormous population and with the Maoist tradition of guerilla warfare cannot be ruled from beyond its borders for any length of time. It seems that the Soviet leadership is aware of this dilemma and has renounced preventive war. In this situation, Kissinger's policy of including China as an equal partner in the dialogue, i.e., the beginning of a deliberate relinquishment of the duopoly, is a realistic policy. But this means that if the duopoly does not end in hegemonic conflict, it will find it necessary to transform itself into a long-term balance of power.

NATO strategy which was designed to deter an attack by

the Warsaw Pact forces in Europe was referred to as deterrence by the incalculable risk of a self-contradictory threat. We will discuss this in detail in chapter 10. Here, we confine ourselves to a thetic presentation of a few fundamentals. During the last few decades, the military stability of Europe was partly based on the confrontation between Russia's superiority in conventional weapons and the nuclear superiority of the U.S., which made war in a vital, sensitive geographic region an incalculable risk for both powers. But it also rested on the absence of a motive for war on either side. The triggering element of local conflicts was almost removed by the Iron Curtain which has been justly condemned for humane and social reasons or, more precisely, it was removed by the exact division of Europe into systems of alliances of the two superpowers. It was logical that only a few states were allowed by either of the two powers to remain neutral, and they were states that did not jeopardize the stability of the division. The reunification of Germany was excluded precisely because both sides had very good reasons to view it as a dangerous destabilizing element. Western Europe justifiably felt threatened by possible Soviet dominance but the idea of countering that danger by a preventive war has always been far from the minds of Western Europeans and, since Hitler's death, from the minds of the West Germans as well. Besides, such a war would be absurd from a military point of view. Conversely, the Soviet Union has an interest in vigorous trade with militarily inferior but economically stronger and more civilized Western Europe, and it would certainly rather seize than miss an opportunity to give this trade the form of a "Finlandization" of ever larger parts of Europe. Russia is interested in a Europe that has not been destroyed by war. For this reason, it is not the genuine ability to defend itself but rather the simple determination to do so that protects Europe from military attack by the East for the time being.

It is precisely this political protection of Western Europe

that obscures the inadequacy of its military protection. Should the Soviet Union ever have strong political reasons for taking a step out of character with its traditional caution, and really test the credibility of European deterrence, it could choose from a variety of limited goals. It would either have to separate Europe from America altogether, or detach a "diseased part of the European body" from the rest of the NATO partners. As American nuclear superiority declines, and especially as Russian superiority becomes more apparent (see chapter 9), the military instability of Europe reveals itself more clearly. England's and France's nuclear armaments were an early reaction to this problem. But politically, that reaction still derived from the mentality of the European pentarchy which actually ceased to exist after the Second World War. England and France are no longer truly major powers. Western Europe might become one if it could take the seemingly impossible step toward becoming a political unit. We will pursue this question in chapter 10. Here, we merely intended to point up the internal logic by which a transition from American superiority to the stabilization of the duopoly obliges Europe to conduct a policy of its own whose very effect it will be to loosen the purely duopolistic structure of regional European politics.

This policy of war prevention encounters obstacles which are rooted in social structures.

This thesis can count on the ready assent of those who hope that war will be left behind as a particular form of social system is overcome. It is this system then which they perceive as their enemy, communism or capitalism, as the case may be. The symmetry of these theses provokes skeptical reflection. In our comments on the first thesis, we expressed the view that neither the convergence of the two social systems nor the victory of one would guarantee the prevention of war. Nonetheless, we believe that fundamen-

tal social obstacles stand in the way of a policy of war prevention. To clarify our meaning, we begin with a thesis
which will then be elucidated step by step.

1. *The obstacles to peace do not lie only in those structures
which distinguish present-day societies from each other, but
predominantly in those they share.*

How are the obstacles to a peace policy perceived on the
two sides, both in one's own and in the enemy camp?

We begin with the self-perception of liberal society, especially in its major military power, the United States. In it,
we note an internal domestic polarization concerning questions of foreign and armaments policy. Their respective representatives are occasionally dubbed doves and hawks.
Viewed ideal-typically, the dove appeals to reason, i.e., the
intelligent perception of the egoistic interest of both sides
in the interest of the whole. It appeals to the reason of its
own side *and* that of the enemy. It is in the hawks in its
own camp that it sees the danger of war, not because they
themselves would start one, but because they give the
enemy reasons for fear, and thus strengthen the hawks in
the opposite camp. The hawk, on the other hand, feels that
this appeal to the reason of the enemy is love's labor's lost.
He believes at best that the strength of the West can make
the enemy see reason. While the dove perceives the parallels in the two systems—hawks and doves here and there—
the hawk perceives the difference between the two. He
points out that in order to retain internal political power, a
communist system cannot afford any kind of weakness, and
that communist Marxism differs from liberal doctrine in believing war to be presumably unavoidable. The Western
hawk perceives the specific social presupposition of the
continuing war readiness of the Soviet Union. This author
must state his own position at this point: when the hawk
argues intelligently (and this is not invariably the case), he
judges those preconditions correctly. He can quote the
many precise statements of Soviet leaders concerning the
meaning of peaceful coexistence. Peaceful coexistence is the

continuation of the class struggle by all means except war. It is inconceivable that someone who adheres to this doctrine about the class struggle should not prepare himself for the eventuality that the class enemy will take the struggle into the arena of war. Besides, Soviet doctrine believes in ultimate victory and has never given a guarantee that the policy of peaceful coexistence is more than a phase in the history of the class struggle.

This has already taken us to the perceptions on the communist side. Of course, Soviet leadership does not delude itself about the lethal dangers of war. There is no reason to doubt that it takes seriously a policy which will avoid it. And a trend toward caution in comments and remarks paralleled the acquisition of nuclear armaments. It cannot be readily decided by an outside observer whether there is an opposition between hawks and doves among the Soviet leadership. Experts deny it. But that entire leadership is perfectly aware that the prevention of war is a desideratum. A Western policy which wishes to come to terms with it over the long run and while maintaining the strength of both sides will find that group to be a realistic partner in negotiations. But can the Soviet leadership expect to find dependable and realistic negotiating partners in the governments of the West?

Let us recall a communist but not a Soviet judgment, i.e., Mao's "the Americans and the Russians are hegemonists, but the Americans don't understand this business. They try to catch ten fleas with their ten fingers." Compared to Russian policy, American policy seems inconsistent (see chapter 9, p. 192). One can put permanent stock neither in its dovish nor its hawkish aspects. Of course, this indecisiveness is even more pronounced in Western Europe. A Soviet foreign policy planner can only react to Western policy by keeping all options open for his country. Within the framework of his political philosophy, he can understand this inconsistency perfectly well: the decline of capitalism is due to an inherent necessity which constantly places the members and groups of the leadership elite at odds with each other because they represent different private interests. If the author may make a comment here: this Marxist analysis contains an element of truth but is too primitive. In this instance also, it is more interesting to criticize the strengths of the liberal system. We are thus led back to the perception we have of our own social system.

The strength of liberalism largely rests on the fact that it involves the rationality of the largest possible number of members of the society by motivating them to actively fight for their interests. In the economic sphere, that is the theory of the transparent market: those who participate in the market are better judges of their own interests than any bureaucracy, and the free interplay of these individual interests creates a social Pareto-optimality.[34] But economic liberalism requires a stabilizing political framework. It is the theory of political liberalism that political decisions are prepared for by free discussion and based on the insight that has been attained. I must insist that a liberal theory which in the political arena also only sees a balancing of private interests according to a constitutional schema does justice neither to the difficulty of the problems, nor to the actual strength of the liberal system. There are fundamental political questions—and the preservation of peace is certainly among them—where the interest of the whole does not lie in a balancing of particular interests. Only insight is useful here. Good policy is impossible without a measure of recognized truth. Political liberalism rests on the experience that truth is more easily found in free discussion than in any other way. It is true that this system produces long, laborious and often chaotic debates. Clear procedures are therefore required so that timely decisions can be made after debate has taken place. As long as these procedures work, the system is probably also more efficient than authoritarian ones which do not have to engage in debate. Even public scandals are preferable to scandals that are swept under the rug.

But freedom of debate in representative democracy encounters its limit when we look at the effects the struggle for domestic power has. Election years are a concentrated object lesson here. Those taboos whose violation by one of the contending parties would insure its failure in an election are respected. And the politician who consciously withholds the truth is less dangerous than the one who permits himself the psychological relief of not facing it. Not the deliberate lie, but self-deception is the innermost citadel of the devil, the father of all lies. One of the means of political self-deception is the projection of the causes of evils. Problems of armaments agreements may serve as an example: it is never we who are at fault in the arms race; it is always the enemy. America was unable to see that its policy of military superiority was a threat to Russian security but reacted with profound fear to the threat Russian military superiority posed to its own security (for the first time in the case of the Sputnik/missile gap crisis before 1960). An example of the repression of truth taken from more recent German history: up until 1969, no party in the Federal Republic could openly admit that the recognition of the German Democratic Republic and the Oder-Neisse line was unavoidable.

The vicissitudinous history of Western security policy could be presented as a function of domestic political power struggles.[35] An analysis of the interests of elements among the armed forces, the ministries, the arms manufacturers, political parties, cliques and individuals, would furnish a great deal of material. To the person who studies the inner history of decision-making in some depth, even the right decision must almost seem an accident. In this respect, the two social systems resemble each other. We summarize the picture in a second sub-thesis:

2. *All the highly developed societies that have existed so far are stabilized by power structures whose representatives are prevented from clearly perceiving or implementing the general interest of their own state as it is embedded in the general interest of mankind because they are subject to the pressure of their own specific interest, i.e., the preservation of their power in society.*

To overcome the obstacles confronting a war
prevention policy requires a comprehensive
transformation of consciousness.

The terms "consciousness" and "transformation of consciousness" mean several different things. Everything depends on understanding them in the precise manner in
which they are necessary to a policy of peace.

In commenting on thesis I, a transformation of consciousness relating to war as an institution was mentioned. This
has already occurred in our century and is still under way.
It means a reorientation and results in the conviction that
war must and can be definitively overcome. This conviction
was called inadequate to prevent war if it fails to perceive
its social and psychological causes. It is not yet a "genuine"
transformation of consciousness but merely the symbol of a
longing for it.

In the categories of social thought, this inadequate inten-
tion to have peace would be called merely subjective. An
opinion of individuals who accept a social structure that is
in fact at odds with that opinion has little effectiveness, and
usually turns into that sort of self-deception, that kind of
obfuscation of one's own private interests that is promoted
by the profession of general ideals and was called ideology
by Marx. Liberalism and socialism are doctrines that make
political demands; they perceive this weakness and insist
on a change in the social structure. In the comments on
thesis I, it was also maintained that neither of these doctrines—even if it were to prevail with all major world
powers—would guarantee the avoidance of war. The argument there was historical and empirical: up to this time, no
shared social system has ever deterred a plurality of sovereign states from pursuing their imperialist competitive interests through war. The third thesis provides a reason for
this observation. Internal power struggles or structures of
domination in all historical societies, and that includes lib-

eral and socialist ones, interfere with the perception and implementation of the public interest.

If this thesis is correct, it is that very same structure of the competition for power which causes war between nations and prevents the implementation of the public interest within them. Of course, distinctions must be made here. We have historical progress and historical corruption, salutary crises and hopeless decay. We will return to these questions in chapter 11; here, we are only concerned with an awareness of the principle.

Such awareness is very old indeed. Every political ethics, whether it be the old, traditional religious or the rationalist secularized one, demands that special interests be curbed. All societies have striven and in principle been able to extend this restraint far enough to avoid bloody, and especially the systematically bloody settlement of conflicts of interest, i.e. war, within society. Of course, this was achieved because varying groups identified their special interests with the public interest, and this identification is called rule. The altruistic ruler remained a regulative idea. Liberalism and socialism developed from the same movement of political enlightenment which attempted to overcome domination as an institution and to reduce it to the rendering of functional services. They reproach each other for having failed to dissolve one particular kind of domination, indeed, for having strengthened it. In the case of liberalism, it is economic domination, the disposal over capital; in the case of socialism, it is the rule of the absolutist bureaucratic state, to use a moderate term. Both reproaches are justified and often also serve those that raise them to divert attention from the justified reproach addressed to them, and especially to quiet their own conscience.

But ideological critique is only indirectly relevant here. However ideological they may be, both liberal and socialist states generally achieve internal peace and avoid civil war. There is no analogous structure which would dependably prevent national and imperial war. To allow such a structure to come into being, though not in the form of a world state but in that of a secured duopoly, a pentarchy, a world organization after the pattern of a more highly developed United Nations, is the goal of today's war prevention policy. Our third thesis merely states that the rational and fundamentally realizable goal of this policy is not attained because competition for power within the various societies continues. The actual problem is not that recognized necessities cannot be implemented but rather that they cannot be implemented precisely because they are not recognized as necessary by the most powerful groups. The power struggle and the preservation of domination direct a considerable degree of attention to one's own, and especially one's own short-term interests while they blind one to the general interest which includes one's own long-term interests.

A transformation of consciousness would have to change our modes of perception, not our opinions. This is possible, but the road toward that goal is almost unbearably painful. Sacrifice—not the sacrifice of cattle or the gift of charity—but the sacrifice of what one considers indispensable to one's own happiness is the symbolic expression of the readiness to assume this pain. If there ever were men who knew why there always are murderous conflicts among human beings, they were the founders of the major religions. Jesus: "Your heart is where your treasure is." Buddha: "That is the illusion, that is the origin of illusion, that is the dissolution of illusion, that is the way that leads to the dissolution of illusion." Even if social forms should be found which allow power struggles to be settled by techniques other than war, it is inconceivable that murderous intentions will disappear without such momentous self-enlightenment. Anyone who does not know this does not know why his own actions constantly sow the wind and reap the whirlwind. The encompassing transformation of consciousness can and must take hold of the entire person.

But it is also necessary that this encompassing transformation which would lead to a policy of peace be distinguished from exaggerated demands. Not the happiness of mankind but the more modest task of preventing world wars is the goal of the transformation here referred to. To achieve this, it must extend to all social groups which participate in the shaping of political decisions, i.e., those in power and those who mold opinion and, in a certain sense, the peoples in their entirety. But it must go no further than to teach them their own long-term interest insofar as it depends on the preservation of peace. This does not involve the transformation of the entire person but the still painful and subsequently joyful perception of the world-political nexus.

The person who believes he knows what is being presented in this book finds himself in a constant dilemma as regards the political behavior he is to demand of himself. He sees that the political mechanisms, which ultimately mean his own fellow beings with whom he is in daily contact, half-unconsciously create the avoidable misery that awaits them. A transformation of consciousness requires a profound fright which one can no longer ignore once it has taken hold. Often, one feels one has to shout at people to make them wake up. But one knows that they consider a person who shouts a fool and therefore chooses the path of sober presentation. An academic contribution finds friendly acceptance but practical consequences do not result. But anyone who has been profoundly affected by the self-inflicted suffering of society, such as the leftist youth movement of the last decade, usually reacts falsely and engages in an ideological diabolization of certain groups and social structures which invariably results in effective, reactive diabolization on the part of society.

Perhaps this had to be said to make clear to readers with what kind of motivation this apparently academic book addresses itself. Given the powers in today's world, we must ask what kind of peace policy is possible so that, should it be successful over the short term, it not deprive itself of the psychological base it needs over the longer one.

A war prevention policy must be conducted in such a way that it facilitates and does not impede the transformation of consciousness.

Like any policy, war prevention policy must be the slow, cautiously proceeding art of the possible. But its criteria must include more than political success. It must permit that transformation of consciousness which always strives for something lying beyond the goal the policy has actually been able to attain at any given moment. In the last part of the book, we will also measure the concrete political steps by this criterion.

7. On the Theory of Power

Halfway along the path, on the summit between the ascent toward an overview of some of the major dangers of our time, and the descent into the valleys of practical politics to prevent war, we stop for a brief, fundamental reflection. Have we brought order to the chaos of today's fears? Do the concepts we used in our analysis permit consistent use? Do we understand our own basic concepts?

We made the attempt not to begin our analysis with theoretical prejudices but by a concentrated exposition of the questions relating to today's economic, political and military practice. We took the practice for granted and first searched for the simplest, still recognizable structures that can cast light on the unsolved problems of practice. Where we began with general assertions (as in chapter 6), they really only had the rhetorical purpose of attracting attention. They were meant as a provocative formulation of the findings the author had come to after an extended analysis of questions of political practice. Everywhere, we proceeded inductively and reflectively, not deductively.

But this procedure has led us to certain fundamental concepts. Current usage, a vocabulary that reflects contemporary thought, suggested them. The most important terms of this vocabulary are perhaps the three abstract nouns: freedom—domination—power. Let us recall how they suggested themselves to us.

As defined by its representatives, today's world economy is a free economy. The doctrine of this freedom derives from the emancipatory pathos of the European Enlightenment of the eighteenth century. Here, freedom is understood as the opposite of domination. History evidences the productive power of this system of a free market, of free entrepreneurs and of the freedom to form unions: today's technological world is their work. But the problems and dangers we encountered also stem from the unregulated, possibly uncontrollable elements of this freedom. We had to demand governmental, sometimes international rules and regulations, and sometimes we had to become utopian and demand that a world government lay down such rules, i.e., we had to demand that freedom be modified by elements of a rule which itself would have to be constitutionally limited.

Marxism criticizes the capitalist system from a different perspective. It sees it as an imperfect emancipation, a continuation of domination though not by feudal lords but mediated by the private disposition over the means of production. It is factually no longer important whether this disposition through the legal institution of property lies with individual entrepreneurs or stock holders or, in large enterprises, with managers who largely escape social control, the Galbraithean "technostructure." [36] But we have advanced reasons for the view that even where its criticism of the system is well founded, Marxism, at least in its original revolutionary form, did not develop an alternative which would have brought us closer to the dismantling of domination. On the contrary, it created systems of domination whose liberalization seems difficult if not hopeless, and this precisely because the means of production are not privately owned.

While the ideological dispute between the systems thus uses varying interpretations of the concepts freedom and domination, we discovered behind the age-old institution of war a structure which we called power, and systems of power. This raises the question whether the three concepts, freedom—domination—power, can be used in a consistent manner.

Every serious theory begins with our surprise about something that had seemed too natural to us because we had always been familiar with it. This philosophical wonderment may seize us when we consider the phenomenon of domination. Initially, we may find it comprehensible that the physically strong rooster should dominate the hens, or the bull the cows. But why do serfs obey the landowner, soldiers the commander that leads them to their death? Louis XV became king when he was barely five years old and died at the age of sixty-four, having lived a life during which he was more interested in beautiful women than in governing. How is it that the monarchy survived him? Why did I accept twelve years of Hitler rule?

These questions lead directly into the ideological quarrel: tell me what party you elect, and I will tell you what theory of domination you find persuasive. Conservatives talk about human nature, progressives about social structures. The views of an intelligent person which are not motivated by his political interests are therefore almost the only ones which have importance in the search for truth. Is ruling and being ruled a natural, innate form of behavior or is it a historical, transformable social product?

It seems to me that domination is a complex phenomenon where one can differentiate at least three components: order of rank, function, power.[37] The science of behavior has taught us to understand order of rank as an apparently innate form of behavior among many animals that live in groups. And it is immediately plausible that life in a social group will produce fewer frictions when there does exist a long-term undisputed order of rank among its members. It is possible to live with such an order; to live without it is extremely laborious. But what is immediately plausible obscures the questions that are not being raised: to begin with, precisely if an order of rank is efficient because it makes for a smooth existence, it will be difficult to determine empirically what about this behavior is innate and what must constantly be learned anew by the individual. Will an order of rank, if innate, also make its appearance where it is not particularly efficient? Secondly: is it not obvious a priori that the order of rank will be the same for all life functions? Humanization has been attributed to the possibility that the same individual may hold a variety of ranks in a variety of functions, in short that rank depends on role. Finally: where do those conflicts emerge which can be settled smoothly because an order of rank exists? Presumably, the formula of classical economics applies here: wherever certain goods are scarce. The primacy of the economic which is condemned by so many conservatives as the mark of Marxism is precisely the explanatory principle for the fact that evolutionary development favored the rise of an order of rank.

It cannot be the aim of a sketch such as this to decide such difficult ethological and anthropological questions. But we can say this: the observation of orders of rank is a behavior pattern that occurs frequently and apparently readily among men and animals. The frequently observable resistance of the individual is not directed against the order of rank per se but against his own inferior place within it. For this behavior in social groups, the smooth settlement of conflicts over scarce goods is a plausible objective reason. It is not necessary that the participants have an insight into the mechanism; the Darwinist argument ad spectatorem is sufficient: social groups which settle such matters smoothly have a better chance for survival in the struggle between groups than do those which have no such mechanism.

The term function, on the other hand, is meant to denote that kind of role distribution which goes beyond a mere super- or sub-ordination in an order of rank, as where one can talk about work, for example, the division of labor. Among human beings, the distribution of functions is generally tied to some insight into their purpose (even if, as in the case of religious functions, for example, that purpose is not evident to members of another culture such as modern rationalists). Human morality in its various phases of development may lead to a recognition of a basic equality of men (as in Kant's categorical imperative), provided that existing differences between them are accepted as necessary differences in function. Peace in rational human orders of rank is the body of an insight into the role of insight in human life. On the other hand, a reasonable order of rank can be justified through the degrees of insight available to its members, which means that maturity, education, ability, a detached view of one's own person are the criteria. But such an order is always relativized by the fact that all its members are treated as human beings, i.e., as in principle capable of insight, and equal to this extent. A sensible mitigation of the order of rank is achieved through functional ordering, through the distinction between the power of the office and the position of the person holding it, through regularly occurring elections to office, in short through limiting the attributes of domination to what functionally makes sense.

But anyone that knows social reality and political history senses the unrealistic and idyllic quality in this description of rational orders of rank. If the phenomenon of domination could be reduced to the two components of order of rank and function, the fascination, the temptations and the suffering connected with it, its affective aspect which pervades all of history would remain incomprehensible. There is a third element in domination and it is that element which introduces the edge, and the compulsion to struggle. That element will be called "power" here.

What is power?

There is a widespread view according to which power is

primarily irrational drive, the striving for power. This view considers interference with the rational order of human life as explicable only if the strength of unreason, of affect, of blind drive is seen as the source of confusion. This way of thinking sights an important phenomenon but its aim is short, as it were. The irrational, the affect that is not directed by reason, is certainly an enormous power in human life. But the irrational also has a reason for its existence and anyone who wishes to deal with it rationally must attempt to understand that reason. For the person that thinks historically and in evolutionary terms, the irrational does not suddenly make its inexplicable appearance, like the serpent in paradise. Affects can be defined primarily as elements that sustain "objectively rational behavior without the subjective perception of reason." Without such behavior, animal life, humanization and human history would not have been possible. The formula of the rationality of the irrational suggests itself in this connection. Then one can also understand in evolutionary terms how affects become disorderly in changed circumstances, how they necessarily destroy what has been constructed by a creature capable of reason when rational control is not exerted.

When one attributes disturbances in rational social orders to irrational forces, two other irrational drives, aggression and fear, are usually also named. A discussion of the psychology of these affects will benefit us as we try to understand power.

In the development of peace research, there was a phase during which the source of conflicts and especially of war was primarily looked for in the psychological mechanism of aggression. Indeed, the use of organized force by human beings against other human beings would presumably not be possible without a generally available aggressive potential. In this sense, the readiness to be aggressive would be a necessary condition of violent forms of domination and of war. But it is not a sufficient condition, for otherwise mankind would never have known peace. Do violent conflicts arise from a heightened aggressive potential, or do socially and politically caused conflicts conversely arouse dormant aggression? Such questions cannot be answered unless one reflects about the causes of aggressive behavior and its meaning in evolution.

Among the intellectual public, a simplified form of psychoanalytic thought which does not always use Freudian concepts and hypotheses as the system requires is very widespread. Tracing aggression to traumas in early childhood is part of this, and this derivation is often conjoined with a socio-critical judgment concerning the domination of parents over children. In its empirical detail, this view contains a good deal of truth. It can contribute to a better perception of the children by parents, and thus to peace between the generations and the capacity for peaceful behavior by adults. But it is a partial truth. Most importantly, its proponents usually forget to ask the real question about the cause of aggression. They confuse the actual release of aggression with the reasons for the capacity for it. How is it that a human being can react to psychological lesions and disappointed expectations (and sometimes perhaps to the disappointed expectation that it will be led) with this specific psychological mechanism, aggression? How, for example, do we explain the frequent inclination of children who have been brought up in an "anti-authoritarian fashion" to manifest pointless aggressive behavior though all ordinary causes for it have been carefully removed?

Sigmund Freud cannot be blamed for not having asked this question. He did not react to phenomena he could not explain by forgetting to ask about their reason, though sometimes by fantastic constructs. In his later phase, he linked aggression to the darker aspects of his view of life, the death instinct, which he felt it necessary to postulate. But the only attempt to make aggression understandable as something positive, as a factor in development, i.e., as the "rationality of the irrational," comes from Konrad Lorenz.[38]

The ups and downs of intellectual fashion initially brought his theory considerable prestige, and then a great deal of criticism. Yet it seems to me that the criticism does not refute the structure of his argument but merely some admittedly ill-considered applications to current problems. As a theoretical model, the structure of his argument merits examination.

Lorenz begins by teaching us to see aggression as a behavior pattern of animals. It is essentially directed toward members of the same species, more abstractly, against "one's own kind," and generally neither against prey (hunger instead of aggression) nor against stronger enemies (fear instead of aggression). The more highly developed the animal, the more discriminating and probably stronger aggression becomes, by and large. Lorenz then inquires into the biological meaning of this behavior or, in Darwinist terms, into the contribution it makes to the survival of the species. Lorenz's answers to the question may be incomplete, but the question itself is correct. He discovers that intraspecific aggression furthers the expansion of a species in the living space accessible to it. Among animals that live in social groups, aggression stabilizes the order of rank. Aggression within a social group is directed at individuals, and sometimes at individuals only insofar as they play a certain role (not at X as a colleague, for example, but as an erotic competitor). As happens often with organs and forms of behavior, so aggression also changes its structure when its use changes. Lorenz even speculates that aggression may sustain individual recognition, even individual ties, i.e., non-erotic friendship.

But already the reasonableness of the question concerning the biological meaning of aggression changes that meaning when we try to explain "irrational" behavior. To the extent that we recognize aggression as a building block in meaningful social behavior, we can no longer consider it the fundamental cause of peace-endangering conflicts. Well known, threateningly aggressive forms of behavior such as anger, hatred, hostility among groups, enthusiasm, are precisely not what is being described here hypothetically as functionally embedded aggression. What is being described is the severance of such forms of behavior from their peace-preserving function. It is only by virtue of this severance that aggression takes on the characteristic coloration which makes it "emotional" or "irrational."

Among the most important factors of this severance are the closely associated affects fear and anxiety. I will not discuss their psychology here (see my lecture "Anxiety") but only quote two attempts at a definition: fear is the affective perception of a danger, anxiety is the fear of our own incapacity for peace. The second, more complex definition will be taken up once again in chapter 11. The concept of fear leads to the question how man reacts to danger. Already in animals, fear can trigger aggression. The individual will usually run away from a danger it can avoid. But what happens when it can no longer flee? Sometimes, it can save itself if it attacks a stronger enemy with extreme aggression, and even if the individual does not survive, its attack may save its group and serve the preservation of the species. In the evolutionary process, such forms of behavior make for survival.[39]

But in the case of man, there exists not only this combination of patterns of behavior of escape and desperate attack but another, structurally more "detached" or "colder" way of dealing with danger which was sufficiently successful to be integrated into traditional and perhaps even into biologically inherited behavior. And it is this which will here be referred to as "power." Its description justifies that we choose a new point of departure for our examination.

As the word is being used here, power is a form of behavior uniquely characteristic of human beings. While it is true that it can only be understood against the background of the struggle for survival which pervades all organic life, it is a form of behavior in that struggle which man "invented." It has a tendency toward boundlessness which is alien to animal behavior. We have to try to understand the reason for the possibility and the functional meaning of this boundlessness and to do so, we must sketch an anthropology of power. Power is a central concept in a study about paths in danger, for in its origin, it is a reaction to dangers.

We shall first discuss the biological background. Danger is omnipresent in organic life. Every creature is threatened. Seen from the point of view of evolution, this is not an imperfection of life. The threat to every individual, every species is a product and a vehicle of evolution. The earth on which organic life developed is no protected garden but a field of battle. Progress in evolution is newly discovered paths in and through danger. Evolution itself produces the pressure weighing on its creatures. It produces the danger which pushes evolution along in turn. It allows the successful to multiply until those possessions on which their survival depends become scarce, and new paths toward new successes are given a chance. This is not intended as that glorification of struggle characteristic of certain forms of popularized Darwinism. One sees deeper into reality when one perceives the suffering of the vanquished majority and not just the triumphant history of progress as the victor writes it. But it is our task here to neither praise nor blame what happens, but to first learn to understand it.

The pattern of behavior of the surviving individual and, on a higher level, the pattern of the surviving social group is itself a product of evolution, an "invention of nature" which favors the survival of the species in question. Simple molecules which can reproduce themselves and which one may assume to be the beginning of organic life make no contribution to self-preservation, for that is a highly nuanced organic achievement. It is only for individuals who try to stay alive that something like danger exists: a situation which is an occasion to protect oneself or, more abstractly, to engage in patterns of behavior that insure survival. A further, very much higher, late level of development is a capacity of individuals which can only be adequately described in psychological concepts: it is the ability to imagine a danger, and is called fear. To imagine danger does not require that it be present; thought can direct itself to what has not occurred as yet. A third, even higher evolutionary step is man's ability to store ideas and forms of behavior to an almost unlimited degree, which is done in language and tradition mediated by language.

As compared to the animal, we can thus say that man has an almost unlimited ability to store ideas. One of the most important ideas man in nature has is the idea of danger and of defenses against it: foodstuffs, implements, weapons. That there is, in principle, no limit to the amounts that can be accumulated corresponds to the limitlessness of notions, ideas, representations. Accumulation has its rational limit at the point where its continuation no longer reduces danger. Dangers resulting from hunger or predatory animals are limited, and a limited quantity of fruits, arrows and other weapons is sufficient to deal with them.

But there is a danger which is potentially unbounded, and that is the danger posed by other human beings. Everywhere in organic life, the most complex patterns of behavior developed in contact with members of the same species, for here any developed pattern of action can produce a reaction in the same species: mating behavior, care of the young, behavior patterns within a social group, are classical illustrations. If the behavior is not innate but learned or even mediated by ideas, the alternation of challenge and response can develop and intensify in the life of two individuals, or over the course of a few generations. Mutual threat through the accumulated means of power is one of these patterns of behavior.

The accumulation of means is one of the most important building blocks of culture. The accumulation of the means of power was an instrument in the creation and preservation of extensive forms of domination. Without such forms, presumably neither cities nor the empires with a high culture would have come into being in the course of history.

But the instances of the constructive role of power in the history of human culture do not prove that power has eo ipso a constructive effect. It is ambivalent, it both hastens and endangers evolution, it is the kind of effect that always results from forms of behavior which meet dangers by creating new ones. According to the theory of selection, no pattern of behavior guarantees unlimited success. Many evolutionary steps were temporarily successful and then led to catastrophe (historical examples: gigantic growth, irreversible specialization). Since its beginnings among the Greeks (and probably also in ancient China), the theory of politics has been a theory of the reasonable limitation of power, of the necessary rule of reason over power.

The necessity of a reasonable limitation of power can easily be demonstrated by an abstract model of the competition for power. The foreign policy of sovereign states is such a model, and it is this model which made clear to us the importance of the concept of power as discussed in the preceding chapter. A state is called sovereign when there is international agreement that it can freely dispose over its means within the framework of generally valid international legal restrictions. It is thus free, among other things, to wage war on its neighbors. How does the neighbor protect himself against this danger? By armaments. In principle, the accumulation of military power is unlimited. What seems to be a limitation of resources is in practice usually a limit to the military effort a state is still willing to make; in economic terms, a question of cost. When will a state feel secure militarily? Strictly speaking, only when its defensive capacity is superior to the combined aggressive capacity of all of its possible enemies. If the state demands this of itself, we get, mathematically speaking, a set of inequalities which cannot be solved. In a system of several sovereign states which are strategic targets for each other, it is impossible for everyone of them to be militarily superior to all potential enemies (even defensively). In the preceding chapter, we discussed models for resolving this situation at some length. Up to this time in history, none of them has been able to avoid periodic wars, i.e., the de facto temporary failure of its defense, except by the elimination of sovereignties and their replacement by a central power.

We describe this structure here for a second time, using the most abstract, simplified language possible, because we want to make clear that its permanent instability is not due to a correctible defect in the system, but lies in its very nature. A pure balance of power is inherently unstable, if only because power can be accumulated indefinitely, at least in principle. Every partner in a competition for power acts rationally in pursuit of his objective when he increases his own power, and this rationality of the parts is the irrationality of the whole. Temporarily achieved stabilizations of systems of sovereign powers always contain an element which does not derive from the pure competition for power, an element of reason, if the use of this somewhat vague term is permissible here. Because of Kissinger's prestige, his example of the European balance after the Vienna Congress is once again being discussed internationally.[40] In Kissinger's formulation, the example demands that no "revolutionary" power be a partner in the concert, and a revolutionary power is defined as one that does not acknowledge the rationality of a policy of balance. But we must not overlook that this particular balance owed its permanence to the export of the competition for power. It shifted to economic and colonial expansion, and collapsed when there was nothing left to divide.

Marx's analysis of capital accumulation furnishes another example of the identical mechanism of power. Capital is that form of power which is accessible to the bourgeoisie. All pre-liberal economic theories considered it proper to subordinate this power to the control of the state, i.e., the control of a central reason. Adam Smith was right when he said that decontrol of the market and of production would give both an exceptional evolutionary impetus. It is no accident that Darwinism took classical economics as its conceptual starting point (see *Fragen zur Weltpolitik*, pp. 112–117). Of course, Darwin went on from the pessimistic version of the economy which Malthus had developed. It is precisely economic success which initially causes a population increase and thus the renewed scarcity of goods. But Darwin also saw the evolutionary impetus of scarcity, and that is how he developed his concept of selection in the struggle for survival. In an almost Darwinian manner, Marx analyzes the compulsion that exists for the individual capitalist to accumulate if he wants to survive competition. His specific immiserization prognosis was false. But that the capitalist world system with its inherent compulsion to growth is no configuration of unlimited stability became obvious in the third chapter, I believe.

For millennia, the phenomenon of power has engaged the imagination of men. The great poets, and especially the great dramatists, have shown us that power is generally tragic for those who have it. Power is unlimited in principle, and the striving for it is therefore ultimately doomed to failure. But this profound psychological insight may induce the temptation to see the striving for power as an aberration, foolishness. Yet the tragedy lies at an even deeper level. It is rooted in the fact that the striving for power in competition has a rational goal in so far as it serves the purpose of defense. Only when we have understood this do we understand the seemingly demonic consistency with which war, political domination and economic competition have time and again involved men in almost irresolvable conflicts.

This insight into the tragic core of power is indispensable for a political analysis. To ignore it means to ineluctably embroil oneself in utopian hopes, for we have tragedy where we are so blinded that we do not comprehend the reasons for our self-created fate. The tragedy of power is not inevitable; power is not the greatest force in human life. It may serve reason. A necessary, though not a sufficient, condition for this is that reason sees through the mechanism of power.

It was the purpose of this chapter to give a basic sketch of this mechanism, but it is not the purpose of this book to provide the utopian plan of a world order where today's powers would function in the service of reason; we are dealing with paths in a continuing danger. We can, however, address the reason of the powerful, and the reason of the public that puts up with them, which means that in a sense, it clearly wants them as they are. We will now turn to the concrete attempt of outlining an integration of military power into foreign policy reason, and will not hesitate to make concrete political proposals. The final chapter will take up the themes sounded here once again.

8. The Armaments Policy of the Two Superpowers

In the last two chapters, we discussed the problem of war prevention in its fundamental and in that sense abstract structure. In the following three chapters, we focus on its specific historical form in the present and examine what it looked like during the last few decades and may continue to be some decades into the future.

Since the end of the Second World War, there have been only two major military powers, the U.S. and the Soviet Union. One can speak of two additional major economic powers, Western Europe and Japan, and of one additional major political power, China. But these five powers do not constitute a pentarchy in the classical sense because a military power that could be turned against the other members of this Club of Five is available at this moment only to the two superpowers. The military situation in today's world is determined by a duopolistic apex.

Theory of the Armaments Duopoly

Before discussing the historical detail, we shall call to mind the fundamental structure of a military duopoly.

The term military or armaments duopoly is used to denote a situation in which there are precisely two states whose military power can only be seriously endangered by the other.

The term "Clausewitzean weapons" is used to refer to weapons to which Clausewitz' comment applies: given an equal quantity of weapons, defense is superior to attack. If there are only Clausewitzean weapons, there is no imminent reason in a duopoly to engage in an unlimited arms race. For if strength is equal on both sides, the defensive position of each is superior to any attack and thus neither need fear it even if it should be launched. The inducement to attain offensive superiority over the enemy by unilateral armaments decreases with the increasing superiority of defense over attack. If, for example, a one-to-two relationship in troop strength is adequate for defense, a potential attacker would have to arm to more than twice the strength of the defender.

It is true nonetheless that historically, duopolies have often been unstable. Presumably, this is due primarily to two factors not mentioned above: external interests, and geography.

External interests: the two duopolists usually live in a complex world of militarily weaker powers. They strive first to maintain their military superiority over the world around them, which means they strive to stabilize the duopoly externally. Secondly, they have interests in the surrounding world which cannot simply be realized by military means.

External stabilization of the duopoly establishes a lower limit for what are viewed as adequate armaments. Total disarmament, a step that is plausible if we only consider the relationship of the duopolists toward each other, is therefore unacceptable to them. It should be added that if the duopolists mistrust each other, even quite minor arms buildups also become immanently destabilizing. For each of the two need only make a small effort to increase his weaponry to such an extent that it becomes superior to the

other's for purposes of attack. In a duopoly, with Clausewitzean weapons, only those arms buildups are stable which
are large enough to make the attainment of superiority in
attack economically or politically more costly than is judged
acceptable by either side. For this reason alone, the armaments of duopolists normally lie close to the upper limit
of what is perceived as economically acceptable.[41]

Interests that are external to the duopoly and are not necessarily military but may be principally economic or socio-
political are often seen by the duopolists as their primary
interests beyond their national borders. Normally, a military duopoly is not a planned structure but the result of a
hegemonic conflict that is as yet unresolved. Precisely in
consequence of the military stability of the duopoly, such
conflict has a strong tendency to be shifted to whatever
happens to be the "Third" World at a given moment. Interests there can frequently not be realized by purely military
means but can be protected by military safeguards. This
leads duopolists to a variety of external military efforts. As
Mao put it, the U.S. wanted to "catch ten fleas with their
ten fingers."

Geography: the external interests of candidates for hegemony offer an example of the bearing geographic conditions
have on a duopoly. But we are returning now to an examination of the purely military confrontation of the two duopolists with Clausewitzean weapons. It is worthwhile here
to ask *why* defense is usually superior to attack. Fighting
men ordinarily must not only subdue their enemy but also
nature, and that includes such elements as distances, obstacles in space, inadequate overview. By choosing his position, the defender can turn space into his ally. Abstractly
speaking, geography is the defender's ally. The attacker, in
contrast, has the advantage that he can choose where to attack, and can concentrate his forces at the chosen target.
Normally, the attacker can conquer part of the territory he
attacks but pays for this by losses which may either make
further conquest too costly or even make possible a coun-

terattack. In addition to this physical element, there is a moral factor: the defender's willingness to fight frequently increases as the threat approaches the area in which he lives. This phenomenon has been demonstrated in the behavior patterns of territorially living animals: the result is that individuals or groups have territories which are roughly proportional to the size of their fighting strength.

This geographic element initially contributes to the stabilization of duopolies (and of power systems generally). What has been destabilizing in the history of power systems is the increase in power connected with the conquest of territory and the people living in it. Large empires usually grew slowly and therefore in a territorially stable fashion. Toynbee has pointed out that ultimately, hegemony in a culture sphere superior to the world around it often falls to a peripheral power whose territorial expansion was favored precisely by its peripheral position and its late entry into hegemonic competition. An example: European preponderance in the world of the last four centuries has brought it about that the European peripheral powers, North America and Russia, are the only ones to remain as hegemonic candidates.

The appearance of non-Clausewitzean weapons—nuclear weapons—initially had a destabilizing effect, as we noted in chapter 6. Non-Clausewitzean weapons are a possible consequence of very advanced technological development. Natural space is no adequate protection against them. The struggle occurs in an artificial world. A duopoly theory as relatively simple as the one just presented cannot be developed for non-Clausewitzean weapons. The history of the Russian-American duopoly so far can be presented as a succession of attempts to establish a stability plateau for the new weapons, and the renewed erosion of that stability. We will use our theoretical approach merely to examine the phases of this history in its structural elements.

On the History of the U.S.-Russian Duopoly

Early in 1945, it was apparent that the following few decades of world history would be governed by a Russo-American military duopoly. There was reason to believe that this duopoly would be stabilized by geography. Nuclear weapons had not yet made their public appearance. To defeat the other militarily therefore necessarily seemed a technically overwhelming task for each of the two superpowers. And for this very reason, the destabilizing effect of geography was also in full force. A war between America and Russia was very likely at that time because it would not be a struggle involving survival or catastrophe but a war for territories that would be of decisive importance for power in the future. Seen from this perspective, the two most important territories were Europe and China. That these local wars were brewing was not seen clearly in the West and especially in the United States. There was the euphoria that the war was over, and hope for world organizations, such as the United Nations. But at the Yalta conference in 1944, Stalin and Churchill grasped these perspectives clearly. Their quarrel arose precisely because both saw the future identically, albeit from opposite points of view. They evaluated it in terms of power politics. Roosevelt, however, was willing to sacrifice Western positions to his hope of winning the Russians over to a worldwide peaceful order.[42] From Yalta to the present, the policy of the two superpowers can be described by the somewhat crude formula: Russia consistently obeyed the rules of power politics, while America did so waveringly and halfheartedly (cf. Mao's judgment).

During the second half of the forties, the two major territorial conflicts were settled by the superpowers without recourse to actual war. Europe was divided between East and West. Through a civil war to which Russia contributed more than America, which mistrusted the party it was allied with, China became communist and thus, initially, Russia's ally.

This analysis which confines itself to power politics does not of course do justice to the perceptions on either side. Both America and Russia acted on the basis of ideologies one of whose aims it was to overcome war as an institution. In this respect, they differed from the mentality that prevailed in the European concert. Roosevelt and Stalin, though not Churchill, felt similarly about this. But in precise analogy to their domestic policy (see chapter 4), they differed in their judgment concerning the path to be chosen toward world peace. Liberal America saw it as a step by step dismantling of power, and communist Russia as the social victory of socialism which would be achieved through power. America's relationship to its own power therefore had to be ambivalent: it had to view its own striving for power critically. Russia, on the other hand, could perfectly fuse its own ideology with the tradition of domination of the Czarist empire. It seems to me that one should not be surprised that the hopes one had for world peace in 1945 were disappointed, and it is fruitless to search for a villain. After the beginning of the Cold War, both sides used good arguments to stigmatize certain acts of the opposing side as resulting from power politics, and justified the need for power politics of their own on that basis. It is a fact that neither of them ever stopped engaging in such politics except that America did so halfheartedly at times.

The resolution of the European and Chinese territorial problem should also be considered in terms of consciousness. One could say that communist rule in Eastern Europe was stabilized exclusively through military power. But in the civil war in China, it had the support of, or at least encountered no resistance by, the masses. If one makes the self-determination of nations the guiding criterion, it must be said that America supported the wrong party in both Eastern Europe and China at that time. The atom bomb produced the global awareness of instability with shock-like effect. But it is also true that it stabilized peace within the duopoly for that very reason. The first impetus to stabilization came from world-political consciousness (see chapter 9). The horror of war was deepened by the atomic bomb. Because people began to understand that the abolition of war was a necessity, they began to think that it might also be possible to abolish it. It is questionable that America could have waged a permanently successful preventive war against Russia when it enjoyed nuclear superiority. Because of their own morality, however, the Americans could not have started such a war in any event. In addition, the bomb was also initially a stabilizing element in strategic calculations. It tabooed all territorial war between the superpowers because there was the danger of nuclear escalation, and thus reduced the impact of the geographically caused instability of the duopoly. It fixed all those borders whose modification contained the danger of direct confrontation between the superpowers. Europe's stability since 1945 is its result. This is the first level of nuclear stability. The doctrine of massive retaliation is its strategic expression, and it attained its fulfillment through the hydrogen bomb.

But this stability did not really rest on strategic rationality but on America's superiority and the American conviction that this superiority must not be used to launch an attack. This situation was a signal to Russia to both undercut America's nuclear superiority and to eliminate it by a nuclear arms race. That the enemy would evade massive retaliation which one could threaten abstractly but would not readily decide on in practice if he engaged in small-scale aggressive moves was a danger that dawned on the Americans and led to the doctrine of graduated deterrence and thus to an inevitable arms race in conventional and tactical nuclear weapons. The arms race in strategic weapons, on the other hand, was the natural consequence of the introduction of these very weapons. Here, our previous remark also applies: a low level of armaments within the duopoly is unstable because it can easily lead to unilateral superiority. Nuclear armaments were one-sided from the very start, and it was indispensable for the Russians to try to catch up. The American hope that superiority could be maintained derived from erroneous estimates of Russian capabilities.

A limitation of the arms race in strategic nuclear weapons is the goal and partially also the result of the second level of nuclear stability, mutual deterrence through second strike capabilities (MAD, see chapter 6). Ideally, this is a genuine military balance whose theory we need not restate here. To the extent that it is correct, this limitation is due not only to the fact that costs are acceptable to both sides, but that the marginal utility of further armaments decreases. Pure mutual deterrence through strategic weapons could, in principle, be guaranteed by a minimum deterrence, i.e., through capabilities which are just sufficient to inflict unacceptable damage on the enemy. Those representatives of the arms control school whose primary goal it was to eliminate the danger of war did in fact hope that they could attain a "radiation of stability" (see chapter 6) from such secure strategic deterrence to small types of weapons, and ultimately disarmament. I remember having often heard in discussions at that time (as during the Pugwash Conferences, for example) that the creation of second strike capabilities was precisely the level of armaments necessary to make possible the subsequent disarmament in an atmosphere of stability and of an easing of tensions. This idea was explained by a plausible comparison. If a tall, dilapidated tower in a town must be torn down, that cannot be done without danger to those living nearby. A solid scaffold therefore must first be put up so that the tower won't topple; then, it is dismantled story by story.

While stable deterrence did presumably result in a slowdown in arms buildups and clearly initiated a phase of an easing of political tensions between the world powers, it certainly brought no disarmament. Retrospectively, this is not surprising. In chapter 6, we discussed the limits of the effectiveness of deterrence. Our fourth point there was that precisely when deterrence to the use of the largest weapons is effective, it cannot solve the problem of agression on a smaller scale and with smaller weapons. This initially results in building other than strategic weapons. In chapter 10 we will discuss the significance this kind of armament has for Europe. But it may be weightier that from the very beginning, the strategic level was not clearly set off against the lower levels, and that consequently strategic deterrence did not become the point of departure for the total stability of the weapons systems, which would be a prerequisite for disarmament.

During the early sixties, in fact, America still had a significantly greater number of strategic weapons than the Soviet Union. Because of its concern about a "missile gap" which surfaced around 1959, it constructed intercontinental ballistic missiles at a pace which Russia could not keep up with at first. There is no question that American superiority in strategic weapons contributed to the Russian pullback in the Cuban crisis of 1962. In such a context, calculations based on a limited strategic exchange directed against the missile bases of the enemy emerge, and the question is then raised how many missiles each of the two sides will have left for a strike against the industry and population of the enemy (counter-value strike). Whoever has a surplus of missiles in such a calculation can use part of it as a threat against smaller transgressions of the enemy in the sense of massive retaliation (exploitable capability). In Europe, where the Russian preponderance in conventional arms was never in doubt, the West maintained a credible deterrence because it had tactical nuclear weapons and a surplus of strategic weapons on which it could draw.

But this superiority, so reassuring to the Western alliance, also guaranteed that the existing situation could not strike the Soviet Union as an adequate point of departure for disarmament. The Soviet Union had to attain strategic balance before it would consent to it, if it was willing to do so at all. This position derives from the logic of the duopoly and requires no recourse to communist ideology for its explanation. As long as America was far superior in nuclear weapons, i.e., during the early phases of the arms race, the Soviet Union characteristically made a propagandistic point by calling for the abolition of all nuclear weapons as a necessary first step toward international disarmament. But it dropped this demand as it approached parity with America.

In American and Russian armaments in strategic weapons, one discovers a structural difference which corresponds to the difference in the relationship the two philosophical systems entertained vis-à-vis political and military power. American doctrine stressed deterrence while Russian doctrine stressed employment of the weapons in case of war. Of course, this difference must not be understood too abstractly. The Russians also did not primarily want to use them in a military situation but were concerned with deterrence of the enemy, except that they obviously always felt that war would ultimately be quite likely. At least that expresses itself in their consistent tendency to limit damage in their own country by using both ABMs and civil defense. The Americans, on the other hand, strove for a stable deterrence as their primary goal but developed weapons for those more limited encounters which cannot be prevented by strategic deterrence, although it was their aim, of course, to obviate such encounters by proving that they were ready for them. As discussed in chapter 6, the difference in these concepts promotes the creation of destabilizing systems such as ABMs and MIRVs. From a technical point of view, SALT is no more than an attempt to forestall an arms race in such destabilizing systems. Diplomatically, of course SALT means more, i.e., the creation of a habit of resolving possible armaments problems through negotiations, to engage in the kind of policy set forth in our fifth thesis (chapter 6) which will promote rather than inhibit the necessary transformation of consciousness.

Present and Future of the Duopoly

The present state of the duopoly is characterized by a continuing Russian arms buildup. It is only against this background that one can judge the new doctrines which were introduced primarily by James Schlesinger when he was Secretary of Defense. These armaments developments relate to land war, the navy, strategic weapons and civil defense. In all four areas, the Soviet Union increased the quantitative edge it already had, and where America was ahead, it either caught up with it or took the lead. The Schlesinger doctrine counters this primarily by maintaining American superiority in many areas of weapons technology and by diversification so that "the options available to the president of the U.S. can be increased." Both sides are thus striving for "stabilization through superiority". The concept of stabilization through symmetry is being progressively eroded.

It is not the task of this book to discuss this process in detail. We shall limit ourselves to pointing out a few quantitatively important elements.

Since 1945, the Soviet Union has consistently maintained superiority in ground forces. During the past decade and a half, China probably feared a Soviet preventive war. Now, the Chinese tell German visitors that they have recently discovered that Soviet offensive preparations are not directed against China but the West. Judging by what we know about the concentration of Soviet troops along the Chinese border these days, we are probably correct in seeing it as defensive (see chapter 5). In Europe, the Soviet buildup was always greater than defense would require. Much of it probably is aimed at remaining superior to any disobedient partner in the Warsaw Pact (German Democratic Republic in 1953; Hungary in 1956; Czechoslovakia in 1968). Even observers familiar with this phenomenon express a certain unease about the continuing expansion of Soviet ground forces. In the 1973 war in the Near East, the world was surprised about the quantity and quality of the Soviet weapons sent there. This arms buildup is in line with classical military logic according to which long-term power is based on the dependable control of territory. On Europe's special situation, see chapter 10.

During the last ten years, the Soviet navy has caught up with the American. The type of Soviet naval construction can be roughly described by saying that it has more but smaller ships than the U.S. The American units are presumably more efficient but the American fleet as a whole is more vulnerable than the Russian. With this buildup, the Soviet Union can show its flag in the Third World wherever the United States does so. In a certain sense, this means that it is merely creating a balance after having been encircled by American naval and bomber bases during the fifties. But in this situation of encirclement, the Soviet Union was largely independent economically while the world market which is dominated by America and of vital importance to the West is very much exposed to the danger of military interference with its lines of maritime communication. Up to now, the Soviet Union has shown considerable restraint in the use of these means. In a relatively inconspicuous manner, it is creating a power which will be available for the long term.

Today, Soviet strategic missiles are superior to American missiles in quantity and throw-weight, and this is reason to consider a selective exchange of strikes. Nitze estimates[43] that due to technical American superiority during the last decade, a counter-force exchange would have left the Americans with a superiority in total throw-weight, and this even though after 1969 or thereabouts, the total Soviet throw-weight (missiles plus airplanes) available before the hypothetic exchange had begun to exceed that of the Americans. But if present trends continue, this will no longer be the case in the coming years, according to Nitze. A counter-force exchange would then drastically increase Soviet superiority. Of course, this is a controversial thesis. K. Tsipis[44] does not base his calculations on throw-weight but on CEP (counter-force effectiveness probability) where the number of warheads and their accuracy enters in, and theorizes that there will be a continuing and increasing American superiority.

Afheldt's book (chapter 4) contains a more detailed analysis of the possibilities in a selective counter-force exchange. As compared to the theory of assured destruction, the situation has changed primarily because strategic weapons no longer merely function as mutual deterrence to a major war which must be prevented at all cost precisely for that reason, but because they now play the role of an instrument that might actually be used for special purposes. It is characteristic for the turnabout in traditional logic which applied to both Clausewitzean weapons and the program of total deterrence that the selective use of strategic weapons only continues to be an effective threat when the enemy still has property that could be destroyed. If, for example, one power (called A) were to destroy the population of the other (B) by a single strike or render it incapable of survival, the counter-strike by B would no longer serve a rational purpose. But it is also true that the remaining and immune military headquarters in B would now no longer be deterred from it by a threat. If, on the other hand, A spares a significant part of the population and other targets in B, A can then deter B from a counter-strike by threatening to destroy what remains. There is the question, however, of whether anyone will continue playing this chess party coldbloodedly after a certain level of escalation has been reached.

The clearest example of the continuing use of traditional war logic on the Russian side is the Russian preparations in the area of civil defense. During the Kennedy era, civil defense was much discussed for a time in the United States, but ultimately little was done about it. The arguments advanced against civil defense at that time merit a fresh look today. It was primarily bunkers within cities that were planned then, a perfectionist protective program, in other words. Bunkers were to be reached very rapidly and to provide good protection even if the city in question were to be under direct attack. This plan was a reaction to the new threat by rapidly flying missiles. It was doomed to fail because of exorbitant costs, if for no other reason. Besides, civil defense preparations are psychologically problematical because they remind people in a painful way of the suppressed reality of the danger of war. They also carry the objective danger that once in place, they create an impression of safety which might encourage the country to an irresponsibly aggressive foreign policy. This last objection permits a less psychological formulation: effective civil defense destabilizes deterrence. With the exception of relatively insignificant fallout safety measures, civil defense was struck from the list of actions seriously called for. Here as elsewhere, America preferred to rely on total protection through deterrence rather than on the highly questionable protection afforded by defensive measures.

In the meantime, however, the Soviet Union has been busy creating a limited civil defense program.[45] It consists in preparing for the evacuation of large cities and the construction of ad hoc shelters in the open country by the evacuated population itself. Using ordinary tools, shelters of timber and earth can be dug and supported by following instructions that are supplied. Allegedly, they will sustain a pressure of one and one-half atmospheres and can be provided with filters against radioactivity. It is claimed that this structure can be put up in two days.[46] There is the question, of course, what strategic concept underlies this program. It offers no protection against surprise attack. But in a tense situation, the Soviet government might order evacuation and then threaten a strike against the American population. Politically, it would not be easy for the American government to forestall such an evacuation by a preventive strike. Wigner has calculated that a strike with the total American weapons potential and with no evacuation having taken place would result in 100 million dead in the Soviet Union, but not more than 10 million after evacuation and bunker construction had occurred.

If we accept these data, Russian civil defense has already destabilized strategic deterrence to a limited though not to a negligible degree. Of course, the relevance of the data is controversial in the U.S. But we must examine the consequences, should the data be correct and should additional factors not considered here fail to render them irrelevant. A significant increase in the number of dead resulting from a strike after evacuation would not be attainable in the view of the experts quoted here, even if a further buildup of American strategic weapons were undertaken. America would then only have the choice of simply accepting this unilateral Russian threat capacity, or of countering it by a civil defense program of equal value. But that the Soviet Union should make such a threat which would also be dangerous to itself can at most be expected in a unique case of enormous world-political import, for the Russians are traditionally cautious. Yet such an eventuality cannot be wholly excluded, and the existence of such a threat contributes to the erosion of deterrence.

This Russian armaments policy which is anonymous for us and gives us the impression of monolithic consistency is countered by a number of American concepts some of which can best be characterized by the names of their proponents. We shall confine ourselves here to Kissinger and Schlesinger. At the moment this chapter is being written, Schlesinger has been out of office for half a year, and most opinion makers do not expect Kissinger to remain in office much longer. But both of them have put their stamp on a phase of American policy which cannot wholly be wiped out even if others take their place. Kissinger's concept relates to foreign policy and has consequences for arms technology, while Schlesinger's relates to arms technology and has foreign policy consequences.

Since his Ph.D. dissertation on the Congress of Vienna, it has been Kissinger's point of departure that peace cannot be the direct goal of foreign policy but can only be the premium for a correctly conceived and intelligently executed policy.[47] Our theses 1 and 2 (chapter 6) may be viewed as an interpretation of his policy vis-à-vis the Soviet Union. For long-term stability, the duopoly first has to be stabilized and then transformed into a more pluralistic structure. The very successful triangular diplomacy with China and the largely unsuccessful effort to secure closer cooperation with Europe served this objective (see chapter 10). Stabilization of the duopoly includes a balanced military buildup and avoidance of a new arms race. This means that American strength must not appear as a threat to Russia. Kissinger viewed communist Russia as a "revolutionary" power, which means that it did not in principle recognize the legitimacy and principles of stabilization of the existing international system but did so only because it had to. This judgment earned him the criticism of the "liberal" wing. He also tried to lead the Soviet Union from its willy-nilly recognition of the balance of the system to a recognition of the necessity and legitimacy of this balance. To do so, he had to demonstrate that the U.S. was prepared to accept a balanced duopoly and would renounce a policy of military hegemony. This can be understood as the kind of policy set forth in the fifth thesis of our sixth chapter: a war prevention policy must facilitate and not inhibit a transformation of consciousness on both sides. During recent years, this has earned Kissinger the growing criticism of the right wing. He finally had to practice his maxim on a worldwide scale and show that a peace policy is not primarily a policy to establish peace but a policy of solving problems. His exceptional personal commitment here contributed to a change in consciousness. The solutions he could negotiate under the pressure of pervasively interrelated foreign and domestic policy power struggles were often not sufficiently constructive to be stable. So far, I have not come across a conception that would be superior to his, and have the chance of becoming a reality.

Schlesinger's central idea is the concept of military options. His point of departure is the stability of mutual strategic deterrence but he recognizes that precisely when it is stable, it solves no other problems. Through war games, the politicians have learned "that in many cases, the most suicidal and therefore the least credible course for the U.S. would be to attack the population in the cities of the enemy. So they quickly see that it is desirable to have the capability to retaliate by means other than a massive attack on cities." [48] The other options must be capable of being carried out in order to credibly deter the enemy from acts which would force the United States to implement them. They refer primarily to three areas: the balance of strategic nuclear forces, the balance of power in Central Europe, and naval balance. We will only discuss the European program in greater detail (chapter 10).

As regards its formulation, Schlesinger's program is not opposed to Kissinger's but its necessary complement. And yet both programs have an inherent tendency to conflict with each other. Actually, the military options are not elements of a constructive, common stabilization in the sense this may be said of the strategic second strike capability of both sides. They represent options for one side and provoke the search for options by the other. From the point of view of Kissinger's policy, the Pentagon's search for options could appear as a perfectionism which has not achieved the necessary transformation of consciousness, and which almost compels the enemy not to achieve it either. Precisely when it is successful, it is an element in the arms race. The reproach that Kissinger's policy neglects necessary safeguards is so false that it could more easily be maintained that it was precisely he who put his finger on the inadequacies of the strategic balance resulting from the growing lead of Russian strategic weapons, and that he therefore es-

tablished upper ceilings for their number in the 1974 Vlad-
ivostok agreement. Kissinger must resist the search for options where it is not vital from a military point of view, and
politically counterproductive.

It seems obvious that the conflicting positions here will
outlast the tenure of their respective advocates.

Consequences

The gradual erosion of the system of deterrence that was
conceived around 1960 does not threaten war between the
two superpowers for the time being. One might say that it
means the transition from a deterrence through assured destruction to a deterrence through an incalculable risk. But
this is precisely the reason it is a temptation to engage in an
arms race, and America did not resist it during the early
McNamara era. When America began to do so, it became
Russia's turn to yield to it.[49] The continuing Russian
buildup now leads America once again into this temptation.
Over the long term, it would contradict all historical experience if this arms race did not lead to war. The mere diplomatic intent to come to agreements cannot suffice to arrest
it; it cannot prevail over the immanent logic of such a race.
A third level with a transparent structure and a dependable
automatism once it had been carefully established and
which would be stable for some time would have to be
worked out. Is such a level at all conceivable, considering
the weapons which are now and soon will be available?

We will sketch such a level here which Afheldt presents
in a book now being published (especially in chapter 4)
without sticking too closely to his formulations. We begin
with a fundamental observation. Irrational consequences of
a power struggle such as an arms race which will ultimately
fail to leave the two enemies more secure than before arise
from the conflict between the realistically perceived desire
of each of the opponents not to be inferior to the other. The

two opponents have a common interest. The appeal to reason and good will (to fair play in classical European society)
should ideally be sufficient to avoid such consequences but
in reality fails to do so. The social implementation of the
laws of a universal morality requires social conditions such
that obedience to these laws would, at the very least, result
in no disadvantage to the individual in society (see chapter
11). In the society of states engaged in a military buildup,
the stable avoidance of an arms race requires that further
military buildup have a decreasing marginal utility for either partner. In the duopoly, this was the idea of minimum
deterrence or of MAD. The erosion of this level results from
the very fact that it has not allowed the marginal utility of
armaments other than those required for strategic deterrence to become sufficiently small.

A new level would thus have to stabilize not only the
strategic level but also those below it (the "substrategic"
levels). But if this demand is very strictly formulated, it is
presumably unfulfillable. Yet one can have the goal to stabilize the strategic level and the two most important substrategic ones. These are Europe and the high seas, and this is
precisely Schlesinger's program. But just as in the case of
the first historical level (Dulles) and the American practice
of the second (arms control), the program has the inherent
tendency to understand balance as American superiority.
Politically, this expresses itself in the postulate concerning
"continued leadership in the world."[50] In at least three respects, even this clear and demanding formula has a defensive meaning in the logic of power. America wants to be in
a position where it can always protect its commerce, its
allies and, wherever necessary, the principle of freedom in
the world. We, as American allies and participants in the
endangered freedom of the citizen have every reason to be
grateful for this American power. But because the Soviet
Union represents analogous (though not identical) interests,
it is evident that a principle of protection through superiority will lead to an arms race and therefore to a threat to what

is to be protected. The question therefore is whether these things can be protected in an arms structure to which the duopoly can agree and which will be self-stabilizing, once created. We will begin by setting up six ideal demands of a stable structure of deterrence and do so before we can know whether such demands can be strictly complied with.

1 / It should efficiently deter the enemy from seizing or destroying those possessions for whose protection it was created.
2 / It should give no occasion for an arms race.
3 / It should threaten the enemy only with acts which its population can survive.
4 / It should give the enemy no rational grounds to threaten the survival of the population in our countries.
5 / It should be capable of being introduced by unilateral action on our part.
6 / Should it erode again, it should not provide an occasion to turn into the opposite of demands 3 and 4.

1. This demand is self-evident. Without it, we are not dealing with deterrence. "Efficiently" is a deliberately vague term. A totally dependable deterrence is presumably unattainable. One can, however, reach the degree of probability with which we are prepared to live today. If one searches for certainty, one must abolish war (see chapter 11).

2. This demand defines a "level" of stability.

3. This demand is a radical departure from MAD. If it can be met, it will answer the objections which have been raised against both the morality and the credibility of MAD.

4. This is the mirror image of demand 3, and actually its prerequisite. If we give the enemy no occasion to take our population hostage, we need not inflict this on him. Otherwise, we will not resist the temptation to give tit for tat.

5. This demand may seem exaggerated. Perhaps our previous formulation that the structure of deterrence should be self-stabilizing once it is in place, is sufficient. That means

that it would have to be introduced through agreement but then lead no side into the temptation to infringe it. But such structures are not adequately definable in a few treaty clauses, and it may therefore be assumed that if they are at all stable after they have been instituted, they will offer advantages even to that side which observes them unilaterally.

6. What demand 5 expresses as regards the period prior to the establishment of the desired level is here being stated for the hypothetical period after its greatest effectiveness. Whether or not this last demand can be met may be wholly uncertain today. But we must never forget that none of these military safeguards can be more than a "path in danger" whose ultimate goal can only be a politically secured world peace if a world war is not to be the end result.

Anyone who is weighed down by the excessive effect atomic weapons have—and that is true of today's public, even the intellectual part of it—will view these demands as absurdly optimistic. They may even arouse the suspicion that they actually reduce those inhibitions to conduct war which are grounded in its huge dimensions. We have to take this suspicion seriously but can only give two answers. We have shown in chapter 6 that deterrence up to this point does not simply rely on the dimensions of the effect weapons have but on their rationally planned use for second strike capabilities. Besides, even such inhibitions are not absolute. General staffs and armaments experts have the obligation to work out many conceivable courses of armed conflict, and the above demands are first of all attempts to regulate these war games. They are the modest attempt to turn the demands of reason into demands addressed to the understanding of the planners.

Viewed instrumentally, however, it would seem that these demands are just as much within today's technical possibilities as was minimum deterrence or MAD some fifteen years ago. From the first development of nuclear weapons to the hydrogen bomb, the dominant technical concern was the magnitude of the effect weapons would have. Today, it is accuracy. The technical ability to achieve excessive effects can no longer be done away with. A war that would result in the practical annihilation of entire nations is possible. But accurate weapons can be used in such a way that such a war will not even be necessary as a deterrent threat.

A concrete model that might meet these demands will be set forth in this chapter, but it applies only to the strategic level. The corresponding model for Europe will be taken up in chapter 10. We will not discuss the problem of the security of the high seas.

The central idea of the model is that wars between sovereign states are neither begun nor ended by populations or armies, but by governments. Deterrence can and should have the aim of tying the interests of the rulers to the preservation of peace. Lichtenberg's powder keg expresses this in the form of an aphorism (see p. 126). It has two inadequacies. The first is that a law is being invented here which imposes on one's government an insupportable condition, and that it will therefore be abolished by that government at the earliest possible moment. The threat must originate with the enemy that is interested in peace. If possible, it must also be in recognizable harmony with the interest in peace of both populations. Otherwise, it can be eliminated by a unilateral act of the threatened government. Secondly, a government is necessary not only at the beginning but also at the end of the war. It is too primitive, not wholly plausible morally (and presumably also difficult to realize technically) to make the physical existence of the enemy government the object of deterrence. The specific vital interest of a government in contrast to the population and often also to the army is to rule the country. Deterrence would have to counter each act of war by threatening the enemy government's capacity to govern.

The second, instrumental concept of the model is therefore to threaten neither counter-force nor counter-population but precise counter-value strikes. Counter-force strategy will only lead to a reduction of the enemy's potential for military action without being able to force his will. If present technological development should lead to their abolition, destabilization would be manifest. A stable deterrence must therefore tend to keep the inducement to such a development small. It must thus let counter-force strikes become as useless as possible. Counter-population is hidden in MAD under the heading "counter-value." We are making a sharp distinction here between these concepts. To hit a population or an industry are two different things. If we ask ourselves which of the two kinds of strike will have a greater effect on a government that has decided to wage war or to persevere in one already started, the answer is unquestionably the destruction of industry. In a country with an advanced technology, this would mean that provisions for the population are no longer guaranteed, and a necessary foundation for the population's readiness to wage war would thus be eliminated. On the other hand, all experience shows that attacks on the population increase the solidarity between that population and even an unpopular government (those who lived through the Second World War in Germany will remember this).

The third idea of the model is not to threaten massive but sharply limited strikes with precise political objectives. This idea comes from the modern American debate about deterrence which we alluded to in this chapter. This requires that objectives which can continue to be threatened always remain so that a feared counter-strike against enemy strikes is still possible. An example would be an idea of Szilard from the fifties: in the case of a specific enemy act, it would be made known that one city would be destroyed in a week's time. This delay would give the population the time to evacuate. In such a case, this population may move on the capital to call on its government to desist. All these "scenarios" have something repellent about them, the quality of something that is both horrible and playful, like science fiction, that literary school of inhumanity. But they are realistic possibilities as long as sovereign states with modern weapons exist. It is the object of the model set forth here to subject these scenarios to the six demands made above, and thus to impose on them that measure of reason and humanity which is possible in this world of technological war.

Because a model such as this cannot be judged without a detailed examination of its feasibility, we refer the reader to Afheldt's extensive presentation. Here, we confine ourselves to this test: is the model reconcilable in principle with our six demands?

On 3—It is the core idea of the model to spare the enemy population as much as possible.

On 4—Morally, it will be difficult for the enemy to take hostage the population of a country which has expressly renounced that option. Nonetheless, there must be no military inducement to do so, be it explicitly or implicitly, as by a threat to material values which cannot be struck without the mass murder of the population. To the extent that the enemy observes the rules laid down here, this would mean that cities, industrial sites and regions etc., are to be advised in time. Our delivery system would constitute the sole inducement to an enemy strike. The continued existence of a second strike capability and its installation far from inhabited centers are thus essential. On this point, the model calls for no change in prevailing conditions. As long as our second strike capability which might ultimately retaliate cannot be destroyed, there is no military and political advantage in answering our limited threat by threatening or implementing the total destruction of our country. It is part of the new strategic development that it is a disadvantage in the system of threats to destroy in a single strike all of the enemy's resources that are subject to the threat of destruction.

On 5—The reflections under 3 and 4 make it likely that this model could be introduced without negotiations and unilaterally, and would carry a strong call on the enemy to follow suit.

On 6—One does not dare say more than that a deviation from its rules will encounter the resistance of caution and morality, once this model is firmly anchored in the consciousness of peoples and planners.

On 2—The arms race is a result of a counter-force strategy. Empirically, this formulation seems to be borne out by the history of arms development in the Russo-American duopoly. The strategic buildup preserved numerical stability as long as the American desire for a counter-force capability (either directly against missile bases or as an exploitable capability against weapons on a lower level) did not take armaments in that country beyond the necessary level and then provoked still continuing Russian countermeasures. Theoretically, this is precisely what must be expected. Our entire theory of power (chapter 7) is based on the unlimited possibility of accumulating weapons against weapons. Weapons against targets which are not being accumulated are not subject to this compulsion.

On 1—The argument that a strategy according to this model will deter effectively depends on the credibility of the threatened acts. For the side that threatens them, none of these acts entails an unacceptable danger either directly or through a prospective counter-strike, or an unacceptable moral or political odium. Yet it is true, of course, that even this strategy does not dependably solve the problem of war prevention. It can only claim to be better than the strategies now in existence. The previously discussed objection that it eliminates the actual war prevention factor, the horror at the enormousness of nuclear war, is incorrect. This horror has not prevented limited wars during the last thirty years, and greater threats have been made (Suez 1956, Cuba 1962). "The continuation of state policy with other means"* can-

---

*This is Clausewitz's definition of war. Translator's note.

not be permanently halted by this one terrifying fact, at least not as long as no political world order stands behind it. Another reflection is weightier: the state whose internal political system is less able to weather strain will be more sensitive to a threat that is directed against the will of the government. It is precisely a government which feels less certain of its position that will be more strongly tempted to choose threats other than those discussed. The introduction of this system may therefore be frustrated by those social structures which are the significant obstacles to a policy of war prevention (chapter 6, thesis 3).

There is another question which was not examined here: can this model do more than stabilize the strategic level? For that had also been achieved by MAD, and indeed by minimum deterrence. The instability and the arms race originated in relationships to other levels. This point will be discussed in the section, "Consequences," in chapter 10.

9. The Spread of Weapons

Danger Zones of World Politics

THE POLITICAL STRUCTURE OF THE THIRD WORLD

In this chapter, we will discuss the danger of armed conflicts whose origin is geographically limited but which may become sizable enough to affect world politics. When we ask ourselves where such danger zones exist today, we think primarily of certain Third World regions. This is no accident. In the belt stretching through the northern hemisphere where the centers of military and economic power are situated today, there has developed the kind of relative stability which often results when large powers border on each other. It is precisely the size of their power which obliges its possessors to be cautious in their dealings with each other. There must be a precise relationship between the danger that exists when armed conflict erupts, and the value of the object for whose sake that conflict is being risked. In the preceding chapters, we have advanced reasons for the view that this caution of the large powers is no guarantee that a major war will be avoided between them, and in the following chapter we will consider the local danger zone in the northern hemisphere most important to us, our European continent, from the perspective of a possible war. But compared to the ease with which revolutions and wars have been breaking out in the Third World for some decades, the northern belt is very stable today.

Armed conflicts in the Third World have a traditional and a modern component. The traditional one is that they are the continuation of a millennia-old condition of power conflicts in all regions of the world. Only territorial states, especially large empires at their height, have been able to suppress such conflicts internally and to some extent along their periphery. The peaceableness sovereign European states evidence today is a singular phenomenon world-historically, and we will examine the reason for it in the following chapter. But no one should be surprised that things in the Third World look as they customarily have in world history. Yet the people there (and here also) do not view their condition in this traditional way but rather as a unique historical process. It is invariably perceived as a process of modernization, and usually also as a struggle for liberation. A particular kind of conflict has become the most frequent and is called national liberation by those engaged in it. It has elements of what we, in the older Europe, would call revolution, civil war, national war.

The form of perception that goes along with this kind of conflict sees the entire world as a single political arena. The fronts have shifted time and again, but time and again, and sometimes to an increasing extent, they interpret themselves in universalistic, usually socio-political categories, and this is what I mean by world-internal politics.* After the military and economic superiority of the Euro-American civilization had been generally recognized toward the end of the nineteenth century, there developed an opposition

---

*The author's term, *world-internal politics,* is his coinage and is explained on p. 243. Translator's note.

between the traditionalists and the modernists in the other countries. Traditional and modernist elements later joined together in anti-colonialism. When political colonial rule ended, the struggle shifted to the economic and socio-political arena. Generally speaking, we now have a well-to-do minority that is allied with international capitalist interests and believes in modernization of its nation along this path. It is primarily socialist intellectuals that are the spokesmen for the impoverished majority. We considered the economic aspects of this development in our third chapter.

It may be assumed that the economic process is indeed the hard core of these events which changing political forms and modes of thought only modulate or at most advance or inhibit in certain directions. What occurs is technical modernization and a generally increasing though very unevenly distributed wealth. Even committed socialist regimes can only alleviate but not eliminate uneven distribution, even if we leave out of consideration the privileges of the functionaries (cf. our comments on China, chapter 5).

The speed of economic progress is always slower than reformers and revolutionaries hope for, but it is nonetheless significantly more rapid than it was one or two hundred years ago in Europe. The creation of wealth leads to the creation of power which, even on a global scale, is not wholly insignificant.

The economic power of the oil producers is an example. It would appear that this power has had no structurally adverse effect whatever on the capitalist system that prevails in the First and the Third Worlds, it merely created a crisis of adaptation for it. The new powers are integrated into the club of those that were powerful before. The effects on consciousness seem paradoxical but are actually perfectly understandable. The anticolonialist front against the First World was a political condition for the rise of the oil cartel. But as the cartel proves economically successful, its members begin to exercise economic and political power according to the traditional patterns. The spiritual front of the poor against the rich has the poverty of the poor as its prerequisite. As the Third World begins to participate in the power of wealth, its political thought which had been world-internal yields to traditional foreign policy thought.

This is very much in evidence in the military sphere. As wealth grows, weapons are bought. Using statistical material, we shall soon look at this process in greater detail. For the moment, we consider the political consequences. But they themselves are twofold, for they relate both to internal and foreign policy matters.

In terms of internal politics, the initial phase of poverty is a result of traditional and/or colonial rule. If the political opposition to such rule wants to organize itself militarily, it can only do so as guerillas. While successful guerilla warfare requires a military structure of command, it functions only on the basis of the strong political motivation of the fighters who are shaped and represented by a stable political organization. For this reason, the organizational form of victorious guerillas not only introduces a marked military component into the new regime but also the stabilizing primary of politics. Even a traditional or technocratic government which has defeated a guerilla movement and developed a military that could achieve such a victory usually remains politically superior to its own soldiers. But after political stabilization, the hoped-for disarmament of the victorious army usually fails to occur. Both domestic and foreign policy reasons favor its continuing strength. While during the struggle, weapons were frequently provided by sympathetic major powers, increasing wealth also makes it possible to purchase them on the open market. When the political leadership is faced by a crisis, the hour strikes where the military can become an internal force. Military dictatorship is thus the typical political form of countries that have been liberated from foreign rule but are domestically and economically unstable. To create and stabilize a functioning technocratic structure the military, being trained in its own sphere, is better suited than any other social group, especially when an experienced, half-way honest bureaucracy does not exist.

The spectrum of the political sympathies of the military ranges from conscious integration into the capitalist world system and the often sincere desire of the military reformers to ultimately turn over (or return) power to a legal, representative democracy, to radical, socialist and revolutionary convictions. Whether these political sympathies of the ruling military will ultimately lead to the political forms they wish to implement cannot yet be determined today. We now find ourselves in a phase where the political stability of military dictatorships is greater than that of systems characterized by political convictions. Outside of the northwestern part of the world where it is a developed expression of old tendencies of the native culture, representative democracy usually fails because it is allied with private economic interests, and especially where these interests do not have the highly efficient form of the technocratic capitalism also rooted in the northwestern part of the world, but the more traditional form of corruption. The sympathy that originally accrued to communist movements because they resisted colonialism and capitalism could not overcome the barrier produced by the antipathy to the imperialism of communist world powers, particularly that of the Soviet Union. Moscow- and Peking-oriented communist parties today participate in the competitive struggle for power in the Third World, like all the rest. But sympathy for them is not nearly as marked as a general, vague socialist sentiment; at best, their chances lie in the military support they receive. Where the test of freedom of expression could be made, no peoples with communist majorities have been found. Only in old-established, communist empires has communism developed an identity without alternatives. But the present opportunities military dictatorships have domestically does not prove that they will be able to solve their internal economic and political problems (cf. the pessimistic version of the economic prognosis, chapter 3). Under these circumstances, the foreign policy aspect of military development becomes important. Viewed in terms of foreign policy, one can say that the different Third World regions are today developing into classical systems of sovereign powers. Increasingly, they avail themselves of the classical techniques of the balance of power, hegemonic politics and limited wars. This is tolerated by the northern powers although it is not a source of delight to them. Of course, power systems already existed in these regions of the world during the precolonial phase and in forms which expressed the culture in question. But colonialism and the economic preponderance of the North suppressed this power structure for a while. The actual world-political power systems that came into being during this era consisted entirely of Northern powers. In principle, this is still true today. Compared to the North, the Third World is still militarily and economically powerless. The only exception, the oil producers, retain their share of power only because they participate in the economic process of the First World. Up to this point, they lack the basis for real power, i.e., a highly developed, diversified economy. That the North should have surrendered its colonial empires in view of all this justified a momentary philosophical astonishment (see chapter 7).

It would seem that the rise of political consciousness was the central element here. The intellectuals of the non-European nations adopted modern thought, especially its pathos of freedom and the organizational model of the nation-state. This development gained strength from the criticism European and American intellectuals, both liberals and socialists, leveled against power and domination. The colonial empires had been established by a succession of strong European maritime powers: Portugal, Spain, Holland, England, France, and Germany. The Second World War weakened these powers decisively. Their successors, Russia and America, had engaged in colonial expansion on their own continents and had integrated that colonial land. They could thus cultivate the illusion that they were no colonial powers and make themselves the advocates of anticolonialism. But the colonial empires were surrendered only because the real power basis of the North, the economic one, had not been shaken, and the maintenance of political rule in the colonies was no longer economically rewarding. Power shifted from the old European center west- and eastward, but not into the south. Otherwise, it would be incomprehensible why the oldest and militarily and economically weakest colonial rule, that of Portugal, survived longest.

Initially, and from the point of view of power politics, the reemergence of the regional power systems of the Third World is almost a luxury which the powerful North indulged in: let the children play! It would be too laborious to stop them. But it is also true that the political and economic interests of the Northern powers in the Third World, and also their political sympathies for the various groups there diverged from the very beginning. The world-political polarization of the North between liberals and communists extends to the Third World. The Northern powers feel impelled to intervene for reasons of ideology and power politics. Vietnam is the significant setback for the policy of intervention of the Western powers of the North. The Eastern powers learn their lesson in a less spectacular form. The powers of the North, in any event, see themselves obliged today to put up with the development of autonomous power systems in the Third World. This tolerance is subject to the continuing and unshaken superiority of the North. But the Northern powers must put up with the effects the power struggles in the Third World have on their own economy and politics, and it may be expected that this will become increasingly difficult and dangerous in the coming decades.

Here, the growing arms buildups in the Third World play a disquieting role. With depressing precision, they follow the pattern of the accumulation of power we discussed in chapter 7. Every one of the old or newly created territorial states has neighbors which restrict it economically or accord the internal political opposition in those states a threatening measure of support. One must be militarily protected against this, and thus the arms race of mutual defensive buildups sets in. And even if considerations of prestige and offensive intentions played a less significant role than they actually do, this process would have no natural limit. It should be pointed out that it is usually not the military dictatorships that carry on such militarist power politics, but rather certain countries where political organization—be it feudal-technocratic or socialist—has a stabilizing primacy. One may assume that the demand that the military be both responsible for governing the country and support an aggressive foreign policy is excessive. The attempt to combine both tasks is usually already a symptom of an acute internal political crisis. In this race, both the political and economic interests of the North intervene, thus hastening it along. For the Northern powers, it is a political obligation vis-à-vis political allies, and it is also big business.

What will be the political consequences? Arguments can be advanced for the view that this process will bring political stabilization. The power vacuum created by the withdrawal of the colonial powers demands new, stable structures. Why should they not develop according to the classical forms of foreign policy? Europe had its great economic and cultural development in the form of a concert of powers. The periodic wars that went along with that concert did not prevent this development. Why should the Third World regions not have a similar historical phase ahead of them? It is indeed possible to conceive of several regional concerts of power in the Third World during the next few decades. But this system is subject to two limiting conditions which did not exist for the old European concert: the overarching interests of the Northern power systems, and the modernity of technology, particularly of the economy. Both conditions are present in the world market and in the spread of modern weapons. It is for this reason that we are devoting one chapter to each of these two phenomena. What will be the long-term foreign policy consequences of the spread of weapons?

DANGER ZONES

The four great regions into which one can divide the Third World will be briefly examined here in relation to the dangers of military conflicts they harbor.[51] In each trouble spot, we have varying configurations of the conflict between the demand of reason and the internal logic of power and the effects it produces. Every one of the conflicts admits of a rational solution, and each contains the danger of a solution by force which would entail terrible misery in the region and a threat to world peace.

The Middle East. World opinion is correct in seeing the future of the state of Israel as posing the most crucial danger of war. The establishment of this state can only be understood through the millennia-old history of the people of Israel. Without the religious hope for the re-establishment of this state, this people would not have survived as a people. If justice toward a people means that it be given the chance to live that form of existence within which it finds its identity, it was just to create the conditions for the establishment of this state.[52] A reasonable, mutually advantageous symbiosis with the Palestinians would have been possible. Perhaps it had to fail in a world-historical phase during which the colonial forms of such symbioses ended almost everywhere, and new ones had not been elaborated. Today, the pathos of justice on the Arab side is almost as inextinguishable as the pathos of survival on that of the Israelis. The logic of power systems obliges Israel to always be stronger than its neighbors, and obliges the neighbors to exceed Israel's strength. The Arabs will win this race, and as long as the conflict cannot be settled in a form accepted as just by both, Israel's only hope will be to restrain its neighbors through the fear of a desperate strike by the weaker.

But the conflict with Israel and the necessity for the oil cartel to be successful has only thinly veiled the fundamental disunity of the Islamic world around the southern and eastern Mediterranean and the Persian Gulf. It is unclear how the opposition between a feudalism that is being transformed into a technocracy, and socialism will be decided in this region, particularly because disunity among the socialist groups everywhere in the world is as traditional as it is among Arabic feudal lords. It seems that over the short and medium term, the future does not lie in a vision of Islamic or at least Arab unity but with the territorial states that are giving themselves a modern organization. For reasons that differ in each case, several of these states are candidates for the role of a "regional superpower." Examples would be Iran, Saudi Arabia, Syria, Egypt and Algeria.

For the world powers, the Middle East is the most neuralgic spot of the Third World. America is inextricably enmeshed in the Israeli conflict and this makes it plausible for its world-political enemies to take the Arab side. Oil is vital for today's capitalist world economy. The Soviet Union has common borders with the region and could be threatened almost as much from Iran as from Europe or Turkey. Outside of its own territory, this is the area where the Western world is most vulnerable.

Southern Asia. India, Pakistan, Vietnam and Indonesia are already "major regional powers." Because spheres of power are not wholly defined and the Indian subcontinent suffers from excessive social problems, this region is a source of world-political unrest. Judging by the number of people and the level of the cultures being subjected to a process of transformation, none of the three other regions listed here is as important as this one. Yet events here probably have the smallest impact on the immediate interests of the great Northern powers (except for Japan, and probably China). There is no economic or strategic necessity for the U.S.A., Western Europe or the Soviet Union to deeply engage themselves in this part of the world. It can probably be said that the extended, indecisive American commitment in Vietnam rested precisely on this objective, relative irrelevance of the region for the superpowers. It was the free decision of the U.S. to intervene here and to pull out almost twenty years later. Only its self-respect and prestige were at stake, but no vital interest of its own which would have made victory at any price a necessity. Nor was there a vital interest on the part of any other power which could have prevented the American commitment.

Of course, the imminent problems of the region presage further armed conflicts whose effect on world consciousness is difficult to predict. In connection with the spread of nuclear weapons, we will return to the Indian decisions.

Africa. Today, the newly formed independent nations of Black Africa mean that there is a power vacuum with its attendant crisis potential. At the moment, it looks as if the strongest world-political interest there would continue to be the economic interest of the First World. As regards internal politics, these nations are today a field for experimentation where military dictatorships now have their chance. Structurally, they are probably less like the military dictatorships of contemporary Latin America than like those of the nineteenth century.

World-politically, the most important trouble spot today is South Africa and the reason is that the European power interest dating back to the colonial period is most difficult to surrender there. Seen within a global framework, there are no great concentrations of power there, and where it was determined to do so, a technically and organizationally superior white minority successfully resisted so far. Portugal gave up its colonies when its military leaders had become convinced that it was an objective mistake to cling to them. The Portuguese could withdraw to the mother country, as the French settlers withdrew from Algeria some twenty years earlier. The white Rhodesians don't want to do this, and the white South Africans can't. They feel that they have their backs against the wall, like Israel. It is uncertain when Rhodesia will fall, it is uncertain if South Africa ever will, should the world political situation remain stable for a few more decades. The governments of the North do not support South Africa overtly, but the economy does, and relations within the Southern world, to Israel, Iran, Australia, are being established.

In Europe, people reacted with comprehensible rather than well-founded nervousness to the seizure of power in Angola by a movement that was supported by the communists. Twelve thousand Cubans were the decisive element there. On the one hand, this shows how little the United States would have had to do to turn events around. A single glance at history would have shown that Angola and Vietnam are not comparable. In the one case, there were tribes which had not as yet been integrated into a nation. In the other, there was an old country that had been steeled in a millennia-old defensive struggle against China. In one case, the communists had to send supplies from across the seas; in the other, China was next door and provided support. But the American Congress did not fear this particular adventure, but the readiness to engage in adventures of this sort. In and of itself, the victory of the MPLA did no harm to any vital American or European interest. There is the question, however, whether this will be a signal for the as yet undefined African future. If I may make a subjective judgment here about a region I hardly know, I would say that Angola also will not escape integration into the world market, and the experiment of a further, more socialist-oriented alternative in Africa may enrich the spectrum of possibilities. If one sees the world of the next few decades as the arena of a struggle between the U.S.A. and the U.S.S.R.—and this may be realistic—it will be less the domestic policy of African states that will contribute to a decision than the chance the Soviet Union has to construct naval bases in West Africa. This takes us back to what was discussed in the preceding chapter.

Latin America. Seen in terms of domestic politics, the military dictatorships in many of the countries there seem to be the hole into which the ball will easily roll, and which it will leave only with difficulty. The question is whether these governments will succeed in technocratically furthering the economy so that social tensions decrease, as they decreased in Europe and North America during the last one hundred years. Nothing can be added here to what has already been set forth in the third chapter.

In Latin America, we already have something like major regional powers, or at least one, Brazil. The continent is lucky, for it has hardly any unresolved territorial conflicts. But economic growth will also lead to the import of weapons, and the political consequences of that will only appear at a later time.

The Worldwide Arms Buildup

Today, the world population is 4 billion. More than 20 million of these, more than 5 per thousand, serve as regular troops in armed forces.[53] The GNP of mankind was estimated at 3.8 billion dollars in 1972, which gives an average of about $1,000 per person. Military expenditures came to more than $240 billion, i.e., 6% of the gross product. The fraction of the gross product that goes to the military is, if calculated in this way, 10 times larger than the corresponding part of the population. Even when one considers that families are fed along with all those soldiers except where they are young draftees, and that the civilians paid from the military budget are comparable in number to troops, the military remains a capital intensive enterprise. For that same year, 1972, worldwide expenditures for education were estimated at roughly 210 billion. If the 136 countries included in the report cited under I (and these are all countries of some economic consequence) are divided into 28 "developed" and 108 "developing" countries[54] the total gross national product of all developing countries came to a little over 700 billion, which means that it was less than three times as much as mankind's total military expenditures during that same year.

As one lets these figures sink in, one feels compelled to call for disarmament. The amount of misery that could be eliminated by the funds now spent for weapons is enormous. And a great many legitimate reasons for bloody revolutions and wars would be done away with. Through a rational utilization of these economic resources, mankind would live infinitely more peacefully and therefore would not need these arms. And this consideration is based on the assumption that the military will not be used, that the money spent for it is thus spent "for nothing," as it were. But when the military does have to wage war, the economic damage will be incomparably greater within a very short time. And how much more limited this damage would be if the armaments had been smaller! If armaments and wars are truly the consequence of mutual fear, how much smaller that fear would be if armaments were reduced, if consequently reasons for armaments became less compelling. And how much smaller the danger of war would then be!

The call for disarmament is thus raised time and again, and always in vain. Historical experience teaches that disarmament was never a way toward the peaceful solution of foreign policy problems but at best the result of such a solution. Abstractly considered, it would of course be possible to implement a proportional reduction of weapons expenditures in all countries to one half, one tenth, and even one hundredth of their present level without materially affecting the present balance of power. As long as we do not see through the mechanism discussed in the chapter on power, we can share the conviction that exists in every nation and every world-political party: it is not us, but the unwillingness of the enemy that prevents disarmament. It is precisely this conviction which the enemy perceives as a lack of will on our side, and it thus produces the evil it fears. One might almost say that it itself is the evil it fears. The first chance for disarmament would be given if this mechanism were universally understood. This insight is neither remote nor difficult for the professional foreign affairs politician or the simple "man in the street." In this vague, general formulation, it is correct, but does not yet constitute a basis for concrete policy. It is necessary to understand the armaments mechanism in its detail if one wishes to counter it.

We will first consider growth rates, both globally and according to developed and developing countries.[55] From 1963 to 1973, the GNP grew by 5.1%, allowance made for inflation. Given an annual 2.1% growth rate of the world population, this gives us an annual per capita growth rate of 2.9%. Over that same period, military expenditures grew by 2.6% annually. The share of military expenditures in the total product thus decreased by 2.4% annually. In the developed countries, the growth rate of the GNP was 4.9%, in the developing countries 5.8%. But in the developed countries, the population growth rate was 1% annually, and in the developing countries it was 2.5%, which means that the per capita growth rate of the GNP in the former was 3.9% and in the latter 3.2%. In the developed countries, military expenditures increased by only 2% annually (relative decrease: 3.2%) while it was 7.2% in the developing countries (relative increase: 2.6%). We thus get a moderate buildup in the powerful North, a rapid one in the South. The economic and military power relationships are reflected in the absolute figures: the 1972 GNP of the developed countries: 3.4 billion per 1 billion population, or precisely $3,378 per capita. The GNP of the developing countries: 708 billion per 2.8 billion population, which gives $251 per capita. Arms expenditures of the developed countries were $211 billion, i.e. $211 per capita; for the developing countries, they were $38 billion, or $13.4 per capita. Worldwide armed forces strength was 25 million, 6.55 per thousand of population. In the developed countries, it was 10 million, almost 10 per thousand of population, in the developing countries 15 million or 5.4 per thousand of population. Expenditures per soldier worldwide were just under $10,000; $21,000 in the developed countries, and $2,500 in the developing ones. We thus still have an absolutely and relatively greater buildup in the developed countries.

The relationships become even clearer when they are broken down. Among the developing countries, China emerges with high absolute and moderate relative figures: estimated military expenditures, 14.5 billion, 9% of the GNP; estimated armed force, 3.3 million or 3.8 per thousand of population. By way of comparison, we take the United States: 77 billion, 6.7% of the GNP; 2.3 million men, 11 per thousand of population. Soviet Union: 81 billion, estimated at 10% of the GNP, 3.5 million men or 14 per thousand of population. Rate of increase of military expenditures in China, 8% annually; in the U.S., 1%; in the Soviet Union, 3.1%. Large military expenditures in the Near East: Israel (1972), 1.49 billion, 21.6% of the GNP; 130,000 men, or 41 per thousand of population; growth of expenditures (1963–1973), 25% annually. Syria: 250 million, or 12% of GNP; 115,000 men or 17 per thousand of population; growth rate, 12% annually. Egypt: 1.1 billion, 14.6% of GNP; 390,000 men or 11.4 per thousand of population; growth rate, 10% annually. India: 2 billion, or 3.6% of GNP; 1.6 million men or 2.7 per thousand of population, growth rate, 2.2%. Brazil: 1.24 billion, 2.5% of the GNP; 410,000 men or 4 per thousand of population; growth rate, 10%. Nigeria: 560 million or 5.3% of the GNP; 305,000 men or 5.3 per thousand; growth rate, 31.8% (from 1963–1973—creation of the army of a state that has been independent for only a short time).

Let us try to understand these figures. In the Northern belt of major powers, balance is temporarily being maintained by arms buildups that are still growing in absolute terms but that tend to be structurally stabilizing. The figures refer to the transition period from the Cold War to detente. In the South, we get large arms buildups and rapid growth in the danger zones and, absolutely speaking, small arms buildups with, in part, significant growth in less endangered ones. Apparently, the tendency toward increasing armaments is irresistible everywhere. Its size increases with increasing political imbalance. Every prediction of political destabilization will therefore entail a prediction of an intensified arms buildup.

What is the upper limit here? Probably economic considerations will everywhere set such a limit. Supply and demand determine price and quantity. Especially as a result of increasing wealth, demand in the Third World is increasing. The Third World is "normalizing" itself by striving for the same share of the military in the volume of economic activity as is customary in the other world power centers. The supply of weapons comes predominantly from developed countries. The volume of worldwide arms trade rose from 4.4 billion (1972 value) to 8.7 billion between 1963 and 1973. The sellers in this trade are also primarily states rather than private firms.

Given such a volume of production and trade, it is evident that there exists a significant economic interest in its preservation and expansion. The much-quoted phrase concerning the "military-industrial complex" as the community of interests of producers and users of weapons was coined by Eisenhower and describes what was obvious to a critical, high-ranking military man. Yet it would be an error to see the "real reason" for the arms race in the economic sphere. The technical possibilities of modern industry and the inducements of the market have made possible an unprecedented increase in supplies. But demand is maintained by a mechanism which is older than the capitalist, and stronger than the socialist, system.

The Spread of Nuclear Weapons

That part of this section which refers to the past deals with events which are widely known and have received considerable comment. In presenting my reflections about this story, I may perhaps be permitted to rely explicitly on my own recollections. Nothing is fully perceived unless one is emotionally involved. The deliberate presentation of emotionally tinged perceptions may perhaps render facts and problems more objectively than an "objective" stylization which hides one's personal motives.

The spread of nuclear weapons begins with the publication of the discovery of nuclear fission by Otto Hahn in January 1939. The terse announcement sufficed to put some 200 researchers all around the globe on a trail which was to lead to the atom bomb. Hahn did not know this at the time. When Joliot recognized and made known four weeks later that fission would release neutrons as byproducts the 200 researchers realized simultaneously that a chain reaction would now be possible. Nuclear weapons were international before they actually existed.

When we recognized these possibilities, people in every group probably asked themselves if it would not have been better, had the discovery remained unpublished. In March 1939, Szilard attempted to persuade the Western physicists to tacitly agree to suspend publications on nuclear fission so that the important details would at least not fall into the hands of the Germans (and the Russians). He failed because Joliot refused. I discussed the problem with Hahn at that time. He was still hopeful that a bomb would not be made and clung to the old scientific ethos that publication was a duty, that keeping matters secret would violate the spirit of the search for truth. He did not close his eyes to the danger of the bomb but also felt that if it were to be made, it would be worst for the entire world, even for Germany, if Hitler were to be the only one to have it. Profoundly disturbed, I discussed the wholly new set of problems with Georg Picht during one evening in February '39. Although not in all its precise detail, we had the sudden insight that this discovery could not fail to radically change the political structure of the world. And it is this change that is being discussed in this book. We saw clearly that from that moment on, the scientists would bear a political responsibility they could not possibly shrug off. It was also clear that this responsibility could not really be born in the existing political structure of the world. Hitler's rule was a drastic example. But we understood the power structure of traditional foreign policy clearly enough to also examine the wars that would occur after the Second World War which was imminent at that time. There may be special cases when it is correct to say that the scientist meets his obligation by keeping secret his discovery or by not making any. But in a general way, the development of the situation at that time, the "spread of nuclear weapons before they had come into existence," showed that this way out is usually impossible. One might envision a cooperative "order of physicists," but that would only be a dream. We were unaware that at that very moment, Szilard had failed in the single serious attempt which was taken in that direction, and when Heisenberg tried to discuss such possibilities with Bohr a few years later, the required exchange under conditions of complete mutual trust was no longer possible.[56] The scientist can only act as the citizen of a state, and as a citizen of the world with somewhat greater awareness than others: he must use his knowledge to work with others to bring about a new global political structure, and prove the seriousness of his efforts by his acts.

But what can this new global structure look like? To a person finding himself at the beginning of an era, its simple fundamental structures may become visible like a distant landscape in the flash of a single stroke of lightning. But the path toward them in the dark is long and confusing. At that time, we were faced with a very simple logic. Wars waged with atom bombs as regularly recurring events, that is to say, nuclear wars as institutions, do not seem reconcilable with the survival of the participating nations. But the atom bomb exists. It exists in the minds of some men. According to the historically known logic of armaments and power systems, it will soon make its physical appearance. If that is so, then the participating nations and ultimately mankind itself can only survive if war as an institution is abolished.

The atom bomb was made six years later, in 1945. The reality of world politics proved to be considerably more complex than the simple logic of our initial reflections. Of course, this very logic also occurred to physicists in America. They were close now to the levers of stable world power. Together with Lilienthal, Oppenheimer drew up a plan for an international atomic authority which would have disposal over all fissionable material in the world. It would have been the beginning of a world-state organization, created around a new, unprecedented problem which would perhaps give the world the courage for an unprecedented political construct. The plan failed because of the predictable Russian refusal and would otherwise have failed because of the almost predictable U.S. refusal. In the preceding chapter, we already discussed the further development of the Russo-American nuclear arms race.

Here, we are concerned with the mechanism of the spread of nuclear weapons to other countries and its impact on world politics. The extensive terrain stretching from the first emergence of the atomic bomb to the distant horizon— the goal of abolishing war—turned out to contain a third possibility, a compromise. One would have atomic weapons and see to it that they would not be used. The point of this compromise is not apparent to the simple logic of the little man. If one is determined not to use the bomb, why build it? There is a nice answer to this question which sometimes is prompted by a measure of unconscious humor: it is built to prevent its use. When this program is followed by two or more players, it does in fact become apparent that it follows almost necessarily from the logic of power systems. Everyone has the bomb to protect himself against its use by others. We have already analyzed the strengths and limitations of this deterrence within the duopoly. We now have to deal with its effectiveness in the pluralistic world system.

The atom bomb has created a new class system among nations. It has divided them into those that have it, and those that don't. Initially, only the U.S. had it. Great Britain was the only country which obtained it by agreement, for British researchers had participated in the American efforts from the very beginning, and the U.S. raised no objection to the production of the bomb by a smaller ally. The bombing of Hiroshima was the most important signal for the Soviet Union to manufacture the bomb. There was nothing of greater consequence to the Russians than to know that it worked. They obtained more detailed information from published reports (Smyth report) and presumably also from their spies. But there can be no doubt that they would have been able to manufacture the bomb without such help, and wholly on their own, within a few years. Technologically, France was also clearly able to do so, and prepared production even before de Gaulle came to power in 1958 and backed the plans by his nationalist determination and his pluralistic world concept.

During the middle fifties, the German Federal Republic was faced with the question whether it should undertake to produce its own atomic weapons. The country was a NATO partner, and there was a large arsenal of American nuclear weapons on its territory. Since 1954, we had been permitted the development of atomic energy for peaceful uses, and while we were not allowed to make nuclear weapons, we could have sought to have this ban rescinded. Nuclear physicists, including myself, who were advisers to the newly established Ministry for Nuclear Energy stated their unanimous view that nuclear armaments would be a national disaster. Our arguments were not as uniform as our conclusion. For me, the principal consideration was that if a war should in fact break out, it would be the very possession of a capability that vitally threatened the enemy that would invite a preventive strike against us. Worldwide disarmament negotiations were soon to take place, and Adenauer was unwilling to make a unilateral declaration that would prematurely surrender the bargaining chip of Germany's claim to nuclear weapons of its own. "No advance concessions, gentlemen." I believed that he was sincere in his wishful thinking that productive disarmament negotiations would come, for he was too intelligent to delude himself about the consequences of failure. But for the reasons stated above, I had no faith in disarmament. There was a combination of three reasons why I felt that the unilateral renunciation of nuclear armaments would be more advisable. To begin with, I did not believe that in times of peace, our real national interests would be significantly buttressed by the possession of nuclear weapons. In the second place, I felt that renunciation would be a contribution to the development of international consciousness, and hoped that it would have some slight influence on French plans. And thirdly, I expected that not having nuclear weapons would mean a small increase in our chances for survival in a possible war, as I stated before. F. J. Strauss was interested in the creation of a large European nuclear force which would be powerful enough to deter the Russians, should the Americans pull out of Europe, as he expected even at that time. The following chapter will deal with this question. After our public declaration in 1957, there followed a confused public debate during which naive friends and primitive opponents made it equally difficult for me to clearly set forth my nuanced understanding of a complex situation. The upshot of all of this was that the Federal Republic of Germany renounced nuclear weapons.

In the early sixties, both the French and the Chinese had atomic bombs. America realized that the atomic monopoly was not just transforming itself into a duopoly based on parity, but that even the duopoly could not be rigorously maintained. The Nuclear Non-Proliferation Treaty was proposed and implemented. The political idea was that the atomic club of the five powers could still be stabilized by arms control since the two superpowers initially had a crushing technical superiority, but that it would be impossible to do so if there were an unlimited number of countries having atom bombs. The signatories agreed not to manufacture, buy or sell nuclear weapons. Clauses which required a good deal of laborious compromise assured free access to peaceful reactor technology under the control of the International Atomic Energy Agency (IAEA) in Vienna.

After I had advocated that the Federal Republic become a co-signer of the Non-Proliferation Treaty as was consistent with my earlier position, I had some very instructive but disquieting talks with its opponents in India and France. When I explained to Indian colleagues (in 1969) why I had recommended that my own country voluntarily renounce the manufacture of nuclear weapons, I was told that that was our business, that India did not want such weapons, but that the Chinese danger obliged it to keep its options open. This argument was linked to a withering criticism of the morality of the duopoly. The division of the nations of the world into those whom one considered sufficiently rational and moral to handle nuclear weapons for the single reason that they already had them (and had used them against civilians!), and those whose rationality and morality one denied because they had lacked that background, is worthy of moral condemnation and untenable, I was told. With Cartesian precision, the French general Gallois, adviser to de Gaulle, presented me with a political and military theory on this position. The possession of nuclear weapons makes their owner cautious, and world peace would be guaranteed at the very moment where *all* sovereign nations (including Paraguay and Upper Volta) owned them. In any event, it would only make sense to use such weapons in the punishment of a life-endangering threat, i.e., the military occupation of the sanctuary of a nation, its national soil. If possession of nuclear weapons were general, all borders would become inviolable. When I asked what would happen if someone should wage nuclear war against a neighbor, I was told that the first would also be the last, for the rest would learn their lesson from the result.

These talks did not convince me of the harmlessness of a further spread of nuclear weapons during the coming decades but impressed me with its probability. I could justifiably have reproached my partners in these conversations for the very thing for which they just as justifiably reproached the superpowers, which is that they were working out a general, political and moral thesis designed to justify their own particular interests, and that they furthermore took a short-term view of those interests. I did not raise this objection for to voice the suspicion that the partner is ideologically motivated does not contribute to the search for truth, even when that suspicion is justified. I would have had to propose a more convincing world order than either the duopolistic or the atomic-pluralistic one. What actually emerges here is that non-possession of nuclear weapons cannot be permanently enforced in a system of sovereign powers, and that the thesis "to have but not to use nuclear weapons" does not dependably guarantee peace. The only solution is to do away with sovereignty. As a very modest extension of the Oppenheimer-Lilienthal plan, the Non-Proliferation Treaty was meant to be an initial step in that direction. But it becomes apparent that, at best, only those that benefit from them will go along with such regulations. I have never really heard a logically more consistent analysis of this situation in today's world than the one Mao has the habit of presenting to his visitors, although here also the Chinese interest shows through the cracks (see chapter 5).

The German Federal Republic is becoming a country that exports nuclear reactors. Plutonium is created in such reactors. We gave in to Brazil's wish to provide a reprocessing plant along with the reactors. This did not involve a violation of the Non-Proliferation Treaty (which Brazil did not sign in any event though Germany did), but it did violate a rule which the U.S. imposes on its own firms that supply reactors: reprocessing must occur only in the exporting country. The treaty between the Federal Republic and Brazil aroused exceptional public indignation in the U.S.,[57] and was the most profound crisis of confidence between the two countries in years. The Germans defended themselves by a mixture of correct and incorrect arguments. It is correct that in its contract with us, Brazil consented to controls by the IAEA which are even stricter than those provided in the Non-Proliferation Treaty. But it is false to allege that the real reason for the American protest is economic, as most Germans surprisingly believed for a time. In many discussions with Americans, I observed the profound *political* concern, while the lobby of the American reactor manufacturers began to suggest that its government imitate German liberality. It may be correct that Germany would not have received the order, had it not agreed to provide a reprocessing plant, and this is an economic consideration. And it is probably also true that the American nonproliferation policy cannot be sustained over the long term. But it is false to believe that such failure would not be dangerous.

The degree of risk one ascribes to such reactor deals depends on the kinds of danger one envisages. It is possible to secure agreement concerning controls against the theft of fissionable material, and this is what a cartel of reactor-exporting countries did in London, in December 1975. It would presumably serve collaborative efforts to create a system of checks if importing countries were allowed to participate in such agreements to the fullest extent possible for without mutual trust, such a system cannot work over the long term. But theft is not the greatest and certainly not the only danger, in my view. In chapter 2, I expressed skepticism concerning the use terrorists could make of stolen plutonium. It would of course be possible for national governments in the importing countries to secrete plutonium and make bombs from it. But we may ask what advantage they would derive from the secret possession of atomic weapons. In a war, they could use them in a desperate situation or in an unexpected attack. But the much more plausible political use of such weapons is to publicize their possession and thus to deter or intimidate enemies by the threat of their use. It therefore makes much more sense to acquire atomic weapons in public view, and not secretly. Politically, the majority of "local major powers" of the world regions could presumably afford to do so today without having to fear active resistance by the world powers. India's example confirms this. Once Brazil has factual and legal possession of a reprocessing plant and has collected materials and know-how, there is no one that could prevent it from simply terminating the treaty that forbids the military use of such material. But if a reprocessing plant in Brazil were to serve all of Latin America and were the legal property of a regional or global authority, Brazil would have to violate international law if it wished to appropriate those materials.*

During the next few decades, it will be difficult to prevent "local major powers" from acquiring atomic weapons if they so desire. The technology is becoming so simple and accessible, and the required quantities of material are so small that they might take this course even without having to break the contract by which they now acquire their reactors. It is possible nonetheless that the concept of regionalization and internationalization could have a braking effect—but only under the indispensable condition that it is introduced in an atmosphere of cooperativeness. The local powers can judge for themselves what problems will confront them, once they have their own atomic weapons, for their enemies will also have them some day. It is still possi-

---

*This was written before the election of President Carter. In the meantime, I have attended several bilateral German-American talks on these problems. This is not the place to go into details. In principle, my view of the problem has not changed. The proposals of the MITRE-Ford Report to forego reprocessing altogether seems to be economically unacceptable to countries like Germany and the policy of denying non-nuclear countries necessary facilities has no chance of success unless these countries are genuinely persuaded that non-possession of nuclear weapons is a better protection for them than possession.

ble to take a step toward the necessary modification of sovereignty via the path of atomic energy (including regional and international nuclear parks). But this presupposes that the superpowers subject their material to the same controls they demand of others. And that may easily preclude any agreements.

We are thus led back to the question whether an unavoidable multiplicity of nuclear powers is so very dangerous. Could it be that general Gallois is right after all? Unfortunately, I must categorically deny this. His thesis is a crystal-clear formulation of the absurdity of the principle: "build weapons to prevent their use." In a purely military sense, all the objections we raised before against the possibility of deterring from minor transgressions by the threat of strategic weapons also hold here. Politically, his thesis presupposes an integrity of the nation state which could only appear plausible to a Frenchman. Both quantitatively and qualitatively, means of power must be adequate to the interests they are meant to protect. In addition to Gallois' bombs, nations would have to have all the other arms, and it is these that would decide their minor conflicts. And the same applies here as in the case of the major powers: escalation may trigger nuclear strikes.

Of course, once local powers own atomic weapons, they will become more cautious than heretofore, just as the superpowers have become more cautious. But all instability arguments apply here as well, and they become weightier due to the multiplicity of the powers and the multiformity of the situations. The only possible conclusion is this: if local nuclear powers are going to develop, local nuclear wars will someday break out. And local nuclear wars will bring with them one of the most serious tests for peace among the world powers.

Problems of Guidance and Control

How to guide world politics has already been discussed in the third chapter, where our perspective was largely economic. Here, we return to the political aspects. The difficulty can be expressed in a simple formula: reason and power. It is reasonable to give first priority to the overall interest of mankind. And this means first of all: survival. Peace, well-being, justice and freedom are values which can thrive under the umbrella of an order that rationally safeguards survival. But opinions differ as to the rational form of this order. The various ideas that have been advanced are all expressions of special interests. Every party is convinced that it furthers, or at least takes account of, the overall interests when it supports its side and promotes its own interests with its help. Today, none of these ideas is backed by a power that would be large enough to make it prevail over all other ideas. The power struggle between special interests also presents itself as the power struggle between concepts. There is no authority which can limit or guide this twofold struggle or that could implement an orderly settlement, as a national government can. We refer to this condition as imperfect world-internal politics.

Concepts are not sharply set off from each other, but we can make three rough distinctions: there is the liberal, the socialist and the nationalist one. We examined them before and advanced reasons for our view that none of them could guarantee world peace (chapter 6). Here, our goal is more modest. We will ask how the balance of power between them can be controlled in such a way that acute dangers are avoided and the world is brought closer to a stable order.

We first return to a thesis of the sixth chapter. A policy which attempts to enforce the supremacy of one of these concepts, even without overt war, is no peace policy. For it cannot be expected that the interest groups behind any one of these ideologies will capitulate without war. This may change at some future time, but that is how things are today. The conception by which world policy will be guided must therefore involve the peaceful coexistence of these ideologies. This must be done with the awareness that at least according to one of them, the socialist, peaceful coexistence is understood to be merely a step toward its own victory. The liberals should have no illusions about the fact that they also intend their beliefs to prevail. Internationally, peaceful coexistence must mean that sovereignties and political systems are respected. But a step-by-step reduction of sovereignty must be prepared for nonetheless. It is not certain that this task can be solved. The fourth and fifth theses are essential for such a task: world politics must be guided in such a way that the requisite transformation of consciousness is facilitated and not inhibited. Given the absence of a central authority, the unity necessary for guidance can only be achieved through an appeal to a common consciousness.

Consequences

We confine ourselves here to listing the consequences which can be drawn regarding the spread of weapons. What actions can our country, its allies and business partners take?

1. The spread of weapons has a negative effect on the development of the kind of consciousness necessary to prevent world war. It is important to see this and to act accordingly although a given shipment of weapons often has no recognizable connection with the danger of a world war and may even contribute to the stabilization of a region.

The spread of weapons in the Third World is in fact a "normalization" in a certain sense, an adaptation to the situation that already exists in the belt of the Northern powers. But it is no stabilization for that very reason. By inducing the false belief that the normal condition between armed powers is a guarantee against war, it actually increases the danger of its outbreak.

2. The prevention of the spread of nuclear weapons must become the subject of an international agreement in which the countries that import nuclear technology participate as partners with equal rights. Every other strategy will be counterproductive over the long term. The unilateral decision of exporting countries to stop the spread of weapons cannot be permanently enforced, and it prevents the timely creation of a basis for worldwide cooperation.

I am aware that especially the second demand is still vague. I do not wish to go into greater detail here because what is essential in concrete proposals is not their abstract correctness but the possibility that they can be agreed upon internationally. It is only in and through negotiating experience that they can be formulated adequately. But such experience will not be acquired if it is not recognized that an international agreement is indispensable.

10. European Defense

The subject of this chapter is the military defense of Europe. It has political preconditions which must first be called to mind.

Politics

Europe is the historical base of today's power system, and it is through that situation that the structural problems in the politics of present-day Europe can be understood. The military superpowers, America and Russia, are powers on the periphery of the European cultural sphere. In continental regions with a power vacuum, they grew into territorial states of more than European dimensions. They are overpowering because they share in the historically superior technical civilization of Europe, and also are geographically sizeable. As a civilization, the old Europe still belongs in the first rank. Economically, Western Europe is still, or again, a major power. The old major European powers, England, France and Germany, however, no longer occupy that rank either world-politically or militarily. Of course, this judgment conflicts with an underlying sentiment today, at least in England and France, which were members of the victorious alliance in the two world wars of this century. The political history of Europe since 1945 can be seen to have been governed by the combination of four motifs: the opposition between the two military superpowers and their ideologies; the striving for economic recovery, dominance and stability; the effort to secure something of the role major political powers played in Europe; the search for a political and cultural European consciousness. These expressions—opposition, striving, effort, search—reflect the wavering self-estimate which stands in curious contrast to the actual political stability of these thirty years. What requires explanation here is not the lability of perception which is natural after the decline from a position of world political leadership, but the stability of the structures.

The stability of Europe was really the result of the Soviet-American duopoly. The two superpowers could stabilize their relations only if there was peace in this area beyond their borders, and vital to both of them. This objective stabilization did not require a policy of détente, it existed even during the Cold War. To insure its existence, it was enough that neither of the two opponents could undertake large-scale action without incurring risks. Each of the two had freedom of action in one of the two systems of alliances, and no influence in the other. The price Europe paid for this stability was partition.

All successful political developments in Europe during these thirty years served the stabilization of partition and that of the parts. There nonetheless does exist a constant counter-movement against this form of stabilization. It is worthwhile to examine the various hitherto unsuccessful steps of this movement. We are thinking of the rollback tendency of the Dulles era, the German demand for reunification, de Gaulle's concept of a Europe *des patries*, the tendencies toward independence with the Warsaw Pact, most visibly in Czechoslovakia, and the policy of the communist parties in Western Europe.

Dulles' rollback tendency had as its starting point the indisputable fact that Russian rule in Eastern Europe did not come about through the free will of the peoples there. It is a consequence of the military defeat of these outposts of the West through Hitler, their occupation by Stalin after Hitler's defeat, and the acceptance of this conquest by Roosevelt. Practically, the rollback remained a dream which was partly responsible for the Hungarian tragedy of 1956. In the tension between the military technological superiority of America and the numerical superiority of the Russian army, NATO and the Warsaw Pact arose on either side as defensive alliances to stabilize the borders.

The partition of Germany was probably an essential building block in a stable partition of Europe. An undivided Germany on one of the two sides would have caused a shift in the balance that would have been disquieting to the other. A neutralized Germany could only have come about by explicit agreement between the two sides, but to create a divided Germany, the occupation zones as set up in 1945 and the later implicit agreement which was called the cold war, sufficed. The reunification of Germany is impossible without the prior reunification of Europe. The Eastern policy of the Brandt era meant that West German illusions about these facts were sacrificed. It thus meant that the foreign policy of the German Federal Republic would gain that room to maneuver which the earlier insistence on unrealistic demands had denied it. This realism also had a moral component: truthfulness toward one's own nation, and the unmistakable commitment to a non-revanchist policy vis-à-vis Eastern Europe, most impressively symbolized by Brandt's genuflection in Warsaw. It thus served the transformation of consciousness necessary to a peace policy. After this, Germany was no longer an obstacle to a possible accommodation between the superpowers, as it had occasionally been during the sixties. The present setback to the public's hopes for détente is merely the compensation for an unrealistic conception of it. Détente does not negate the imperialist opposition between the world powers but merely provides a chance to maintain its stability through diplomacy and a gradual change in consciousness.

In a way, de Gaulle really wanted what we called the reunification of Europe above. He wanted to dissolve the blocs and do away with partition by making the nations the ultimate units. In part, this involved the traditional component, France's role as a major power, in part the future-oriented idea of transforming the duopoly into a pluralistic structure (chapter 6, thesis 2). De Gaulle proved his realism by his progressive treatment of non-European problems: the voluntary and planned transformation of the African colonial empire into a structure that would be closely tied to France, and that has since proven itself remarkably stable; the fact that, at an early time, he took seriously the position of the Arabs, and the timely establishment of relations with Maoist China. But while all these steps were in fact elements of an anti-duopolistic policy, they presupposed the stabilization of the duopoly (see chapter 6, thesis 1). In practice, de Gaulle implemented his European policy under the American umbrella he scolded. That policy failed because, with the exception of that France whose spokesman he was, no nation that would have had a say in these matters felt that its security was better protected in his plan than in the stability of a divided Europe, and because the French power base was insufficient to make France an equal partner of the superpowers.

In Eastern Europe Russian rule is not consented to, but reluctantly put up with, and there is no prospect that this condition will change. The Russian leaders presumably have no illusions about this either. As society becomes increasingly modern under communism, there is a growing need for liberalization which has deep roots in those countries whose intellectual strata always looked toward Western or Central Europe. The striving for liberalization thus arouses a longing to overcome Europe's division. The Soviet leadership can perceive this longing only as a danger to its power. That the representatives of the reform movements were sincere socialists did not change this fact. A variant of socialism is no less dangerous to the Soviet system than a foreign policy initiative of one of its allies.

The communist parties in Western Europe, and especially in the Mediterranean region, find themselves in a mirror image situation. They want to overcome the domination of a political and economic system they perceive as regressive and opposed to human dignity. For them, support from Moscow is almost as ambivalent as was Western sympathy for Nagy and Dubcek. If the Russian armored brigades and the experience of a subversive world communism did not stand behind them, the American government and Europe's conservatives would face them with less worry. From the perspective of liberal thought, the integration of the communists into representative democracy, the gradual reduction of their intolerance by incorporating them in a system of tolerance, the utilization of their social and moral impulse as they share in governmental responsibility, would be the correct form of dealing with them. Such voices have long been heard in Italy. Precisely for this reason, Western European communists have a burning tactical interest in detaching themselves from those aspects of Moscow's communism which are unacceptable in a liberal system. They must reject the doctrine about the dictatorship of the proletariat and commit themselves to freedom of speech and a pluralistic party system. There can be no doubt that this is the sincere conviction of many Italian and French communists. (As early as 1942, Frederic Joliot told me: "We will show those backward Russians what a humane communism looks like.") But it is precisely the fact that such detachment is tactically expedient that makes it impossible to say whether it will continue to be observed.

Here, the author feels obliged to express a personal view. In my opinion, the debate is off to a wrong start when it runs a course between two positions: the communists cannot be tolerated and certainly not form part of a government for they are dangerous, or, they can be tolerated and allowed to participate in governing the country because they are not. It is my own view that they are dangerous and that, knowing this, one should tolerate them and even allow them to participate in a parliamentary government if certain precautionary measures are taken. Of course, one can only hold this view if one feels that the liberal system is strong enough. The basic thesis here is (see chapter 6) that government is impossible without insight, and insight is gained best in open discussion. Liberality is the readiness to learn something from an opponent. The test of liberal tolerance is tolerance vis-à-vis intolerant people,[58] for how else can they ever learn tolerance? A liberal state can adopt such an attitude only if it is politically stable. It is my personal judgment (see chapters 3 and 4) that the social structure of highly industrialized capitalist countries can really not be upset by internal change as long as economic problems do not get out of hand. The liberal state will not preserve its stability by suppressing critics but by solving its problems in one way or another. Every chapter of this book demonstrates that I am not very optimistic that these problems can be solved, but I expect nothing from the projection which blames the political enemy for their existence. If we succeeded in tolerating and integrating our domestic political opponents, that might be the test of the claimed superiority of our system over that of the communists. But that presupposes the foreign policy stability of our system. We can only be tolerant toward communists if we are strong and do not invite the Russians to engage in military or subversive machinations. Our domestic politics thus depends on military and foreign policy conditions.

We begin with foreign policy:

The factual stability of the division of Europe does not mean that either of its two parts has a unity that developed from within. The parts were unified from the outside, Eastern Europe by Russia, Western Europe by the U.S. Anyone who knows Eastern European countries is aware how weak communication between them is, and this obviously facilitates Russian rule. Economic and cultural intercommunication in Western Europe has become very strong and it is not its lack that is responsible for the small progress that has been made in the way of political unification. The media of political unification are NATO and the European Community, and the effectiveness of both is quite limited.

NATO was set up under American dominance because there was a concern over Russian dominance, and before today's economic independence and the stabilization of the duopoly by second strike capabilities had been achieved. If we judge by the results—that war has been prevented up to now—it solved its military problem but no other. We will soon turn to a detailed discussion of the former. To view Western European defense globally is probably easier for informed Americans than for Europeans whose perspective is always dominated by their own interests. More decisively in quiet conversation than publicly, Europeans have been criticized by Americans for at least two decades because they make an inadequate defense effort, let themselves in effect be protected by America, and use the money saved in this way to compete with America on the world market. The American desire for stronger European efforts in the alliance conflicts with the European conviction that Europe must not allow itself to become entangled in global American conflicts of interest. It is a fact that Western Europe has not allowed itself to be integrated into American global politics, most obviously by its non-participation in the Vietnam war. But if Western Europe, which calls itself Europe, really wished to be independent of America, it would also have to assume full responsibility for its military protection. The political condition of Western Europe precludes this for the foreseeable future. In the second section of this chapter, we will also state the view that Western Europe's military self-sufficiency would perhaps not be desirable even if it were possible. Under present conditions, America will in fact have to continue shouldering part of the burden of Europe's military defense, and Europe will have to conduct a policy which takes this dependence on America into account.

The European Community also has its origin in the years after the war when Russia's threat was felt more acutely than it is today. The economic consequences of this unification are not without ambivalence. For the community as a whole, they are probably positive. But the market is cruel, even the Common Market. For some partners, the harm may outweigh the usefulness, at least over the short term. In view of such conflicts of interests, the decision-making mechanism of parliamentary democracy makes voluntary unification a balancing act for the leading statesmen. The political union of previously sovereign powers, some of which still consider themselves major powers, almost requires the pressure of acute danger or the hegemonic position of one of them. Hegemony by one of the three old major powers in Western Europe is a political impossibility today. European unification thus presumably hinges on the perception of the Russian threat. Precisely for this reason, it is clearly in the Russian interest not to let us perceive such a threat.

In this situation, it is not impossible that Europe may ultimately be unified under Russian hegemony. This book is based on the premise that Western Europe does not want that. Its presumed readers are probably largely persons who do not want that. The question is what policy will be necessary to avoid it, and is such a policy feasible. In the discussion of the communist parties, it seemed to emerge that Western Europe can only achieve internal stability if it is stable in foreign policy terms. This requires both an unwavering common foreign policy and a degree of military protection that is judged adequate. But does such protection exist? Can it exist?

Armaments

By way of introduction, I am taking the liberty of quoting a passage from *Fragen zur Weltpolitik* which I can comment on in greater detail here than in that book.

Within the global framework, the problem of European security is the most important example of war prevention below the level of strategic weapons. Of course, the NATO doctrine of flexible response ties deterrence in the lesser weapons systems to a possible use of strategic weapons. NATO is to be in a position to respond to an attack by the Warsaw Pact nations on any level with weapons of the same type. If the Warsaw Pact commits its quantitative superiority on a given level, NATO is to be in a position to escalate to a higher level. The credibility of this deterrence depends significantly on the possibility of passing on to the highest level of escalation, the full use of strategic weapons.

Perhaps I may describe the picture this problem presents to me today in a somewhat anecdotal manner. In 1973, I participated in a discussion of Western military experts about NATO armaments. An American said: "The United States has given the Europeans the nuclear guarantee, and we stand by our word. The Europeans have to realize, of course, that we can use strategic weapons only if our own country if vitally threatened. The European NATO countries therefore have to acquire conventional armaments of their own which permit them to carry on a conventional war by themselves, and for an indefinite period. That is possible with modern 'smart weapons.' "

A European answered: "The previous speaker is correct in his premise but not in his conclusion. Today, every maneuver of the Warsaw Pact begins with the assumption that tactical nuclear weapons have already been used. Europe needs nuclear weapons of its own, and the full spectrum of nuclear weapons."

After a day's discussion, I said: "I am confused. We have been having peace in Europe for almost three decades, and obviously no one here expects a European war for the foreseeable future, at least not during the seventies. But if the two previous speakers were right, the reason for that is not the present defensive capability of NATO but presumably the fact that neither we nor our Eastern neighbors have an interest in this war. The two previous speakers do not wish to rely on that alone. But I assume that neither they nor other participants in this discussion believe that any one of the proposals made by the two earlier speakers will actually be implemented. I should like to hear those proposals that they seriously entertain."

I was given no comprehensible answer. An American colleague, like myself a physicist by training, said: "Professor Weizsäcker comes from a discipline where clear questions can be answered clearly." Afterwards, I went to him and said: "You know that I did not ask from scientific but from political interest. What is your answer?" "You are right, the question has to be thought through again," he told me.[59]

This anecdote contains three assertions for which reasons can be advanced:

1 / The experts gathered at the meeting felt that European armaments were inadequate.
2 / The assertion that an arms buildup which the experts consider technically possible and adequate would not be carried out was not contradicted.
3 / There was no fear of an impending attack by the Warsaw Pact against Europe.

In this formulation, we are only dealing with expert opinion. I will now attempt to interpret each of the three assertions in a way I consider objectively correct.

1. Today's European defenses are inadequate by the criteria of the strategy of deterrence. Deterrence is credible when it meets two conditions:

• If the counter-measures threatened in case of an attack are implemented, they must be sufficient to make the attack something that doesn't pay from the attacker's point of view (adequacy).

- It must be sufficiently probable for the potential attacker that counter-measures will actually be taken if he does attack (credibility).

Adequacy can be attained in two ways. Counter-measures consist either in a defense sufficient to turn back the attack, or in a counter-attack which inflicts a measure of damage on the attacker that is greater than the advantage he hopes to gain by his attack.

The weapons which could be used in Europe can be roughly divided into three categories: conventional weapons, tactical nuclear weapons, strategic nuclear weapons. The Warsaw Pact has always been superior in conventional arms. If the two sides were to strictly limit themselves to such weapons, the deterrence posture of NATO would not be credible. It would be adequate neither for defense nor the counter-attack. This was the starting point of the two speakers in the anecdote told above. In the special case of the German Federal Republic, we have stated elsewhere: "The German Federal Republic cannot be defended by conventional arms." Since this thesis has sometimes been misunderstood, I shall explain it. There is no doubt that the Warsaw Pact could attack limited objectives in Western Europe (and thus in the Federal Republic) and so limit its weapons that the conventional NATO forces could repel it. Our weapons protect us against this kind of attack. If the enemy has no adequate motive to conduct an attack with his total conventional potential, our conventional weapons can defend us against his. But assertion 3 states that the Warsaw Pact has no adequate motive for such an attack in the foreseeable future. We will discuss this below. At the moment, we are dealing with the purely military question whether a conventional attack by all of the Warsaw Pact forces could be repelled by NATO with its present conventional means. And here the answer is no. A

rapid thrust by Russian armor toward the Rhine or the At-
lantic is a possibility if tactical nuclear weapons are not
used by NATO.

Since its creation, NATO has therefore threatened the use
of nuclear weapons to deter a large-scale conventional attack, and since the introduction of the strategy of flexible
response with whatever limited use of nuclear weapons
might be appropriate. On this level, it becomes more dubi-
ous whether the attack would overwhelm the defense, particularly since every defensive failure on a given level of
escalation could be dealt with by passing on to the next
higher one. But as the degree of the adequacy of escalatory
counter-measures increases, its likelihood becomes problematical. As regards the highest level of escalation, the use
of American strategic weapons, this is expressed in the anecdote when the American speaker says that his country
will not risk its own destruction to save Europe. Of course,
the strategy of the largest weapons is now developing toward limited options with defined political objectives (see
chapter 9). Below (under III), we will discuss a strategy for
Europe where such an American strategic covering force
does indeed have an essential function. But it is evident
that America will be guided by the desire never to find itself in a situation where it can prevent danger to Europe
only by directly threatening the use of strategic weapons.
The American proposal in our anecdote and Schlesinger's
later tendency both had the objective of making unlimited
war in Europe possible by keeping open maritime routes of
transport.

But if the European theater of war is to stabilize itself
through tactical nuclear weapons, the question arises
whether the European nations would be willing to engage
in this kind of defense, should the situation demand it. As
regards the German Federal Republic, we formulated the
consequence in the following thesis: "The use of nuclear
weapons with the intent of defending the Federal Republic
would lead to nuclear self-annihilation." This thesis also

requires comment, and it is almost the same as that relating to the earlier one. It is possible, of course, to use so small a number of nuclear weapons and to aim them so precisely that damage will be limited. Should the enemy not be determined to win the war, he will let himself be deterred by such a limited employment. But the question is whether he *can* use the means against which only a massive counterstrike of nuclear weapons which would destroy our own country would afford a possible defense. There is no doubt that the enemy can, and without the readiness for such employment, he would not begin a war in Europe. Like NATO, he will have the desire to avoid large-scale use, although he is ready for it. The point is to gain time for negotiations through slow and flexible escalation, as NATO doctrine formulates it. But historical experience suggests that the time gained will only be used for negotiations when the war has already been decided (1918) or when its continuation has become insupportable for one of the parties (Vietnam). It is thus overwhelmingly likely that even a successful defense of Europe with tactical nuclear weapons would leave Germany wholly devastated, and would not seriously affect America or Russia. It will not be obvious to the Russians that the European nations, should they have the freedom to decide, would be willing to really implement this level of threatened escalation.

This entire set of problems has been formulated in the following thesis: "For the Federal Republic, there is only one, self-contradictory deterrence (deterrence by a risk that is incalculable for both sides)." One may believe that such deterrence is adequate. Their traditional caution will keep the Russians from taking even a small risk (1%–5%) of escalation to the strategic level. And under the umbrella of this deterrence, a political stability which will finally eliminate the inducement to wage war can develop. I unhesitatingly admit that we live under the umbrella of this very deterrence today, and it is strengthened by the Soviet's lack of interest in a military conquest of Europe (see 3 below). Nor did the military experts quoted in our anecdote contradict this. But this does not do away with the hegemonic conflict between Americans and Russians, and in Western and Southern Europe the internal political situation is not wholly stable. Above, we maintained that this internal political situation could only be stabilized if Western Europe enjoys external stability, and this requires adequate military defense. Should the Western European alliance weaken, the Soviet Union might have the opportunity of detaching individual European nations from the alliance by military threats or political offers, and would thus ultimately dissolve the alliance without recourse to arms. Seen from this perspective, the desire for a genuinely credible deterrence is comprehensible.

2. There are political reasons why a technically possible deterrence which would be adequate in terms of present deterrence theory will not come about. We have to inquire first whether a deterrence that is adequate in this sense can exist at all. What would it have to look like? The primitive argument that an adequate deterrence should be possible rests on a comparison of production figures and population sizes in Western and Eastern Europe. The West is technically superior, its population no smaller. If Western Europe were to shoulder the same per capita burden for armaments as the Soviet Union, it would probably be militarily superior to it. The counter-argument is equally plausible in a primitive way: look at the political state of Western Europe and you know that that won't happen. Both arguments call for close examination.

Can an adequate deterrence for Western Europe exist at all? We have looked into deterrence between the two superpowers. The history of its development wavers between levels and erosions. The United States and the Soviet Union are quite distant from each other, and both have extensive, very thinly settled regions. Western Europe is small and densely populated, and therefore highly vulnerable. And it borders on Russia. A war of movement between the two is possible. In order not to suffer unacceptable damage, Western Europe would thus have to either create a conventional and a tactical nuclear force which could carry the war into enemy territory, or invent a technical defense concept which deters the enemy without creating great damage at home. The former seems financially insupportable by today's criteria, and would lead to the arms race characteristic of Clausewitzean weapons, which means that it would be feasible but certainly not advisable. The latter seems conceivable to me with modern technical means. The American speaker in our anecdote referred to this possibility. Models for such a defense are frequently discussed today. Below, we will consider Afheldt's version of one such model.

To survive a war of movement without self-destruction, a strategic deterrent force with second strike capability would also be necessary. To be "adequate" in the real meaning of the term, it could not be the American strategic arsenal nor some part of it in the sense of an exploitable capability. For de Gaulle was presumably correct in his initial assumption that the lethal weapons of a nation can only protect that nation. Situations are conceivable where America might be deterred by a Russian threat from using its strategic weapons in Europe's support, and that was the initial assumption in our anecdote. Europe would thus have to have its own second strike capability. Because of the vulnerability of the continent, that capability would presumably have to be carried by submarines. If such a capability were to be a single one for all of Europe, Europe would have to be sufficiently unified politically to be able to react like a single nation, both militarily and in its foreign policy. The decision to use the capability could depend neither on a veto nor even a majority decision. This is something that can be seriously discussed when the political unification of Europe is sufficiently advanced. But only a sizable Russian shock would bring this about, and such a shock would not occur in a situation which would then allow an additional ten years to calmly go about setting up these weapons. Another possibility would be strategic forces belonging to each of the larger Western European nations. This is a recommendation General Gallois made to me in a discussion in the early sixties. My counter-argument was that, should deterrence fail, our possession of nuclear weapons would mean that we become the targets of nuclear strikes. It was the survival argument which we will take up once again under III. This objection might be eliminated by missile-carrying submarines. But world-politically, a national nuclear armament of the German Federal Republic hardly seems a possibility today. That is known in Germany, and that's why we have for so long been the most loyal European allies of the U.S.

These considerations do not prove the political impossibility of an "adequate" European deterrence but they do prove its extreme political improbability for the period for which we can plan today. Would this deterrence be desirable if it were possible? Those sufficiently optimistic to believe that deterrence would reliably prevent war would have to desire it for Europe. But we have arrived at the view that world war remains likely unless a profound change of the political structure and of global consciousness occurs. A unified Europe with an adequate nuclear force would be a genuine major power. It would not fail to participate in a hegemonic conflict. And because of its extreme vulnerability, it would be the most endangered major power. We have reason to believe that to strive for a great military power role would be tantamount to striving for its own destruction.

3. For the time being, the Soviet Union and its allies have no reason to attack western Europe. This does not mean that the Soviet Union does not engage in power politics but is a view based on the interests of such politics as we see them. Compared with Western Europe, the Soviet Union is economically backward. It has profound political fears of China and every reason to seek stable cooperation with at least one of these dangerous neighbors. A political reconciliation with China which would presumably be in Russia's

interest today is blocked by the attitude of the Chinese. Besides, it would not be helpful in the area of modern industry for a long time to come. The Soviet Union would probably be interested in the political domination of Europe although that would burden it with exceptional problems, but it would mean that the most important American base would cease to exist. As long as it has no reason to fear Europe as an aggressive competitor for hegemony, the Soviet Union would not be interested in its destruction. Under these conditions, Western Europe is already protected against a major Russian attack if the destruction of large parts of Western European industry would be the result. In this very specific sense, Western Europe is protected today, not because it can defend itself—that isn't really the case—but because it is willing to do so. The insanity that defense would destroy one's own country deters the potential attacker who is interested in utilizing that country. In this situation, détente is the real interest of the Soviet Union.

Consequences

In spite of the considerable military stability of Europe during the last thirty years, and which will probably continue for some time, there are two reasons for taking seriously the critiques of our system of deterrence: the danger of political blackmail with the military threat in the background, and the danger of the destruction of the country, should deterrence fail. Both dangers are causally connected: it is precisely the danger that the country may be destroyed in a war that will cause the European nations to hesitate to carry out the threat of military resistance. But both dangers also harbor a tendency to trigger contrasting reactions in armaments policy. Those who are primarily afraid of blackmail will call for armaments, and those who fear destruction for disarmament. But a military buildup increases the dangers of destruction, while disarmament increases that of blackmail. The normal reaction in such a dilemma is a compromise which claims that both problems can be solved when actually neither can. The question arises whether there exists a European defense model which does solve them. It would have to threaten defensive measures which would adequately deter the enemy, yet leave the country without unacceptable destruction, were they to be carried out.

In connection with the section, "Consequences," of chapter 8, we will here provide a brief sketch of the Afheldt model of European defense. This model must also satisfy the six demands outlined there. We will first recapitulate and explain what we just set forth under the sections on armaments by measuring present realities and proposals against those demands.

1. So far, deterrence has been successful. But as one of the reasons for its success, we listed the danger of the destruction of the economy of Western Europe, which would violate demand 4, below. It should also be said that deterrence to a major attack on all of Europe is not the same as deterrence to an attack on some part of it that can be politically isolated.

2. Up to this time, one could not speak of an arms race by Western Europe. But the growing Soviet conventional arms buildup leads Western Europe into the dilemma of either keeping up or facing the necessity of political capitulation at some time in the future. It is my view that NATO is more worried about this than it lets appear. The temptation for the Soviet Union to strive for clear superiority arises from the classical logic of an arms race with Clausewitzean weapons of the same type. A Panzer army which would unfailingly win the war in Europe is certainly more attractive to the Soviet Union than an army that would not, even if there should be no intent to launch such a war for the time being.

3. The conventional weakness of NATO, particularly in connection with the principle of defending advance posi-

tions, obliges it to threaten with tactical nuclear weapons which, in certain scenarios, might also have to be used for purposes of interdiction in the rear areas of the Warsaw Pact nations. To avoid the destabilizing effect of this threat (i.e., the implicit call on the enemy to escalate to the level of a lethal blow against Western Europe), NATO has for years been discussing the possible uses of nuclear weapons which would be strictly limited to its own territory. A field of atomic mines or mini-nucs would be examples.

4. If the war were to be carried into one's own country, only its short duration would assure that destruction would remain below a tolerable threshold (i.e., only in the case of a quick Russian victory). The American plan mentioned above by which America would secure the possibility of supplying Europe for a war of unlimited duration is therefore not in our interest. It is dangerous to us precisely because in a limited war against Russia, such an option might be in America's specific interest. We must do everything in our power not to create options which might produce a sharp conflict of interest between Europe and its American ally. The just-quoted proposals (3) regarding interdiction with small nuclear weapons on our own territory near the border are designed for the very purpose of preventing mobile war and its destructive effects on that territory. It is typical of public sentiment that, so far, public resistance has invariably doomed such proposals. The use of nuclear weapons in one's own country is feared even when the experts' correct calculations demonstrate that the damage will be minor. I assume that it is public opinion which is right in this dispute. There is precisely *one* easily comprehensible and definable threshold whose passage can be tabooed, and that is the one separating non-nuclear from nuclear weapons. Hiroshima created this taboo, and it retains its irrational force even today. It is perfectly conceivable and must indeed be feared that the day will come when it is violated. But there is no chance that a new taboo can then be instituted elsewhere. Once it has been violated, all that

remains will be the limited hope that both sides will obey the military rationality of restricting the use of weapons. Anyone who suggests a defensive position that violates this taboo from the very beginning must prove that purely military rationality precludes further escalation by either side. It is not my impression that such proof has been furnished. This means that such a defense may increase the effectiveness of deterrence but that it threatens an action which endangers the very survival of the population of our country although it is its intent to avoid that very thing.

5. The positions NATO has adopted up to this time have always been based on unilateral decisions. This would also be possible for the proposals just mentioned.

6. More probable than a military test of the credibility of our deterrence would be the political erosion of Western Europe. Such a process would be survived by human beings but by free institutions to only a limited extent. The less secure we feel about a military test, the more this danger will grow. I have to say this although I do not tend to share today's widespread gloom concerning the Western European communists.

The alternative model about to be presented here can most easily be introduced by a quote from E. Spannocchi: "To begin with, it is a historical fact and therefore not necessarily a new insight of the nuclear age that it is invariably the quantitatively and qualitatively weaker that will be defeated in a war by the stronger side in a very short time if he enters the conflict according to the same maxims but is backed by a smaller potential—with what may be called proportional inferiority . . . That means that the weaker side made the mistake of allowing the stronger to impose his conduct on it." Spannocchi is thinking of Austria here. That country will essentially have to prepare for the possibility of a non-nuclear attack by a Panzer army of the Warsaw Pact nations. The army reorganization proposed by Spannocchi and being carried out today does not envisage opposing this armor with armor of its own. The tank battle

which would certainly be lost is replaced by hundred of en-
gagements between the invading army and localized small
units with modern armor-piercing weapons. If the enemy is
so inclined, he can win those hundreds of clashes, for everyone knows that Austria is far inferior to the Warsaw Pact
nations. But they will cost him many tanks and considerable time. Given Austria's recognized neutrality and a possible military involvement with the West, the enemy would
have more reason to consider whether he wants to start
such an undertaking than if there were to be a single tank
battle (or the surrender of the Austrian armor before the
battle) that would settle the issue. And the dispersed
carriers of these armor-piercing weapons are no targets for
large weapons. At most, they could be engaged by infantry
beforehand. The temptation for the enemy to destroy the
country he conquers would be small.

It is no accident that it is precisely Austria that has already begun this restructuring of its armaments, for in Austria's position its advantages are evident. So far, Brossollet's
analogous proposals for France have found no acceptance
and Afheldt's suggestions for NATO are just now becoming
topics for debate. We discuss his model here on the basis of
our six demands:

1 and 2 will be taken up at the close of the chapter.

On 3—The plan calls for a transformation within the
NATO framework of the German army into small, mobile
techno-commandos distributed all over the country (these
will be regular troops, not local militia, in order to protect
the population from retaliatory measures). There will be no
armored troops and no tactical nuclear weapons but there
will be a tie-in with an American "covering force"
equipped with strategic nuclear weapons. The network of
autonomous techno-commandos constitutes no threat whatever to the territory of the Warsaw Pact nations, its purely
defensive function being obvious. The covering force would
merely constitute the counter-threat to a threat against the
Federal Republic of Germany (or NATO generally) by a stra-

tegic nuclear strike, according to the pattern discussed in the section on consequences in chapter 8. The target of this covering force would be the East European allies of the Soviet Union, for in response to a threat to their West European allies, the U.S. cannot take the Soviet Union hostage without itself running a serious risk. But it can do so in the case of its East European allies.

Also, a threat of the kind described in chapter 8 would not threaten the population of these countries which is not responsible for these threats but it might jeopardize the stability of Soviet rule there. To this extent, this threat would satisfy demand 3.

On 4—NATO would lose a purely conventional Panzer battle against the Warsaw Pact nations if it were to be fought today. For Western Europe as a whole, a technically possible arms buildup that would result in parity is neither to be expected politically nor advisable, as mentioned before. If our argument above is correct, protection by tactical nuclear weapons violates demand 4 not to expose one's own population to unacceptable danger. Defense by techno-commandos cannot wholly repel a Panzer attack but it can prevent a lightning-like thrust and inflict heavy tank losses on the enemy. At the same time, it spares the population in the home country and does not constitute military targets which would justify an enemy strike that would affect our population. For this reason, it satisfies demand 4 more adequately than any other defense concept.

On 5—It can clearly be conducted unilaterally.

On 2—Being purely defensive, it furnishes no reason for an arms race.

On 1—A strong objection against this form of defense can only come from the concern that it is no reliable deterrence since it could be overwhelmed by the enemy though not without sizable losses on his part. And we would not propose this defense if we did not share the opinion of the experts quoted in II that this also applies to the present NATO defense. If it were certain that the American strategic force would not intervene, the risk in an attack would in both cases be equally calculably small for the Warsaw Pact nations. One question is whether intervention by American strategic weapons is more likely in one case than in the other. A rationally planned, limited use as just explained above (3) is more likely than a large one of indeterminate size that would threaten America with counter-strikes. It can be assumed that today's secret NATO plans include such limited strategic strikes. Dispute would then center around the question whether deterrence by publicly stated, limited threats is more or less effective than deterrence by deliberately veiled ones. But this matter can be wholly detached from the form the substrategic conduct of a war would take.

All that remains of the assumption that this deterrence is less credible than what we have today is the idea expressed above, i.e., that the madness that lies in a defense readiness which risks the total destruction of one's own country might deter a superior enemy who is interested in keeping Western Europe's economic capacity intact. Two principles confront each other here: threat of suicide, or threat of rational conduct. The former can be more impressive but it is our position in this book that such irrational positions cannot be indefinitely maintained. Some day, we will be compelled to make good on our threat or to allow it to be unmasked as a bluff. Compared to that, the rational threat is strong enough, in my view. Those who do not believe this should search for a politically feasible way of achieving a stronger rational threat which would be an equally good guarantee of survival. Such a path may exist. But it will certainly not be found as long as we delude ourselves about the degree of our present security. Those who publicly disseminate or cover up deceptions about this may act with the best of intentions but objectively speaking, they endanger our future.

11. Politics and Consciousness

Review

We are casting a critical backward glance. What have we achieved? At the end of the first chapter, we announced analyses and proposals concerning a reformist development of existing structures. The conservative aspect of the goal stated there, the tie-in to existing structures, has been set forth. We accepted the goals of a technicized society and mentioned critiques such as those of Illich but did not even discuss them. We criticized the capitalist form of our society only immanently, with the object of preserving it. We relativized the socialist alternative by recognizing the communist ("revolutionary") form as appropriate at best for economically underdeveloped countries, and the social democratic ("revisionist") alternative as a variant of the liberal order. We referred to radical hopes for doing away with war as utopian at this time, and made proposals concerning the prevention of war by deterrence and classical foreign policy. We consider them practicable in principle, but they promise no more than a temporary stabilization of the present system and an, albeit very important, increase in the chances for survival, should war come.

235

Nowhere have we attempted to hide the varying degrees of our conservatism. Our commitment to political liberalism was spontaneous and direct, as was our commitment to the constitutionally governed state of representative democracy. The commitment to the goal of war prevention and the protection of human life was a matter of course. At other places, we emphasized that we limit ourselves to what is practically possible today, and thus accept structures which stand in need of a fundamental critique. It is my belief that in all of these cases, no better practicable alternative exists today. This is true of the technocratic management of the energy problem, the "early capitalist wildness of the world market," war prevention by deterrence, particularly by outsized weapons, the shape of world politics as the oligopoly of sovereign powers.

Did we at least make proposals regarding reformist development? In part, the proposals we did make were reasonably precise but lack the effectiveness required in the handling of large problems, such as energy. In part, they were not sufficiently precise but really no more than criteria by which proposals could be judged, as in questions of the world economy and the spread of weapons. In both cases, we pointed out one of the reasons for this inadequacy. What is involved here are economic and political problems which cannot be regulated without a global authority with powers of enforcement. This is just one of two reasons, for who would guarantee that a world authority or even a worldwide agreement would have the requisite wisdom? The creation of a world order of whatever kind encounters the political obstacle of a system of sovereign powers that is pregnant with war. The most far-reaching and precise proposals in this book are Afheldt's models for a stable deterrence (chapters 8 and 10). Even if they were to be successful, they would only stabilize present conditions, and are no more than a base for a policy that would go beyond them. But we did not project such a policy (except for our remarks on the world economy), we merely added the criterion that it should further the necessary transformation of consciousness (chapter 6, fourth and fifth theses). What does transformation of consciousness actually mean?

One could maintain that all of the problems listed by us could be solved if all of the agents involved allowed themselves to be governed by reason. This is a rather far-reaching thesis, of course, and universal consent will not be instantaneous. Later, we will examine it more closely and then be obliged to formulate more precisely what we mean by "all agents" and "reason." But we have always proceeded as if this thesis were true, for we have tried to find rational solutions to the problems and offered them to the reason of the reader for judgment. Which means that we have constantly appealed to reason.

But that made it necessary for us to inquire why rational regulation cannot be implemented. We believe we found the cause in the structure of power (seventh chapter). To understand this idea, it is decisive that we do not view power as a devil, an irrational scapegoat, but as a structure of societies of conceptually thinking beings, a structure of human societies, which arose for understandable reasons in the course of evolution and always re-stabilizes itself. In power structures, occasions will always arise again which make it expeditious for one part to act in a way which disadvantages the whole. Time and again, we are faced with the practical problem of either stabilizing or doing away with power structures.

This final chapter begins with renewed theoretical reflection that connects with the chapter on power. What happens when structures in society are stabilized or overcome? In a book which does not set forth a general social or systems theory, such a reflection can at best cut a path through the woods. The final section returns to the starting point: what transformation of consciousness is necessary today?

Levels of Political Consciousness

EVOLUTIONARY LEVELS

What happens when structures are stabilized or overcome? Once again, we should appeal to philosophical wonderment. The history of nature, not to mention the history of man, is enormously complex. Actually, there is no repetition in history. Every event is individual, every individual is unique. How do stable structures arise at all in history?

We will not make the attempt here to answer this question causally. We only use it as an occasion for a more precise description of evolution which brings out the startling phenomenon of stable structures. We maintain: normally, historical development occurs through a succession of relatively stable "plateaus" or "levels" on the one hand, and through unstable, often fatally dangerous "crises" on the other. In organic evolution, the species, for example, are levels, and crises the transitions from one species to another. In the history of science, Kuhn introduced the distinction between the levels of normal science and crises which he calls scientific revolutions.[60] In capitalist development, economic history refers to levels of steady growth and to periodic crises or recessions.

The history of organic life shows that levels can stabilize without the intervention of consciousness. The condition itself produces processes which stabilize it. There are even examples of this in the inorganic sphere, such as the stability of an unruffled surface of water, the spherical shape of a star or, in a somewhat more complicated form, the stability of a wave pattern along the border area between two media (waves, sand dunes) which is accompanied by the perpetual change of individual forms. In our examples from human life, levels do not stabilize without accompanying human intent, though not by virtue of this intent alone. In the sciences, one looks for stable convictions but they can only be preserved if they successfully solve problems, are true (in a sense we will not analyze here). In economic development, one strives for stable growth but it required the insights of Keynes to master a particular type of crisis. There was no desire for an arms race, but a form of armaments had to be found which would offer no inducement to engage in a race.

When the stabilization of a social level or the discovery of a new one is involved, human thought appears in two functions: instrumental and integrative. The old distinction between reason and understanding may also be used. Then, understanding would be characterized as conceptual thought, and reason as the awareness of the whole. For purposes of illustration, we will shortly examine a power system. The individual partner in a system (a human being or a nation as represented by its decision makers) can perceive his special interest instrumentally, with his understanding. It is possible that he also perceives the conditions of existence of the whole whose part he is, and this we call the integrative achievement of reason. Normally, the power system stabilizes itself via the conflicts of special interests in which every partner in the system acts rationally. As we saw in chapter seven, however, this stability is not permanent. Monopolistic tendencies in the economic power system, arms races, war and hegemonic formations in the power system of states endanger this stability. Market controls, international agreements and similar things are the result of common reason. It was Hegel's idea that that agent in the historical process whose special interests are closest to the interest of the whole will be the representative of historical progress as long as that condition obtains. His temporary victory is the cunning of reason; his ultimate defeat which occurs when world history no longer stands in need of his special interest proves that world history is not the terrain of happiness. Reason, as we use the term here, is a relative concept. It may be the perception of a whole which, from a more comprehensive perspective, is itself only part of a larger whole. Here, we will examine only those levels of integration which are the most important for the questions raised in this book.

In our reflections on the theory of the market and political liberalism, the state emerged as the representative of the whole. Its parts are the citizens with their special economic and other interests. The liberal theory of the ideal market furnishes a representative example how a whole can stabilize itself without the intervention of consciousness. The individual market participant merely has to rationally pursue his own special interest to bring the whole to an optimal condition (chapter 6). But even according to liberal theory, this only happens within the framework of the state, and governmental actions must take account of the whole to be appropriate. The core of political liberalism is the activation of the reason of the citizens through freedom.

The justified skepticism vis-à-vis the reality of this process serves conservatives, technocrats and socialists as they justify a more extensive regulation by the state. But the more the state regulates, the more the demands made on the reason of its representatives, i.e., those who govern, increase. Each of the three has its own view of why it has more reason on its side: the conservatives because of experience, tradition and historical inheritance, the technocrats because of training and individually tested intelligence, the socialists as the avant-garde of historical progress. This suggests that each of these theses, taken generally, is no less ideological than that of the liberals. The fact of the matter is that the objective form of a social system does not suffice to guarantee the reason of its representatives. The effort to be rational remains a moral demand on each of them.

We are not trying here to develop a theory of social systems. It is enough that today's state shows us an instance of a relatively successful level of social integration which so far has always re-stabilized itself. Of course, it is no more than an example and a building bloc for the problems we are concerned with in this book. In every area, these problems transcend the limits of the individual state. The crises of contemporary states are presumably largely connected with the fact that the states have not caught up with the real problems of contemporary mankind.

FOREIGN POLICY

Foreign policy is as old as the state. It is that relationship between states where they appear as individual units on the one hand, and have no higher unity above them on the other. It is therefore the locus classicus of power politics. But the awareness of the necessity of an overarching reason has always accompanied foreign policy. It has created a variety of forms, three of which we will mention: alliances and diplomacy, international law, international organizations.

Agreements, especially bilateral ones, may easily be no more than instruments of power politics. But the existence of a signed agreement teaches consideration for partners. Diplomacy is a type of conduct where even between enemies, the possibility of an agreement is never lost sight of. The disparaging manner in which the word "diplomatic" is often used only rarely derives from the sincerity of reason but more often from the crude directness everyone feels entitled to where his own interests and prejudices are at stake. Vis-à-vis the egoism of governments (and of opposition parties craving power), the professional diplomats on both sides are frequently the unfortunately powerless representatives of reason.

Within the state, the law is a level where interests are reconciled. We will not discuss its specific nature here. What is essential for such domestic law is that it can be enforced. The power of the state stands behind the legal order. International law is the attempt to regulate the relations between states according to the model of the law within states. Its limit lies in its unenforceability, which is not merely a "malfunction" but constitutive of classical international law. Norms of international law must respect the sovereignty of states, but it is precisely the meaning of sovereignty that the state acknowledges no authority above itself. International law only has the de facto validity which the reason of the partners in concert with a possible harmony of interests within a given power structure accords it. The sovereign state and the guarantors of international law are *on the same plane*. They are equals.

International organizations which go beyond agreements between individual states and in which memebership is either general or contingent upon admission are primarily the work of this century. That they are functionally useful and indeed necessary has been shown many times, especially in the economic sphere. But they also express the growing political consciousness that a system of sovereign states is never sufficient to preserve the peace and is therefore inadequate to future world-political tasks.

The most important international organization was the League of Nations as conceived by Woodrow Wilson, and its continuation in the United Nations. This organization has a limited value which is underestimated if it is judged by what have always been utopian goals. Even the history of its failures is important for the future. Wilson hoped, of course, that the World War which later turned out to have been the First would be the "war to end all wars." He was interested in a democratic cooperation of nations in this new organization. In practice, it became a club where the leading politicians of nations regularly met, a useful political stock exchange, though its majority decisions were not complied with by the most powerful states. When it was reestablished in 1945, the creation of the security council with veto power by the major powers was a step toward realism. The interest the major powers had in the organization was to be enhanced by according them a privileged position within it. In actual practice, the organization became increasingly the forum of the weaker nations, particularly of the Third World. The core of a world government is precisely what it did not become. Instead, it turned into a sounding board for one aspect of world-internal politics.

WORLD-INTERNAL POLITICS

This word is my coinage and requires explanation. To begin with, it is meant descriptively, not normatively. It denotes a spreading mode of perception of world-political events, a developing level of consciousness. To think in terms of world-internal politics means that one judges global political events as if they were internal politics. One thinks of the world in these terms when one sees it as a potential or developed market, for example, where the states are perceived as no more than partners or guarantors of trade and production, or as interfering with trade. Similarly, a person who sees world history as a struggle or evolution of social systems where the governments of states primarily represent the interests of domination of their class also thinks in terms of world-internal politics. To this extent, the first four chapters of this book rest on world-internal political categories. The fifth chapter can be interpreted as a discussion of the question whether these categories can suitably describe the reality of present-day China. World-internal politics is no less controversial than any form of internal politics, but it sees its conflicts as differently localized, and as resolvable by means other than those of classical foreign policy. Seen from a technological perspective, the spread of world-internal political thought is a result of worldwide communication. Next to world trade and the international communication of intellectuals, of socialists and other groups with common convictions, television is probably its most important impetus today.

But we saw in our sixth chapter how this perspective is frustrated by the continuing existence of sovereign states. Today, war prevention is practicable only in cooperation with these states, not against them. All the great hopes that war can be overcome are world-internal-political, and all of them are utopian today. The arguments presented in the balance of this book are therefore clothed in the traditional foreign policy and military terms. To the extent that the book pursues its original goal and addresses its pragmatic analyses and proposals to those that carry responsibility in today's world, it cannot proceed differently. Its proposals are meant realistically.

But the realism demanded of this presentation also includes the admission that the system of sovereign powers which has not overcome war in the past will also fail to do so in the future. Yet the necessity to do so is a part of a necessary transformation of consciousness. It is not enough to stabilize the level of world politics we are familiar with. A crisis and a transition to a new level are required. Today's world politics is an incomplete world-internal politics. Will it be possible to call world politics on a new level a perfected world-internal politics?

Consciousness finds itself in a state of unresolvable tension as it always does when a transition to a new level is demanded but not carried out. It is impossible to correctly anticipate the new level theoretically, for too many of the stabilizing elements of one level remain unconscious or are not matters of the will, and therefore unforeseeable. We perceive the tension as a tension between reality and demand, between is and ought, power and reason, politics and morality. Before we pass on to a concrete discussion of the task we face today, we will therefore evoke the fundamental relationships between politics and morality by using the image of evolutionary levels.

MORALITY AND SOCIETY

We first touched upon this theme in the sixth chapter when we discussed the question of a transformation of consciousness. The reader is asked to look once more at these two pages (107, 136). Here, the author must acknowledge his subjectivity. When, almost two years ago, I wrote the first version of the essay which is now the sixth chapter, and I had finished the analyses of the tendencies that ineluctably make for war, the text of those two pages burst forth like a shout. What has been said spontaneously should be left unchanged so that it can be taken in the same way. At this point, however, we must try to understand what is said more calmly so that it can be transformed into acts. We will not begin with war and peace, but with the role of morality in society.

Even in the smallest social groups, power is a central problem. In chapter 7, we passed from the discussion of the concept of domination to that of the concept of power by first looking at an imaginary (idyllic) society where only two of the three elements of domination, order of rank and function, enter into play. We said that an order of rank is really functional, as animal societies show. It is a stable level of behavior. Though constantly and inevitably overturned by struggles for dominance, it always reestablishes itself. The rank of individuals varies, but the structure is restabilized. Ideally, among human beings, it is relativized by the recognition of the equality of all men insofar as they are capable of reason. We can explain this now by our more precise concept of reason. In principle, all men are capable of perceiving the whole of which they are a part. "In principle" has a normative meaning here. We *should* treat all men as if they were capable of perceiving the whole. To treat them like this is one way of satisfying the conditions that will assure the stability of the whole. For if everyone treats everyone else in this fashion, the whole will presumably be stable. To bring this about, it is not necessary for everyone to understand the conditions for the existence of the whole. No one understands them in their entirety. But everyone who has understood something essential about them— whether it be a general or a specific insight—can at least count on being listened to by others, if all abide by this norm. Where the willingness to perceive the whole exists, the optimal conditions for its continued existence are given for thinking beings. What we have just said may be viewed as a version of the categorical imperative (although it is not discussed here in all its philosophical detail). This is what we meant by the sentence above that all problems can be solved if all agents allowed themselves to be guided by reason. Reason as a capacity also demands respect for reason as a capacity in our fellows. And it is this respect that justifies hierarchies in a twofold sense: to the extent that they are orders of rank of realized reason, for potential reason will respect actual reason. And to the extent that they are functionally useful and do not jeopardize the fundamental equality of all men.

This picture of a rational society is idyllic, as we said in chapter 7, because the third element, power, is absent. How does society deal with the accumulation of power by its members? The idea is the taming of power by reason, the reality is the taming of power by domination. Domination is the power of one part of society over the rest, and is used to stabilize the structure of society, and thus itself. This stabilization is impossible without a certain perception of the whole, i.e., without reason. Domination thus needs reason. Yet its perception is almost always one-sided. It almost always perceives the interest of the rulers as if it were the common interest. To the extent that domination guarantees stability, and stability is in the interest of the whole, this perception is not incorrect. Precisely because of this, one form of rule can almost never replace another by orderly evolution but only in the crisis which usually occurs between two levels of historical existence. Such transition is frequently demanded in the name of a transition from domination to reason, but in actual fact it has always been the transition to a new form of domination which, in favorable cases, was more rational. It is the rational idea of the system of representation to accord rule only through delegation and for a limited time, and to ritualize the transition by elections. Precisely for this reason, all sides are obliged during election times to represent themselves as rational, and the opposing side as irrational. When one sees through this compulsion, one will no longer succumb so easily to the intended deception.

But no objectified political system, no constitution, can be better than the reason of its representatives, and none guarantees that reason. To strive for rationality remains a moral demand. In the relationship between reason and morality, we must distinguish two levels. Following Kohlberg,[61] Habermas and his collaborators discuss three major steps of morality: the pre-conventional, the conventional and the post-conventional. Roughly speaking, the first of these orients itself by the real consequences of acts, the second by traditional moral precepts, the third by reason. The third step thus judges moral rules themselves by rational criteria of morality. The first two apparently only guarantee what is really an unconscious stabilization of society, the first through the biologically inherited "reason of affects," the second through historical custom or, at best, the "reason of the forebears." Reason as we ought to find it in society corresponds to the third step.

We note a phenomenon here which modern social theory has paid much too little attention to, in my view. Provisionally, I should like to call it the indispensability of moral rigorism. This term is not meant to be definitive; it is intended to correct the temptation of idyllic utopias present in the postulate of reason which I have called moral. Anyone who reads classical texts such as the Sermon on the Mount or Kant's *Grundlegung zur Metaphysik der Sitten* can only react with fear to the rigorism of the demands that are made there. One sees with horror that the authors are really serious about universal morality. One can rid oneself of this horror by concluding that the authors are impractical rigorists. This protects one against the crisis preceding a new level of insight which manifested itself precisely in this horror. What results from such protection is the continuing laxness in the use of reason which leads to that series of catastrophes which we call universal history, and whose continuation into our future is the theme of this book. Moral rigorism (not, of course, on its conventional but on its rational level) shows us that in everyday practice, we constantly violate the demands of reason. How do we react when this insight dawns on us?

One possible reaction is the social implementation of moral rigorism. Some of the most significant historical events are due to it. Only the prophetic and legal rigorism of the Old Testament (Moses and the Prophets) enabled the Jewish people to survive to this day. It established the level of stability of a nation that had become homeless. Its continued effect in Christianity changed the world. In modern times, the Calvinist Puritans are the outstanding example. America owes them essential characteristics, and Holland and Switzerland (the latter with Zwinglian components) a stamp which is still recognizable today. There are good reasons why Max Weber traced the efficiency of early capitalism back to them, and this is an aspect we did not accord the importance it deserves in this book because our theory of power is close to Marx. Without the element of moral rigorism, the socialist movement up to the present is not conceivable. Mao's China is an impressive version of it.

But moral rigorists incur the disfavor of society, and not without reason. It is true that they are usually right in the reproaches they address to it. But so is society in the reproaches it returns. As a social reality, moral rigorism is almost impossible without self-righteousness. In political practice, self-righteousness imperceptibly turns into the justification of the means by the end. It is for this reason Heisenberg said that a political movement should never be judged by its ends but only its means. That is the reaction of a morally sensitive individual who was no rigorist.

The morally sensitive person who recognizes the self-righteousness implicit in the claim to change the world has at least three choices, it would seem. He is on his own. Before he can make further demands on his fellows, he must try to straighten himself out. One alternative leads to a historically very effective human type who makes the most severe demands on himself and therefore feels entitled to make similarly harsh demands on others. Such individuals are tragic heroes. Even when they do change the world, they fail in what was important to them, the creation of a new human being, moral man in a moral society. Despite all their good will, indeed because of it, conflict and not love emanates from them. Their unceasing struggle against themselves creates this effect and also hides from them the reasons for their failure (it should be clear that an ideal-typical description such as this is not precise in any given instance. It can only point to one component in the immeasurable complexity of every human being).

The second path avoids what is heroic and tragic in the above figure by greater modesty in what he requires of himself and others. When this involves no loss of moral sensitiveness, it will be a path toward maturity and thus toward kindness. Those who have taken this route do not seem to change the world. But anyone who has retained his moral sense will not conduct himself in their presence as he normally would. While the real transformation of the world does not occur without the will, the will itself cannot bring it about. It occurs when the will has pushed aside obstacles and by a power that is unattainable to it.

The third path is really nothing other than the explicit experience of what happens imperfectly and gently along the second path. Historically, it has been taken almost exclusively in religion. Entrance to it is probably always an internal drama, a crisis, where a new form of perception struggles for admission. These crises also are as multiform as the individuals and the cultures which furnish them the means for self-interpretation. This would be one way of describing the crisis: Anyone who clings to radical demands on himself and cannot deceive himself about the fact that he does not live up to them must fall into despair about himself. This despair is an experience of death. In it, the moral self discovers what it means to die, to choke. A resurrection waits within this death. In the language available to us, the experience of a new life expresses itself only in an image, and indeed paradoxically. It is an awakening to a different reality, to reality. It turns out that the ego was only an organ of the true self. I became what I have always been, someone I did not know and yet knew, for otherwise I would not have searched for him. This experience is the basis of religion.

It should not be assumed that the problem of politics and consciousness, of morality and society can be solved if the path moral rigorism discloses is not taken in actual life. Once it has been taken, a perspective on social problems opens up which quite simply shows, as it were, why they had to be unsolvable. Let us turn once more to the conceptual field of power and reason. As we used the word, power is something human, an accumulation of means which imagination and conceptual thought make possible. We called conceptual, instrumental thought understanding. Understanding and will belong together. The will can want what the understanding can conceive of, and the understanding can conceive what such a will can want. Reason we called awareness of the whole. Reason does not reject understanding but comprehends it, indeed makes it possible. For what I can want is part of the whole, and without what is usually an implicit awareness of the whole, I do not have the orientation a rational will requires. Reason in the narrower sense is explicit reason, conscious perception of a whole as a whole. The automatic stabilization of a power system through the interaction of its rationally acting members lacks reason *as* stabilization and is never permanent, as we have seen. Power is the work of *imperfect* insight. It lacks precisely what would be essential to conscious stabilization. We are simply restating the analysis given above when we say that what is required is not a complete insight but merely the readiness of all members of any given society to submit to the perception of the whole. All that is required is "reasonableness."

Moral rigorism formulates the demand of reasonableness in the only form accessible to the understanding, that of logical generality. But stated in this form, the demand will not be met. The moral will does not prevail over the affects, and both sides are at fault in this. Affects by themselves are unilluminated. They perceive what is at hand, but not the whole. At best, they could stabilize the life of creatures that were not yet capable of the immense generalizing achievement of the understanding. But generalizing moral understanding does not perceive the always unique role of the given within the whole. In their conflict with it, the affects frequently defend the right of real life. If man only had affects and a rational will, he could only fail; he would be an aberration of nature. All the social and moral theories which confine themselves to these two modes of conduct have to gloss over things in order to escape the perception of the failure of their constructs. Their conflict thus becomes eternal, for each clearly sees the gloss of the other.

But reason as that kind of human perception that is adequate to the whole is possible. We will not explain its origin causally, as we did not explain the origin of affects and the understanding. We merely describe how it is experienced. We characterized both affects and reason as perceptions, which means that our starting point lies beyond the common distinction between theory and practice. What is normally called theory is itself a practical achievement: a conceptual distancing of the idea from the immediate, an effort of the understanding. Compared to this, reason as perception has something in common with the affects. But its "affect" does not reflect an interest of the self. In the language of the Christian tradition, the affect which makes reason possible is called love. Faith in the sense of Christian tradition is not believing that something is true, i.e., a hypothesis of the understanding, but an openness to love which overcomes anxiety. Anxiety is the fear of one's incapacity for peace. Modern theologians have stressed the difference between biblical and Greek thought which has led to a wrongly conceived antithesis between faith and reason. Here, reason is not understood as perception but as a conceptual structure. Love as the affect which transcends and redeems the moral ego makes reason possible. And love demands reason, for it demands that I really perceive the human being I love.

The reader who has come this far will ask what this theological anthropology can contribute to the solution of social problems. The answer is that, being a theory, it cannot solve those problems but only make comprehensible why they ultimately remain unsolved in the succession of levels and crises. The real problem of morality and society only begins here. We have come to a crossing of the ways.

One way or path is the withdrawal from the attempt to save or change the world through the will and the understanding, through "theory and practice." It is the concentration on the readiness to straighten oneself out, and the concentration on everything the willing to do so experiences. For more than three millennia, this has been a level of human behavior which was entered time and again by hermits and monks, sects and inconspicuous human beings. The mere mention of this historical life style shows that even the person who leaves what society views as real retains a social place. The hermit also is nourished, either by his own efforts, or those of others. The sociology of monks would be a significant subject. Religious societies, however, have usually known that those who withdraw from society in this way achieve something decisive for it.[62] Even in the vague language of modern anthropology, one can say that distancing is one of the significant human achievements that shape consciousness. And we also permit distance to those who distance themselves in order to think something that is comprehensible in modern times, like scientists.

The other path is the attempt to shape society in such a way that the life of reason can be lived in it. The self-sacrifice of the martyr is always possible, of course. But it makes sense to stabilize customs and laws in the society which will permit precise demands of rational morality to be obeyed without self-sacrifice. Perhaps the Hippocratic oath was needed to make a moral medicine possible, for this elitist knowledge contains any number of temptations to seek power. But the Hippocratic oath is meant to be known and approved of publicly so that the physician can invoke it, should he resist a temptation or a demand. Science also must be public. It must publish its findings because truth is discovered in dialogue, in mutual criticism. And its discoveries should not establish private power but promote the public weal. It can only be public, however, if its freedom of expression is guaranteed by a constitution and public consensus. What was repeatedly advocated in this book as the theory of political liberalism is the extension of this principle of the social protection of the search for truth to all citizens and all affairs. Of course, by its very nature, liberal regulation remains formal. To create a space for rationality is not enough. It is equally necessary to implement special, rationally perceived contents in society.

Those who choose this path move from compromise to compromise. They must provide a power base for reason and thus acknowledge powers which are intrinsically unreasonable. They must create a space for neighborly love by sometimes attacking and sometimes sparing egoisms. They must take on allies they can hardly approve of, and will make enemies of some whose motives they must respect. They not only enter into compromises with others but even with themselves. They harness their ambition in the service of what they see as reason. They discover that a victory of their ambition is a defeat for reason, and that their defeat makes room for progress.

Such has been the nature of politics for millennia. In the medium of this torment, mankind has taken steps that have substantially changed its history. Only one of these steps, the one that must be taken now, will concern us in the remainder of this book.

What Transformation
of Consciousness is Necessary Today?

CRISIS AND TRANSFORMATION OF CONSCIOUSNESS

The levels and crises of human existence correspond to levels and crises of consciousness. On a stable level of existence, we generally have modes of perception and views which contribute to stabilization. A person who is stabilized in a role normally perceives precisely what is appropriate to that role. In its extreme forms, this phenomenon is a theme for comedies and tragedies. During a phase of "normal" science, the theories that successfully solve problems are simply considered true. The philosophical inquiry without which the prevailing theory would never have come into existence is judged superfluous and irritating during the phase of the stable dominance of the theory. In a stable society, the prevailing form of rule is usually accepted as legitimate, even by those that are ruled by it. Recognized legitimacy presupposes something like a rational renunciation of reason. Rational, because one is correct in believing that the prevailing state of affairs guarantees the continued existence of the whole and should continue for that reason. To this extent, what is and what ought to be are the same. Renunciation of reason, because one does not even seriously consider that other conditions might be admissible. But this means that one lacks the conceptual breadth to understand *why* existing conditions are stable. The stability of a finite system presupposes a limited self-perception, a not wholly rational reason. The finite system is a whole within a larger whole, and especially also within the framework of its own history which transcends the present stable phase. The stabilizing reason inside the system does not take adequate cognizance of this larger whole.

In a crisis, the relationship to reason becomes ambivalent. On the one hand, traditional self-perception fails, and insecurity spreads. On the other, demands are made on reason which were superfluous before the crisis and may be superfluous once more when that crisis has been overcome and a new level has been attained. A human being in crisis is often closed to rational arguments to which he was open before and will be open again. But a person in crisis can also be open to profound insights to which he closed himself before, and will again close himself afterwards. Philosophy is as essential to scientific revolutions as it is alien to normal science. Social crises manifest themselves in the loss of legitimacy of what exists, in an unusual chance for rational new creation and an opportunity to think far beyond existing possibilities. The actual solution of the crisis usually makes only limited use of the reason released by the crisis, but even this limited use would not have been discovered unless the horizon had opened more than was practically necessary. While stability tends to be irritated and indeed jeopardized by fundamental thought, it is of vital importance to think such thoughts while the crisis lasts.

This is the place to deal with a question which was raised in the first chapter and postponed until now. So far, we have only taken up six of the seven key terms describing our present fears as they were listed there. We postponed the question concerning the fear of a cultural decline. We already suggested that this concern expresses the conservative perception of a real phenomenon. It is true that the legitimacy of our traditional values has been undermined and that men, particularly young people, are breaking out of traditional forms of behavior. A bare ten years ago, this disengagement had the force of a global landslide. Today, we have a regressive phase but it has all the earmarks of a stabilization based on fear rather than insight, and therefore does not promise to be of long duration. Throughout this book, we have discussed objective problems in today's world to which traditional behavior patterns cannot be adequate for understandable reasons. We should not blame the stabilizing forms of perception and conduct of the past because they do not solve today's problems. It is our task to find new solutions. But we must not reproach our contemporaries, and especially our youth, for sensing the inadequacy of tradition in solving present tasks, and for refusing to believe in the legitimacy of tradition even when that refusal itself solves no problems. That is the typical conduct of a necessary but as yet unresolved crisis of consciousness.

We must thus ask about the kind of transformation of consciousness that is necessary today. In so doing, we have to think about principles even if we know that the principles that have been uncovered will again only be put to limited use at a later time. The opening up of reason during a crisis is comparable to the opening of the enchanted castle in fairy tales. All the doors of the castle were locked, and suddenly all of them open. One believes one can see through a succession of rooms all the way to the end of the castle. But as one enters the next room, all the doors close again and will remain closed until the time has come when we are once again to leave that room and another appeal to openness has to be made. The political and economic substance of today's crisis revealed itself as the need for a worldwide order. We now have to ask what kind of consciousness goes along with such an order. What does reason in a global order look like? Reflectively, we now follow the thread of the themes we have dealt with substantively.

RATIONAL USE OF TECHNOLOGY

Throughout this book, it was in technological progress that we discovered the origin of the problems and of the means being tried to solve them in technological progress. It is only in chapter 2 that we thematized technological progress itself, although only by way of an example. We will return to this question. In chapter 3, we sought the source of three complexes of problems (world market, growth, demand for labor) in technological progress. Technological progress does not automatically stabilize the economy. The choice between the optimistic and the pessimistic version is that the rational self-interest of all economic agents with its consequences may be either rational or irrational, include the awareness of the whole, or be blind. The socialist critique of capitalism sees the basis for the necessary unreason in the private ownership of the means of production. But even according to the doctrine of historical materialism, a communist economy where everyone has what he needs, would only be possible if goods were no longer scarce, which would be a result of technically developed productive means. Modern war prevention doctrines fight against an evil, war waged with the technical means for mass destruction, by the planned use of technology, by deterrence through those technical weapons. We have examined these doctrines in detail and made certain proposals for improvement, yet have come to the conclusion that war technology does not automatically stabilize peace but can only do so under the guidance of political reason and through the creation of rational political structures.

For centuries, mankind's attitude toward progressing technology has wavered between optimism and worry. In our century, technical optimism is more widespread than ever before. Its victory in public opinion was so complete that the youth protesting against it usually no longer knew how close its protest was to the conservative criticism of technology voiced throughout the centuries of the modern era. But it is a fact that the criticism of technology, and indeed the fear that technical civilization may destroy itself, is a component of the current crisis in consciousness.

In chapter 2, under the aspect of the protection of the environment in the special case of energy technology, we discussed the criticism of technology in some detail. As elsewhere in this book, we did not join in with those who criticize technology in principle, but neither did we elevate optimism about it into a principle. What characterized our attitude was the thesis that there are technical means for dealing with technically caused dangers, and that the real dangers are caused by man himself. In our present vocabulary, we can say that technology is a means of the rational will. It can be controlled by reason but it cannot compensate for the failure of reason. What is unique in our present situation is that the development of technical means places hitherto unknown demands on reason. We must perceive the whole of technological civilization and its effects on the life of man and nature, whose child man is. But it is questionable that we can, certain that we don't, and essential that we try.

Technological civilization did not come upon us like an unforeseen fate.It is the logical result of a central process in modern occidental civilization which today is victorious on a worldwide scale, the rise of a world of the will and of the understanding. The associated capacities, the will and the understanding, are developing in the individual and society at large to a historically unprecedented degree. The automatism of technological civilization is the automatism of a training of the will and of the understanding that lacks the guidance of reason. We are accumulating means without regard to integrative ends. This world is the purest representation of the phenomenon of power that has ever existed. The power of despots rested on the powerlessness of the ruled. Today, everyone is drawn into the power struggle. It begins with the children as they struggle for admission to higher education. Illich is perfectly correct in his critique that the apparent diffusion of techniques such as schooling, means of communication, technical medicine, all of which are meant to have an equalizing effect, actually threatens to perpetuate social inequalities, for it transforms these gifts of the mind into weapons in the social power struggle.

If our analysis is correct, nothing would be gained by rejecting technology. Technology furnishes means. To use these means without an insight into ends is really nontechnical behavior. But the required transformation of consciousness is very difficult to achieve. The success of technology has turned our consciousness away from traditional reason and changed it into an irrational push and press. The crisis of consciousness necessary here cannot occur without fear and dread. Without these affects, we will not re-learn how to reflect. The new reason cannot be the old, pre-technical reason. Especially, it must integrate modern science. We will return to this question in the final section.

Conscious planning must attempt to direct the unavoidable crisis of the technological world along the gentlest possible course. Fear and dread are ineluctable but they are not good counselors. We demanded that a war prevention policy facilitate rather than inhibit the requisite transformation of consciousness, and this demand applies equally to technology policy. This is how the recommendations in chapter 2 are to be understood. They are inadequate for solving the problems of saving the environment in a technological, affluent society, but they give important examples so that we may school ourselves in the habits of the rational manipulation of technology. What is demanded there is a bare minimum and would do no more than spare us the experience of fear and terror in one limited sphere, energy technology. But presumably not even that will be done, and dread at the consequences will not fail to set in.

If we wish to integrate technology into a new form of reason, we must not see it merely as the cause of economic, social and military occurrences but must simultaneously understand it as their result. Using concepts from individual psychology, we called it the consequence of the development of the will and the understanding. This development in turn is both the effect and the intensifying cause of social power struggles. Insight into the social conditions underlying the creation of technology is part of the necessary transformation of consciousness.

CAPITALISM AND SOCIALISM

In our immanent critique of capitalism, we tried to learn something from socialist criticism. We did not reject that criticism but could not subscribe to the socialist hope. Here, we can do no more than formulate our arguments in the language of this closing chapter.

The anthropological assumption underlying economic liberalism might be defined in this way: we can expect human beings to understand their own interest, but cannot expect them to be aware of the conditions for the survival of the whole. The economic theory of the market rests on a further thesis, i.e., that rational self-interest is all that is needed for the exchange of goods, that an optimal condition is automatically realized in an economically acting society of rational beings. The political object of this thesis is to criticize rulers for usurping the nimbus of reason. The philosopher of reason, Hegel, emphatically affirmed this thesis. According to him, world reason does not require incarnation in a Platonic philosopher king. But our concept of reason is not Hegel's, and this is not the place for a discussion of his work. Hegel's interpretation of the politics of his time, in any event, saw the state as a reality that is necessarily superordinate to bourgeois society. Following Adam Smith, we had to demand a government framework for the market, and had to insist that the state act deliberately and reasonably. We are skeptical of the ability of the world market to achieve stability because a global framework is lacking.

Our critique of capitalism sees it as one power system among others. It parallels Marxist criticism in the sense that we see the accumulation of capital as the accumulation of power. But we agree with laissez-faire economists in believing that the impact of political power factors on the market creates distortions and all those consequences set forth in the pessimistic version. There is no need to believe with the Marxists that it is economic interests that underlie these political factors, that the state bureaucracy, for example, are agents of the capitalists, for in our conceptual schema, the effects of political and economic power are similar in any event. From our point of view, capital is merely one of the means of power in an ineluctable struggle for power. Like

Marx, we see the consequences of this struggle as ambivalent ("dialectic"): they increase production and are temporarily stabilizing but unjust and unstable over the long term.

The acuteness of the struggle for economic power which is a characteristic of modern times derives in part from the preponderant power of the state. Except for terrorism, it could enforce its claim that it had the sole right to use the means of armed conflict. That the citizen should be permitted to exercise no power other than economic power is of course a humanizing element in politics. But the theory of the total freedom of economic agents, of the legitimacy of economic egoism, also played an important role in reducing respect for reason. Men in capitalist society have learned to view human life as a perpetual conflict of private interests. The curious peacelessness of the affluent in our society in particular is certainly connected with this miseducation by the economic system. *Homo economicus* is an abstract fiction used for purposes of theoretical explanation. Free competition is bearable, provided it is not what ultimately counts in life, but fair play. We have stylized our society in such a way that neither the perception of the affects nor that of reason is taken account of. The disintegration of affects and the silence of reason are the result.

If we consider the change in consciousness, those that are adversaries in our world can often be seen as close to each other. Using different means, they struggle with identical problems. Like the liberal movement, the socialist movement wanted to supplant existing domination, produce material goods, and let all benefit from them. Like the liberal movement, it used mechanisms of power whose effects threaten to turn those goals into their opposite. Neither of the two movements has clearly understood the perpetual recreation of power systems, and both have failed to adequately criticize that power they themselves used to realize the progress they aimed for.

As regards the necessary transformation of consciousness,

it is precisely the strength of socialism that its rule is not worldwide at this time, and that where it does rule, it cannot harbor the illusion of having reached its goals. The unfulfilled socialist demand comes closer to an insight into the necessary transformation of consciousness than does liberal self-assertion. It is not impossible that the coming decades will see a major political victory of socialism. In that case, could the language of socialism provide the vocabulary in which the demand of reason, the possibility of neighborly love, could be formulated? To avoid being a historical regression, a victorious socialism would have to satisfy two conditions: it would have to preserve liberal achievements, and break out of the narrow consciousness of the world of the will and the understanding. These two things are connected.

The liberal constitutional state is the greatest political invention of the last few centuries. In the historical sequence, it follows the technico-bureaucratic, efficient state the age of absolutism created. For those nations which were modernized by socialism, it is therefore a future postulate. This does not mean, of course, that future liberal constitutionalism there ought to have all the characteristics of the Western bourgeois world. The liberal state in its bourgeois form is itself merely a historical experiment, an example of the norm of a state which combines the peaceful balancing of interests with institutionalized free dialogue, i.e., with the intent to institute public reason. Socialism can only avoid being a world historical regression if it preserves and develops this norm where it exists and paves the way for it where it doesn't. Otherwise, it will be taken over by groups which will usurp the claim to reason but will not make good on it, as has happened so often in world history.

The principle of the market is also a liberal achievement which need not necessarily take the form of classical capitalism. Purely economically, the much disputed convergence thesis has a strong basis in the developmental tendencies inherent in the systems on both sides, namely the tendency toward planning and the increasing share of the state on the one hand, and the striving for economic liberalization on the other. That convergence does not occur has primarily political causes. Both sides are aware of the extent to which their political system needs their respective economic form as a power base. This power struggle has no natural tendency toward peaceful resolution. That is also why the discovery of the most suitable economic structure, which would seem to be a task of organizational optimization, actually hinges on the transformation of consciousness which would make possible political peace.

The demand that socialism preserve and develop liberal achievements is here and today a conservative demand (though revolutionary for Russia). This is the conservatism without which no progress is possible—the new level must not be worse than the preceding one. But it is also true that the moral impulse of socialism is one of the few great hopes for a transformation of consciousness in our time. The demands for solidarity and justice are such that they might burst open the narrow consciousness of institutionalized power struggles. How could they become a reality? As mere demands with a frequently marked and even politically necessary undertone of hatred, they are affects but not yet reason. Given continuing lip service, such affects are normally frustrated by political reality. The kind of failure varies with the doctrine. Observation shows that the danger of victorious capitalism is cynicism, the danger of victorious socialism the lie on command. The change of consciousness would have to transform the affects of solidarity and justice into reason.

Theory is one of the ways one is schooled in reason. This accounts for the extraordinary historical effect Marx has had: he taught the socialists to look at the whole. But as almost the entire modern era, and socialism as well, understand theory, it is not perception but conceptual thought. It is an effort of the understanding to comprehend the whole. A theoretical error can therefore be fatal. It creates the illusion that a reality is being seen, and blinds the person to existing reality for precisely that reason. We attempted to analyze certain errors of Marx which are fundamental to communism (chapter 4). We must agree with the basic criticism that is made of Marxism: politically correct conduct cannot be derived from a theory of history. But it is equally true that the categorical imperative does not prompt a morally motivated pragmatism. The socialist who is morally serious in his demands must come to terms with moral rigorism. A social theory which is ignorant of this experience cannot be true. Religious socialism once saw its task here, but it probably did not have the strength to create a secular theory. At this point, we come up once more against an unfulfilled demand on our thinking.

OVERCOMING WAR

Nothing less than the overcoming of the institution of war is essential. This would be true even if the next world-historical crisis merely took us to a level where just certain forms of war were excluded. For a historical moment, we can cast a glance through the entire succession of rooms and see that the next one we will enter can no longer be taken for the last one.

Two insights are part of a necessary transformation of consciousness: that overcoming war is necessary, and that it is possible. The logical statement that the necessary is eo ipso possible does not apply here, for what is involved is a conditional necessity and possibility. Both insights presuppose that historical human culture will continue to grow and not be destroyed. It is an additional assertion that this condition can be met. If that were not the case, what is necessary might still be impossible.

That overcoming war is necessary seems obvious to today's mankind only as regards one form of it: world war with the use of strategic weapons. That does not contradict our theses in chapter 6. They merely state that this has not been achieved so far. Even the argument that war can be waged because survival is possible does not do away with the necessity of overcoming it. Like all historical predictions, this cannot be strictly proven. But a world with major sovereign powers which engage in periodic wars with the most modern weapons available is not at a stable level. It will pass over into global peace or global destruction. Here as elsewhere, this argument is based on the irreversible change of the technological possibilities in modern civilization. But should it be possible to overcome major war by a political world order, that order will have an effect on local wars. For if they were to continue unchecked, they would destabilize the overarching order.

But is it possible to overcome war as an institution? Haven't we seen that the conflict in power systems is an anthropological, deeply rooted form of behavior? Here, it is essential to divide the question into two steps. A change in behavior which would overcome power struggles is historically conceivable over the very long term, for we have seen that power is a product of imperfect insight. The step that must and can be taken today, however, is precisely not the overcoming of power conflicts generally, but the overcoming of one specific way of settling them. What we said before about the necessity of fundamental thought in a crisis is applicable here. The step toward overcoming the settlement of conflict by war between sovereign powers is well defined. It is so large that our imagination can hardly encompass it, but it is a finite step from level to level. To make it possible to think about it, we have to understand the bases of political behavior and address ourselves to motives which aim at much more, namely the overcoming of power struggles altogether.

Every modern state furnishes us with examples how the forms of the settlement of conflicts can be changed. In today's states, private feuds and civil war as institutions have been abolished. That does not mean that they never occur. But they are proscribed and rare, and when they become too frequent, the state cannot survive. Why are cities no longer walled? In part, because artillery was invented, in part because within a territorial state, the law provides protection. Both of these things go together. Artillery made the modern state necessary and possible.

Our parallel raises the question whether the world state would be a way for overcoming war. In the political chapters of this book, in the sections dealing with economic and military matters, we twice came to a point where a demand for a state-like world organization would have been a logical step. But we did not take that step there, and that for two, almost antithetical reasons. For one thing, it is still too radical. Today, it is utopian, and thus no guideline for practical politics. On the other hand, such a demand is not radical enough. It retains the recipes by which problems are solved today and merely extends them on a planetary scale. But at this point, and in spite of these objections, we must understand how likely a state-like world order is. Precisely because of its conservative features, it is a possible political level which might well be the result of the next major world-political crisis, especially of a Third World War.

It requires only a jolt in our thinking to transcend the lack of imagination which cannot conceive of something that is historically unprecedented. The introduction of agriculture, of towns, of large empires, of churches, of technology were no smaller steps than would be the step toward a world state. More powerful weapons usually lead to larger territorial states, and hegemonic conflicts to world empires which comprehend a culture sphere. The reciprocal cultural assimilation of the regions of the world is under way today. It is a process that cries out for political and organizational unity. That unified world might be difficult to govern, and therefore methods of government will not be gentle.

It is obvious that the world state would be a danger to freedom, that it would promote the leveling of cultures and thus be a danger to the sources of reason. The goal we assign to our transformation of consciousness should therefore not be the world state, but neither should it be its prevention. The goal should be to allow structures to develop which might perhaps be a substitute for it, and which would make it bearable, should it become a reality. They would have to be structures which elicit and facilitate the application of world-political reason. The "consequences" of several chapters of this book should be measured by this criterion.

We will not pursue the political consequences further at this point. In closing, we ask what step in the structure of a rational consciousness can be taken today.

THE LIGHT OF CONSCIOUSNESS

In all older cultures of the world, the perception of the whole—a philosophical concern—had its social place in religion.[63] This is true in the three-fold sense of the perception of the entire person, of the entire society, of all of nature. The highest form of religious perception was illumination, revelation, which are light metaphors. In eighteenth century Europe, religion was confronted by the social force that is called the Enlightenment. The term "enlightenment" is also a light metaphor. The development of consciousness is reflected in metaphors of seeing, perception. The confrontation of religion and enlightenment will be succeeded by a confrontation of world religions. As compared to earlier centuries, this process is facilitated by modern communications but is far from being achieved. In these two confrontations, a process of consciousness got under way which could also some day be decisive for political consciousness.

What is enlightenment? As a social process, it sees itself as emancipation, as a coming of age. The person that has come of age perceives himself as deciding freely. He knows himself as a moral self. Enlightenment is the moral self interpretation of the world of the will and the understanding. Reason in the form of general thought is accessible to it. It formulates rational insight as theory. It changes the world through concepts. Technical progress which has come about through the connection with science is its work. Today's world with its achievements and problems, its necessary crisis, is thus a product of enlightenment.

The crisis is also a crisis of rationalist self-consciousness. Do our problems come from the opaqueness of our world, and can they be resolved through more enlightenment? Or are they, conversely, a result of enlightenment, perhaps of a growth of power that is inappropriate to human nature, or even of an essentially false conception of reality by enlightenment? Both views may contain some truth. An opaque world will not accept what enlightenment brings, and will react destructively to it. But it seems that even with conceptual thinking, enlightenment cannot master the problems created by conceptual thought. As long as the artificial world of civilization consisted only of islands in a historically grown, long since stabilized world, it could adapt to the conditions of its environment. But as the artificial world becomes the whole on whose stability the parts depend, it becomes increasingly difficult to control. It can protect itself against natural events, but how does it protect itself from the free will of its own agents? Here, the difference between conceptual thought and perception becomes decisive. Enlightenment taught man concepts, but not perception. Perception is no less fallible that conceptual thought but it is not the same. To think something correctly, and to see it, however one-sidedly, are two different things. Affect is perception that precedes conceptual thought. Reason is perception which can avail itself of conceptual thought. Conceptual thought is no substitute for reasonable perception, it is a different capacity, a different light. It is amazing how much people that have trained their understanding can grasp conceptually, and how strong their affects remain. But how blind they are when they conceptualize their affects. In today's world, it is at most the artists that perceive. What they perceive and body forth is decay. This decay is not a symptom of decline but of the approaching crisis. It is no accident that drug addiction spreads and asiatic schools of meditation flourish in this situation. Drugs produce a kind of substitute perception, the coloration, as it were, the emotion of self-perception, but without its structural and productive content. Meditation, on the other hand, is the readiness to allow the will to become calm, and to see the light that only shows itself when that condition prevails. It is a school of perception, of allowing reality to manifest itself. The desire for it is therefore right. But the traditions of meditation must themselves pass through a transformation. Up to now, they were embedded in a mythical world picture. In today's world, they come into the light of enlightenment.

This transformation of consciousness occurs among many individuals today, and usually far away from politics. It finds it difficult to understand itself. It has to think both the traditions of scientific theory and of meditative perception. Here also, we have a task for conceptual change, for philosophy. Does this slow work which is remote from politics make a contribution to politics?

We will not answer this question directly. Instead, we return to a simple description of the task a transformation of political consciousness sets. If all agents let themselves be guided by reason, all the problems discussed in this book could be solved. We defined reasonableness as the readiness to listen to reason. Presumably a general reasonableness would suffice to solve practical problems. Everybody knows that it cannot be created by appeals. Political systems tend to believe that if that is so, reasonableness is of no consequence, that instead organizational, economic or social conditions have to be created which either automatically insure reasonable reactions, or do not require reason. This is true in the sense that there are objective conditions which prevent the development and confirmation of reasonable perception. Reason, however, is not elicited by material conditions but by the call of reason itself.

Notes

1. Horst Afheldt, *Verteidigung und Frieden, Politik mit militärischen Mitteln* (München: Hanser, 1976).
2. Guy Brossollet, "Das Ende der Schlacht" and Emil Spannocchi, "Verteidigung ohne Selbstzerstorung" in Spannocchi and Brossollet, *Verteidigung ohne Schlacht* (München: Hanser, 1976).
3. H. Afheldt, A. Künkel, A. Pfau, E. Rahner, K. Rajewski, U. P. Reich, H. Roth, Ph. Sonntag and C. F. v. Weizsäcker, *Kriegsfolgen und Kriegsverhütung*, editor C. F. v. Weizsäcker (München: Hanser, 1971).

   H. Afheldt, Ch. Potyka, U. P. Reich, Ph. Sonntag and C. F. v. Weizsäcker, *Durch Kriegsverhütung zum Krieg?* (München: Hanser, 1972).

   C. F. v. Weizsäcker, *Fragen zur Weltpolitik* (München, Hanser, 1975).
4. In France, the Institut français d'opinion publique did such a poll in October 1973. It furnished the basis of the international colloquium "Perception nouvelle des menaces" which the Fondation pour les études de defense national held from the 29th of November to the 1st of December 1973, in Paris. See contributions in *Le Monde Diplomatique*, March 1974, pp. 7–17.
5. On the mode of expression adopted here: the author uses "we" in most of those cases where he proposes that the reader think along with the author; he uses "I" when he makes statements for which he assumes sole responsibility, and "the author" when he refers to his role as the author of this book.
6. See also von Weizsäcker, *Fragen zur Weltpolitik*, pp. 51–85.
7. A three percent growth rate in per capita GNP (see figures p. 196) will mean a doubling in two and one-half decades, a tenfold increase in eight decades.
8. Figures from R. Paqué, "Die Energieversorgung der Erde, technische und wirtschaftliche Aspekte insbesondere mit Blick auf die BRD," in *Stiftung Wissenschaft und Politik* (Ebenhausen: SWP-M 2051, July, 1974).
9. B. L. Cohen, "Perspectives on the Nuclear Debate, *"Bulletin of the Atomic Scientists"* 30, no. 7 (1974), pp. 35–39, as quoted by Alvin M. Weinberg in "Is Nuclear Energy Acceptable?" 1975 lecture. (Manuscript.)

10. U.S. Nuclear Regulatory Commission, *"Reactor Safety Study: an Assessment of Accident Risks in U.S. Commercial Nuclear Power Plants,"* prepared for the U.S. Atomic Energy Commission Task Force by N. C. Rasmussen, chairman (Washington, D.C.: Government Printing Office, Oct. 1975, WASH-1400, NUREG-75/014).

11. R. Hagemann, G. Nief and E. Roth, "Études chimiques et isotopiques du reacteur naturel d'Oklo," and "Le phénomène d'Oklo," *Bulletin d'Informations Scientifiques et Techniques,* no. 196 (June 1974), p. 76.

12. Weinberg, "Is Nuclear Energy Acceptable?"

13. *Reviews of Modern Physics,* vol. 47, supplement no. 1 (summer 1975).

14. W. Sullivan, "Long-Term Reactor Peril Stirs Physicist's Concern," *The New York Times,* April 29, 1975, pp. 1, 12.

15. Medical Research Council, *The Toxicity of Plutonium* (London: HMSO, 1975) is considered the best report. In the meantime, the U.S. Environmental Protection Agency, *Proceedings of Public Hearings: Plutonium and the Other Transuranium Elements,* vol. 1 (ORP/CSD–75–1) (proceedings of hearings in Washington, D.C., Dec. 10–11, 1974) have appeared in print.

16. Cohen, "Perspectives on the Nuclear Debate."

17. Marchetti, as quoted by W. Hafele in "Future Energy Resources," IIASA research report, Nov. 1974.

18. I am indebted to my son C. C. von Weizsäcker for important pointers on this problem, but I am responsible for the formulation.

19. See my lecture "Über die Kunst der Prognose," 1968, printed in C. F. v. Weizsäcker, *Der ungesicherte Friede* (Göttingen: Vandenhoeck und Ruprecht, 1969) and reprinted in *Fragen zur Weltpolitik,* pp. 102, 118.

20. See C. F. Bergsten, ed., *The Future of the International Economic Order: An Agenda for Research* (Lexington, Mass.: Heath, 1973) and C. F. Bergsten and W. G. Tyler, eds., *Leading Issues in International Economic Policy* (Lexington, Mass.: Heath, 1973).

21. See "The Oil Crisis in Perspective," *Daedalus,* fall 1975.

22. I. Illich, *Energy and Equity* (New York: Harper and Row, 1974) and *Tools for Conviviality* (New York: Harper and Row, 1973).

23. U. P. Reich, Ph. Sonntag, H. W. Holub, *Arbeit-Konsum-Rechnung: Axiomatische Kritik und Erweiterung der VGR* (Koln: Bund Verlag).

24. J. W. Forrester, *World Dynamics* (Cambridge, Mass.: Wright-Allen Press, 1971) and D. H. Meadows, *The Limits to Growth, a*

Report for the Club of Rome's Project on the Predicament of Mankind (New York: Universe Books, 1972).

25. M. Mesarovic, and E. Pestel, *Mankind at the Turning Point, the Second Report to the Club of Rome* (New York: Dutton, 1974).

26. M. U. Porat, "Defining an Information Sector in the U.S. Economy," second year project (manuscript) for the Institute for Communication Research, Stanford University, Nov. 15, 1974; and E. B. Parker (of the Institute for Communication Research, Stanford University), "Social Implications of Computer/ Telecommunications Systems" (Paris: OECD, DSTI/CUG/ 75.1, Jan. 27, 1975).

27. C. F. v. Weizsäcker, *Die Einheit der Natur, Studien* (München: Hanser, 1971), p. 346ff.

28. Maréchal de Saxe (Moritz Graf von Sachsen, 1696–1750— served with the French), quoted in G. Brossollet, *Essai sur la non-bataille* (Paris, 1975), p. 113.

29. R. P. Suttmeier, *Research and Revolution, Science Policy and Societal Change in China* (Lexington, Mass.: Heath, 1974), p. 29ff.

30. G. Schwarzenberger, *Power Politics, A Study of World Society*, third edition (London: Stevens, 1964); idem, *Civitas maxima?* (Tübingen: Mohr, 1973).

31. P. Nitze, "Assuring Strategic Stability in an Era of Detente," *Foreign Affairs* 54, no. 2 (1976), pp. 207–32.

32. Karl von Clausewitz, *On War* (New York: Modern Library, 1943), p. 318ff.

33. We do not in fact consider all forms of damage limitation to be destabilizing. Cf. Afheldt's proposals in the sections on consequences in chapter 9 and 11.

34. In economics, Pareto-optimality is a condition where none of the participants in the system (such as the market) could still acquire an advantage without at the same time and necessarily creating a disadvantage for another participant.

35. See J. Newhouse, *Cold Dawn, the Story of SALT* (New York: Holt, Rinehart & Winston, 1973).

36. J. K. Galbraith, *The Industrial State* (New York: New American Library, 1968), p. 71ff.

37. See von Weizsäcker, *Fragen zur Weltpolitik*, pp. 136–138, and chapter 4 of this book.

38. Konrad Lorenz, *On Aggression* (New York: Harcourt, Brace & World, 1966).

39. Ibid., pp. 28–29.

40. H. Kissinger, *A World Restored: Castlereagh, Metternich and the*

Restoration of Peace, 1812–1822 (Boston: Houghton, Mifflin, 1957).

41. In the case of non-Clausewitzean weapons, the small marginal utility of further armaments may sometimes be judged differently; cf. MAD or Afheldt's model, discussed in section IV.

42. This is reflected in the judgments of Soviet propaganda: Roosevelt is seen positively, as the Great President, but Churchill is disparaged. V. M. Bereshkow, *Mit Stalin in Teheran* (Frankfurt/M: Stimme, 1968) is an example.

43. Nitze, "Assuring Strategic Stability."

44. K. Tsipis, *Offensive missiles*, Stockholm Paper 5 (Stockholm: Stockholm International Peace Research Institute).

45. This assumption is based on Soviet publications known in the West which deal with civil defense instructions for the Soviet population. See references in E. Wigner, "The Myth of 'Assured Destruction,'" *Survive* 3, no. 4 (1970), pp. 2–4; C. H. Kearny, "Expedient Shelter Construction and Occupancy Experiments," Oak Ridge National Laboratory, *ORNL*-5039 (March 1976), and also consult his earlier studies listed there. I did not investigate how adequately the proposals set forth there satisfy the demands of their own authors.

46. A test was conducted in the U.S.: six families were given an English translation of the Russian instructions and financial inducement for rapid construction: $600 for participation, $900 if completed within two days. Five of the six families finished in two days.

47. See St. Graubard, *Kissinger, Portrait of a Mind* (New York: Norton, 1973).

48. Report of the Secretary of Defense J. R. Schlesinger to the Congress on the FY 1976 . . . FY 1976 . . . FY 1976–1980, Washington: US GPO, February 5, 1975, p. II-1 f.

49. See McNamara's famous speech in San Francisco in 1967 where he openly admitted this and advanced the incalculability of the risk as the reason. *Department of State Bulletin* LVII, no. 1476 (Oct. 9, 1967), pp. 443–51.

50. Schlesinger, "Report to the Congress," pp. 1–7.

51. See my essay "Die heutige Menschheit von aussen betrachtet," in *Fragen zur Weltpolitik*, pp. 13–50.

52. Of course, religious Jewry hoped that its Messiah would not only reestablish its kingdom but would also free all of mankind from its subjection to the power struggles of world history. This idea also entered Christian millennialism. There are

Christian prophecies that the Day of Judgment, the most terrible and blissful end of world history, would come when the Jews had returned to Israel (see V. Soloviev, *Three Conversations on War, Progress and the End of History*). I relegate this comment to a footnote because to the political rationality of our time, such ideas appear as dangerous or anachronistic delusions. Yet one should not underestimate the reflection of reality in mythical images, the rationality of the suprarational. Only the connection with the expectation of the redemption of mankind enabled the highly rational Jewish people that were guided by theologians to cling for millennia to a religion whose central tenet was the expectation of its own salvation. I believe that in addition to its political suitability, it needed a secularized trace of Christian respect for this expectation, a respect also extended in a tolerant, modern manner to the Jews then living, to prompt a statesman such as Balfour to make his promise to the Zionists, a promise that was so fraught with consequences. But it is not the secularized remainder of the Kingdom of the Messiah, the Zionist state, that fulfills the expectations for justice of the myth. Though subjectively they were almost blameless, it became the destiny of the Jews, who only wanted to be a nation among nations with a country among countries, to be decried as the enemies of justice and to repeat, as it were, the situation of exile in their own country. Seen from the perspective of the myth, it seems probable that only a worldwide victory of justice will solve the problem of Israel.

53. These statistical data come primarily from three publications: (1) U.S. Arms Control and Disarmament Agency, *World Military Expenditures and Arms Trade 1963–1973* (Washington, D.C., 1973); (2) Ruth Leger Sivard, *World Military and Social Expenditures 1974* (New York: Institute for World Order, 1974); (3) Idem, 1976.

54. The "developed" countries include all North American and European countries except for Greece, Bulgaria, Albania, Yugoslavia, Portugal, Spain, Malta. Japan, Australia, New Zealand and South Africa are also developed countries. All others are "developing" countries.

55. Data from source 1 in note 53. (See p. 14, table I.)

56. See W. Heisenberg, *Physics and Beyond: Encounters and Conversations*, World Perspectives, vol. 42 (New York: Harper and Row, 1971), p. 182.

57. See *The New York Times* editorials of June 9, 13, 24, and 29, 1975. (An answer by the German embassy in Washington appeared in the edition of July 7, 1975.)
58. John Locke, *Epistola de tolerantia* was prepared to grant religious tolerance to sects but not to the Roman church because it refused to be tolerant of other churches.
59. von Weizsäcker, *Fragen zur Weltpolitik*, pp. 97–98. What is referred to here is the round of discussions, "European Security," of the European-American conference in Amsterdam, March 1973. The American speaker quoted first was David Packard, the European quoted next was Air Vice Marshal S. W. B. Menaul, and the American colleague was Albert Wohlstetter.
60. Th. S. Kuhn, *The Structure of Scientific Revolutions* (Chicago: University of Chicago Press, 1962).
61. L. Kohlberg, *Zur kognitiven Entwicklung des Kindes* (Frankfurt: Suhrkamp, 1974).
62. His fellow monks asked Francis of Assisi to permit them to study theology so that they might preach as effectively as the Dominicans. When he finally consented, after having refused this permission for a long time, he said: "But don't ever forget that no one would have anything to preach about if he had no brethren too humble to dare preach."
63. We are using this term here in a broader sense which also includes non-theistic systems.